The Nature of Value

NICK GOGERTY

The Nature *of* Value

How to Invest in the Adaptive Economy

Columbia University Press
Publishers Since 1893
New York   Chichester, West Sussex
cup.columbia.edu
Copyright © 2014 Nick Gogerty
All rights reserved

Library of Congress Cataloging-in-Publication Data
Gogerty, Nick.
The nature of value : how to invest in the adaptive economy / Nick Gogerty.
pages cm
Includes bibliographical references and index.
ISBN 978-0-231-16244-9 (cloth : alk. paper) — ISBN 978-0-231-53521-2 (ebook)
1. Value. 2. Economics. 3. Investments. I. Title.
HB201.G56 2014
332.6—dc23
2014006664

Columbia University Press books are printed on permanent and durable acid-free paper.
This book is printed on paper with recycled content.
Printed in the United States of America

c 10 9 8 7 6 5 4 3 2 1

Cover design: Fifth Letter

This book is dedicated to my loving and very patient wife, Mercedes Kelemen. Honey, I love you beyond measure and by the time you read this, the book really will be done. Promise.

Contents

Contents

Contents

Preface

THIS BOOK PUTS A theory forward of how and why economic value works, starting with the first principles of tiny innovation sparks and scaling all the way up to the full scope of the economy. This story of value borrows from many other disciplines, including anthropology, ecology, psychology, math, physics, biology, and sociology. Most of all, it examines how evolution's processes help us understand the economy, and how we can take this new understanding to invest in the economy for growth. Examining value creation through behavioral and systems-thinking models will explain the ebb and flow of capital, energy, resources, knowledge, and value over time. After finishing *The Nature of Value*, I hope you'll have a fresh view—or thoughtful criticism—of how value creation works. This won't make market prices predictable, but it hopefully makes one more effective at investing or allocating capital as a manager. And although I don't provide a list of 50 hot stocks to buy, I do aim to show how to spot patterns and processes found in the rare firms that provide long-term, sustainable value creation. Together, this theory and the practical applications are a philosophy that I call—no surprise here!—the nature of value approach.

Throughout the book, I favor the term "allocator" over "investor." They are very similar terms; after all, investing is the allocation of resources in the hope of growing value. However, the typical representation of an investor is someone who mostly looks at prices when planning his or her actions; price-only investors tend to underperform value investors. Effective investors, on the other hand, think like businesspeople, allocating capital within the firm to projects with high expected returns. Allocators—individuals making calculated capital allocations to projects or firms—play a vital role in growing the economy for us all by directing resources to the most effective value-creating organizations. We would all be better off if more investors thought like allocators.

So how did I come to start thinking and writing about value? My past includes adventures in software start-ups, founding roles at strategic risk firms, and time as the chief analyst for a European multidisciplinary science research institute focused on bits, atoms, neurons, and genes. In finance, I performed value research and portfolio management for a small New York–based long/short hedge fund, building risk and foreign exchange models for the world's largest banks, and I have also run in the pits on the floor of the Chicago Board of Trade. Most recently, I worked with the world's largest hedge fund, Bridgewater Associates. My lifelong interests have been in understanding sustainable economic development for poverty reduction and fighting corruption to improve governance procedures.

My hope is that after completing *The Nature of Value*, readers may pose fresh and interesting questions about the value all around them. My second hope is that in understanding the value process better, human, material, and energy resources may be allocated more effectively and efficiently to enhance the collectively linked human condition.

The Organization of the Book

Value is a contextually subjective part of an adaptive economic process. In order to introduce these ideas, I start with first principles and then build up to recognizable models and systems. Many diagrams, metaphors, and real-world examples are used to show patterns and help readers understand what value looks like and how to find it. At each step of the way, I emphasize how these new ideas can inform allocation and investing strategies. The following is a brief overview of the topics covered in the book, to serve as a roadmap of what is to come.

Chapter 1 starts by answering a question that's fundamental to the nature of value theory, that is, why is value important? I show how value differs from price—a close cousin with which it is easily confused—and explain the dangers this confusion presents to both an investor's portfolio and the health of the economic system as a whole. Chapter 2 examines value more closely, showing how a better understanding of value can lead to a better understanding of the economy's behavior. The economy is presented as an evolutionary system, with comparisons made between the economy and the ecology—a theme present throughout the book. Since many readers are already familiar to some degree with how evolution works in the biological realm, this comparison should help shed light on what it means for the economy to "evolve." Chapter 3 presents the theoretical underpinnings of this ecology/economy comparison.

Chapter 4 introduces the fundamental building block of the adaptive economy—the ino, short for an informational unit of innovation. Just as a gene is the unit of information that determines the possible traits an organism can express, an ino is the information that determines the possible capabilities an organization can express. If a company has inos that give it a competitive edge, these inos will start to spread throughout the economy. The chapter examines the various types of innovation that can help companies succeed, and points out what allocators can look for when assessing sustainability in innovative firms.

Chapter 7 introduces the next level of the economic process—clusters, which are the competitive spaces in which firms fight for survival. Like the niches within ecosystems, firms within clusters compete with each other for resources and dominance. Chapter 8 explores the life cycle of clusters, showing how they're born, how they mature, how they die, and what happens to the firms within them throughout these stages. Chapter 9 looks at how value flows within and through the cluster to a downstream consumer. Some clusters are inherently stable and promising for allocators, whereas others may look promising and lucrative on the surface but are actually unstable and should be avoided.

Chapter 10 looks at moats—the combination of capabilities that can help firms achieve long-term positive returns. Chapter 11 explains how these advantageous moats can be measured, and how they can expand or erode over time. It also looks at the various types of moats and at the competitive advantages—such as a strong brand or a geographic edge—that can help firms stay on top. Since moats can be such a lucrative source of value to investors, chapter 12 describes how to evaluate the management of moated firms and how to allocate capital to promote moat health and longevity.

Chapter 13 provides some final tips for the allocator and makes closing points about the differences between the nature of value approach and other investing strategies, such as index buy and hold strategies.

Chapter 15 puts all the pieces together to show the economy as a whole networked system. It shows how a nature of value understanding of the economy aids in predicting what's about to come—and it explores the things that still make the economic system so unpredictable. Going back full circle to chapter 1, I use the nature of value approach to further explore the relationship between money, value, and price in chapter 15, and show what this means in the face of large-scale economic shocks, like debt or fiscal policy–driven inflation and deflation.

Chapter 16 offers some bigger picture, closing thoughts.

The book is best read as an open-ended theory of adaptation, innovation, and economic value creation. You don't have to agree or fully grasp all of the book's concepts to receive a fresh way of thinking. There may be as many "a-ha!" moments in the book as "huh?" moments, depending on your interest in the various roles of value across evolution's economic domains.

A website with extra materials is available at www.thenature -ofvalue.com.

Acknowledgments

This book started as a collection of ideas for a blog post; it became a four-year journey spanning multiple disciplines with each question chased by an even deeper question of "why?" My original thesis about value at the company level (based on my hedge fund research) led me to information theory at the micro level and (surprisingly!) thermodynamics at the macro level, with evolution's selective adaptive processes as the ultimate theme. I would like to express a special thank you to my polymath friend Dr. Ed Reitman for listening to my ideas and introducing me to *Into the Cool: Energy Flow, Thermodynamics, and Life* by Eric D. Schneider and Dorion Sagan, and to *Cosmic Evolution: The Rise of Complexity in Nature* by Eric J. Chaisson. Both books provided a useful way of framing the "why" of adaptive economic complexity as a process of thermodynamic and information flows.

I would like to thank the anonymous reviewers who looked at this manuscript through its various iterations and provided very useful feedback. Many gifted managers at hedge funds also provided insights. Special thanks to Peter Bernard at D.E. Shaw and Daniel Roitman at Greenlight Capital, Joe Zitoli at Bank of America, and Andreas Deutschmann at JP Morgan. After submitting a proposal to Columbia University Press, good fortune smiled upon me as renowned publisher Myles Thompson expressed interest. For a first-time author writing about value, it was like being drafted off the street to be a professional athlete—equal parts thrilling and intimidating. My good fortune was compounded when I was paired with the ever-patient and incredibly gifted Bridget Flannery-McCoy as an editor. Her gifts for creating order out of chaos are seemingly boundless.

I would also like to thank the people of Niger who taught me during my travels across West Africa as an anthropology student to value the riches I have in my friends, family, and freedoms.

Finally a big thank you to my family, Mercedes Kelemen, Zoe Nady, Terry Gogerty, Margaret D. Nady, my twin brother, Alex Gogerty, and the late Robert M. Nady and Irene S. Dutton, for their love, support, and encouragement over the years.

The Nature of Value

PART I

Value

CHAPTER ONE

The Problem with Price? It's Not Value

What is a cynic? A man who knows the price of everything and the value of nothing.

OSCAR WILDE, "LADY WINDERMERE'S FAN," 1892

ON MAY 6, 2010, the shares of technology services consulting firm Accenture crashed from $40 to $0.01 in three minutes, wiping out 99.99 percent of its $35 billion market capitalization. Simultaneously, other companies' share prices gyrated wildly. The combined impacts reflected a $1 trillion loss, measured in share prices, or 9 percent of the index value. Minutes later, the share prices had mostly recovered.

This speedy decline and subsequent bounce back was called the "flash crash." Although this flash crash was notable for its size, miniature flash crashes of 5 to 30 percent, with subsecond price recoveries, occur surprisingly frequently. And during more common single-share flash crashes, prices can decline 30, 50, 80, and even 99 percent in seconds, only to recover moments later. Similar booms in price can also occur. The day of the 2010 flash crash saw Apple's shares trading briefly for up to $100,000/share, making Apple's market capitalization a robust $93.2 trillion—greater than the combined gross national product of all the countries in the world.

Nothing shows the folly of price better than these recurring flash crashes. There was no major change in the intrinsic economic value of Apple or Accenture on May 6, 2010. The crazy prices were the result of algorithms that didn't know a thing about the true value of the underlying companies. For all the algorithms cared, they could have been trading the price of dung balls in New Delhi. The algorithms were focused not on the value of the underlying companies, but on exploiting and harvesting statistical price anomalies, reacting in a matter of microseconds.[1] When algorithms working at that speed start to feed on each other, crazy things can happen. If you own a great company like Coke and algorithms start trading it at $0.02/share, although it traded at $40/share moments before, the distinction between intrinsic corporate value and price is pretty easy to spot.

The flawed prices created during flash crashes showcase a computer-driven, time-compressed version of a flawed price-making process that goes on all the time, namely, a process in which prices are set by two parties, neither of whom understands the long-term economic value of the underlying asset they trade. When a stock price declines, it means that for a given moment most human or algorithmic traders believe a firm's value has lessened. This doesn't mean a firm's value has changed at all, it's just a belief expressed as a number. Day to day, however, most people forget this and instead equate price with economic value. But price is a mere reflection of true value, like Plato's shadows on the cave wall.

In flash crashes, mispricing only lasts for a few moments. But in many cases, mispricing can last for months, or even longer. The tech bubble of the late 1990s, for instance, lasted for years. On the other hand, bargains—like Costco during its early years—may sit quietly, underappreciated for years before gaining momentum to reflect their true value.

Many asset valuation estimates rely on models that use only historical prices or other flawed inputs. Applying price-based models to assets can lead to large losses. Flawed and poorly applied price models were used to structure and price mortgage bundles in the 2000s. These bad price models contributed to the $6.7 trillion U.S. real estate bubble and the subsequent losses associated with the U.S. housing crisis of 2007. Common sense about value and risk was replaced with a statistical pied piper called a Gaussian cupola model, which, along with other problematic models, was then used to rate and evaluate the value of securitized mortgages. Behind many financial crises is a large group of people creating credit based on bad models or other false beliefs confusing upward price momentum with value creation. With so much misunderstanding of the relationship between price and value, the allocator who truly understands a firm's value will find herself at a significant advantage.

The Misunderstanding of Price

The line of thinking that equates prices with value naïvely assumes that everything is worth its current price. Imagine, for instance, you have a goose who lays golden eggs. Outwardly, it looks just like a normal goose. If you asked people how much they would be willing to pay for the goose, and they did not realize the secret of the golden eggs, the answer would not reflect its true value. People would instead price it just like any other goose.

This is illustrated in figure 1.1. Price is pictured as a balloon hovering over the goose, connected to it by a stretchy string. As the goose's intrinsic value wanders slowly forward (increasing) or backward (decreasing)—depending, let's say, on the changing number of golden eggs it's able to produce—the price balloon gets bounced to and fro by gusts of hot air and opinions expressed as traded prices. The winds of opinion push the balloon in front of (trading at a premium to) or behind (trading at a discount to) the intrinsic economic value of the goose.

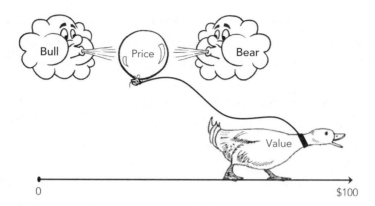

FIGURE 1.1 The Goose and the Balloon
Price is created by opinions of value.

These daily opinions and price changes don't change the nature of the goose's value; thus a company's intrinsic value, like the value of the golden goose, is often different from its price. The farther price gets away from value, the more likely it is to snap back. When the price balloon is far behind value, there may be a bargain in buying before price eventually moves forward to catch up with value. At other times, the price balloon is blown too far in front of the goose by excited traders. Most people obsess about the active and highly visible price balloon. In the long run, however, price activity doesn't matter; the goose—value—takes price to where it belongs. A goal of this book is to shift the reader's thinking from price to a deep understanding of value. I call this the "nature of value" perspective.

As shown in figure 1.2, different groups rely on price in different ways and to different degrees. Investment decisions are made based on price expectations, and are greatly influenced by an investor's time horizon. In short-term time horizons, price reflects opinions of value, but as time horizons stretch out, price tends to more realistically represent the competitive nature and value of the firm's earnings and assets. Famed value investor Benjamin

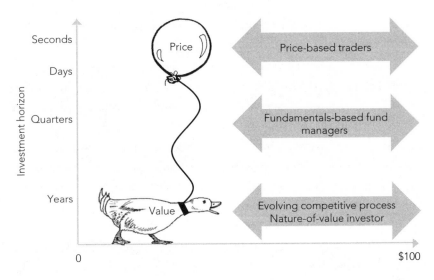

FIGURE 1.2 Time Horizons and Decision Factors Used by Various Investor Types

Graham correctly stated that in the short term, the stock market acts like a voting machine, and over the long term, it acts like a value-weighing machine.

Individuals from various schools of thought apply many methods to rationalize the price–value relationship. The trader's approach to price attempts to identify patterns in historical price shifts, focusing on past price rather than a company's actual value. Efficient market theory posits that price is value, and that price correctly reflects all possible known information about value at all times. Traditional behavioral economic models understand price as being based primarily on past price beliefs. Some analysts use comparative metrics of comparable firms and yields to justify prices. Each of these approaches has limitations, and each fails to grasp the importance of expected value in the firm's changing, competitive context. Let's delve a little deeper into these approaches to price and value, and the possible economic dangers they pose, in order to see how the nature of value perspective differs from and may improve on each one.

Traders: The Entropy Enablers

Most trading activity has little to do with an understanding of value. Traders add liquidity and greater statistical noise into price returns, as measured over time. Another way to say this is that traders introduce more entropy into the system.[2] Entropy is a measure of statistical complexity. Short-term traders use statistical tools or intuition to identify patterns, trending behaviors, and mean reversion from the seemingly random historical noise of price. Each time a trader repeatedly exploits a price pattern, he or she introduces entropy into the short-term price.

A simple price pattern might be that for 20 weeks in a row shares in IBM went up on Tuesday. A person seeking to take advantage of this might start buying on the next Tuesday morning at the open and selling before the Tuesday close. As more people pursue the strategy, entering earlier and exiting earlier, the "predictable" low entropy pattern—or arbitrage opportunity—disappears. Arbitrage typically refers to taking advantage of a price difference between two markets, but arbitrage in the statistical sense involves taking advantage of simple price patterns to such a degree that only highly complex or seemingly random non-exploitable price patterns remain. As the earlier pattern disappears, the price time series appears more random as it gets more statistically complicated. At some point, entropy increases to a level at which easily exploitable patterns disappear in a cloud of white statistical price noise. This process is illustrated in figure 1.3.

Short-term trading has a legitimate economic value in providing liquidity, but trading's economic contribution is overhyped when considered as the mechanism for performing value discovery and economic signaling. A firm's economic or intrinsic value rarely changes in microseconds or minutes—but algorithms and opinions do. So although active trading produces some useful liquidity, most of it just produces statistical noise. Traders make

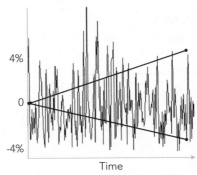

Low entropy = Predictable-path, straight-line market
High entropy = Unpredictable, random-white-noise market

FIGURE 1.3 Traders Increase Price Entropy
Traders consume predictable low entropy patterns, arbitraging them away and creating increased unpredictable price entropy.

money by identifying low entropy patterns and end up creating high entropy price patterns as residue. As we shall see later on, processes like this that consume low entropy and create high entropy are universal.[3]

The Efficient Market Hypothesis

Because of the "noisiness" of price—caused in part by traders exploiting simple patterns, as described above—a price's next bounce can't be predicted. In short time horizons, academics will tell you that price's movements approximate the Black-Scholes equation, derived from a method originally created by physicists to model heat diffusion, and shown in figure 1.4. In its total focus on price, Black-Scholes ignores the goose entirely. Although models like this may be accurate in the short term, the approximation becomes dangerously irrelevant as time horizons lengthen. Many financial problems have resulted from misapplying the Black-Scholes approximation of price over longer time horizons.

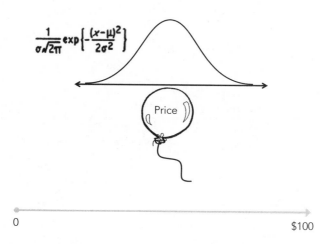

FIGURE 1.4 The Black-Scholes Model Ignores the Goose
Short-term price balloon movements approximate a heat diffusion process.
Black-Scholes–based finance and risk models ignore the goose entirely.

The dominant academic economic model is the efficient market hypothesis, which basically states that price always reflects all available information about value at a given time.[4] For believers of versions of efficient market theory, the balloon is always equivalent to the goose.[5] Any errors in this equivalence are unpredictable and not economically extractible. The efficient market hypothesis and its variants are frequently disproved, but despite this, many advocates of it continue to present it as a hard economic fact.

One problematic aspect of over-reliance on price models like Black-Scholes or the efficient market theory is that they lead to erroneous views of economic risk and asset values. With a focus on price as equivalent to value, modern finance theory dangerously confuses movements in price with true economic risk (the loss of economic value or the potential to generate economic value).[6] Modern financial theory incorrectly states that the faster and more volatile the price balloon moves, the riskier an asset is and therefore the less valuable.

FIGURE 1.5 Most Risk Models Confuse Price Volatility and Risk
As the price balloon wiggles backward and forward faster, modern portfolio risk
models get nervous. The fast wiggling balloon model of volatility won a Nobel
Prize in economics and underpins many financial risk models.

When nonvalue opinions and factors impact price, price-driven
risk models become even more flawed. Figure 1.5 highlights this.

Modern financial theory incorrectly teaches that economic risk is
measured by price volatility. To return to Plato's cave metaphor—
economic risk isn't how fast the shadows (price) flicker across
the wall. Economic risk is about changes in the underlying forms
(value) that actually cast the shadows. Economic risk is the chance
that you permanently lose the capacity to generate or receive
future economic value.

The Behavioral Economic Model of Price

Price can also be understood as a naïve behavioral outcome. Imag-
ine, for instance, that tomorrow you are to meet a stranger in New
York City. Neither of you has a way to communicate in advance.
Where and when do you meet? Nobel prize–winning economist
Thomas Schelling asked a group of students this question. He found

the most common answer was "at noon under the clock at the information booth in Grand Central Terminal." Nothing in particular makes Grand Central Station a better location than any other. Theoretically, one could meet at any bar or coffee shop in New York at any time. But Grand Central Station as a traditional meeting place raises its awareness and likelihood for successful agreement between the parties. This type of problem is known as a coordination game. The solution—assuming there is one—is an equilibrium outcome. Grand Central station at noon is an intuited focal point—referred to in economics as a Schelling point. Schelling points are effective equilibrium or meeting and coordination points for two or more parties.

So how does this apply to price and value? Barring new information, the last price traded for something becomes a logical Schelling point for the next likely price transaction.[7] What does this have to do with the nature of economic value for the underlying asset? Not much. It just explains a lot of stickiness in price behavior. Price mostly meanders around recent price until a big shift in opinion occurs, causing price to jump up or down. This is crudely modeled by quants using something called a jump-diffusion process model. Again, what does this have to do with an asset's true intrinsic value? Not much.

Fortunately, the value-focused investor doesn't have to worry about these statistical methods and jargon. Stochastic calculus, information theory, GARCH variants, statistics, or time-series analysis is interesting if you're into it, but for the value investor, it is mostly noise and not worth pursuing. The value investor needs to accept that often price can be wrong for long periods and occasionally offers interesting discounts to value.

Fundamental Comparative Metrics

Many investors justify a price using the comparable price-based metrics of competitors. If firm X is priced at 120 times revenue, then seemingly similar firm Y must be a bargain when priced at

80 times revenue. This dangerous analytical shortcut—in essence, using a priced-based model to compare apples to oranges—was popular during the Internet bubble of 1997–2000. In that case, both the apple and orange turned out to be rotten pieces of fruit. Being less rotten doesn't make something more edible.

Grouping and comparing businesses with Standard Industry Classification (SIC) codes confuses the map with the competitive territory. Comparable metrics may tell a person that something interesting is going on; for instance, if businesses compete directly, comparable operating margins and ROC may speak to the effectiveness and efficiency of a firm's relative capabilities and strategies. But comparables on their own won't explain why, how, or for how long value creation may continue.

Bubbles

The danger of an over-reliance on price-based approaches is especially clear in bubble situations. In bubbles, price momentum and excitement push prices significantly ahead of value, as investors rationalize their assumptions of increasing value using models based only on momentous recent price increases.[8] This is shown in figure 1.6. The perception that peers are getting rich from rising

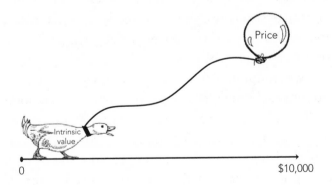

FIGURE 1.6 Bubbles

asset prices becomes a dangerous form of psychological confirmation, amplifying the price and value confusion.

Another danger of bubbles is that they can lead to the creation of money in the form of credit issued against the overpriced asset, as the credit issuer confuses the credit-inflating asset purchase activity with real value creation. The underlying inflated price becomes a justification for extending credit to purchase more of the inflated asset. Cheap debt, used for such asset purchases, is the gasoline fueling the false belief that rising price equals rising value. This feedback loop eventually ends as price crashes violently back down to intrinsic value or below, leaving people and economies with debt that can become increasingly difficult to service. Crashes define bubbles postfact, and reading a bit of history reveals how common they've been in our economies for hundreds if not thousands of years. As the financial turmoil of the last decade has shown, crashes can affect entire countries and populations.[9]

The $6.7 trillion U.S. housing asset bubble relied on increasing prices to justify more money in the form of debt to be allocated to housing. The reckless behavior was caused by two flawed beliefs about the relation of price to value. First, consumers used behavioral rules, by looking at peers' increasing home prices as proxies for value creation. Second, institutional investors, such as banks and pensions, invested in esoteric structured mortgage securities, relying directly on price-based statistical models and the risk ratings provided by agencies that were also using flawed models.[10]

These two misapplications of price-based models of house value fed into each other, creating a positive feedback loop. Soon, overpriced assets were being used to justify debt creation, which inflated house prices further. This in turn made the recently issued debt command higher prices as it appeared even safer. In total, U.S. home prices got $6.7 trillion ahead of their historical value, based on income to home price ratios. As the ratio reverted to relative norms, there was a tremendous paper loss that represented more than 40 percent of U.S. GDP. Variations on the U.S. bubble occurred globally in many countries' consumer real estate markets during the 2000–2009 period.

The reflexive relationship between price and value can have real consequences. Confusing price and value can lead to severe economic resource misallocations and distortions. As the economy shapes itself to the distorted money flows, resources and lives focus on unsustainable value-destroying pursuits. When the bubble bursts, millions of lives are severely affected by joblessness as the economy slowly reorganizes itself.

Summary

Price is an overrated metric, and is dangerous if relied on too heavily. In the short term, price is not predictable or absolutely linked to value. Price simply reflects opinions of an asset's ability to deliver value in the future. That price is easy to measure and model doesn't necessarily make it helpful or explanatory in regard to understanding the nature of economic value.

Value is complicated, idiosyncratic, and difficult to model, but it is fundamentally important because value is closer to economic truth than is price. Ignoring opinions and forming one's own understanding of value is crucial to good investing. Price reflects value over longer periods of time, but in short periods, price reflects many people trying to predict price. So let's leave price behind and try to discover the confluence of sources, processes, ever-changing forms, and fascinating behaviors that create the nature of value.

CHAPTER TWO

Value and Why It Matters

The voyage of discovery lies not in finding new landscapes, but in having new eyes.

MARCEL PROUST (1871–1922)

VALUE, IN THE SIMPLEST sense, is the human perception of what is important. As such, it is subjective and context dependent. Value is experienced in many forms, from the physiological—food, water, shelter—to the experiential—music, art, sport—to the psychological desires for social position, freedom, creativity, and love. The individual and group choices we make to organize and collectively maximize value are the major concerns of the economics field.

Economic value starts with basic physical needs. Food keeps you alive, clothing keeps you warm, and shelter keeps you safe. These things provide functional physiological value, and are found at the base of psychologist Abraham Maslow's hierarchy of human needs, shown in figure 2.1.

As one moves up Maslow's hierarchy, the sources of human value become less physiological and get more abstract, subjective, and personal. Many of the higher needs, such as confidence, creativity, and acceptance, sound like brand attributes. This isn't surprising. Companies create product origin stories and promote brand attributes in an attempt to satisfy our higher-level

Self-actualization: morality, creativity, spontaneity, problem solving, lack of prejudice, acceptance of facts

Esteem needs: confidence, achievement, respect of others, respect by others

Love/belongingness needs: affiliation, acceptance, affection, sexual intimacy

Safety needs/security of: body, employment, resource, morality, the family, health, property, psychological well-being

Physiological needs: breathing, food, water, sex, sleep, homeostasis, excretion

FIGURE 2.1 Maslow's Hierarchy of Needs and Value

needs. Drink Hennessy Cognac, the message may say, because you want to feel like a person of good taste and sensibility. If the advertising is effective, drinkers will seek out Hennessy because they believe it is a way of satisfying or publicly signalling these esteem needs and values.

As Maslow's hierarchy illustrates, we perceive, assign, and ascribe value to goods and service experiences based on real and imagined contexts that go far beyond their mere physical functions. The flexible, subjective, and contextual nature of economic value has confounded fixed absolute models of economic value from Karl Marx to John Maynard Keynes. There is no economic value other than that beheld and experienced. It is all relative experience. This subjectivity poses challenges when it comes to defining, measuring, and managing true or intrinsic value.

Many economic artifacts, such as shares, bonds, paper money, and gold, don't have value in themselves, but rather represent value within their respective social and legal systems. The representational value of these cultural artifacts is equal to what others will pay or trade for them. They are economically valueless outside of their social context. Imagine, for instance, trying to use Icelandic Krona to buy a drink at a bar in New York. Without an Icelandic context, the Krona won't be believable or useful as payment for your martini.

Ice serves as a good example of the flexibility and chimeric nature of value. In the nineteenth century, the Boston merchant Frederic Tudor—known as the Ice King—built a fortune by cutting ice out of frozen Massachusetts lakes, storing the ice in caves, and shipping it to summer hot spots around the world. As the first Boston ice shipment arrived in London, Tudor had a bar set up at the harbor to show off the benefits of his Boston ice. Soon, Tudor's ships were voyaging from Boston to Bombay as the luxury ice trend spread. This was no mean feat. Even with technological advances like stronger wooden hulls, clocks, and riggings, ship journeys were expensive and dangerous. This may sound like a ridiculous extravagance, given the extreme cost and effort. But the 3,000-mile journey made financial sense because the luxury value of ice as perceived by Tudor's customers exceeded the cost of his efforts. Indeed, although the danger and effort involved made the ice very costly, expensive luxury ice was rare and exclusive, and thus all the more appealing and valued. Being seen at the right English gentleman's club drinking the right cocktail with the right kind of ice cube became de rigueur for the Victorian smart set. The nineteenth century social cache of luxury ice disappeared as prices declined due to the innovation of twentieth century refrigeration. Ice lost its perceived luxury value as it stopped being an expensive object that had traveled long journeys across foreign lands.

Social prestige signaled visually with money spent still delivers value today—think designer handbags or expensive sports cars. Premium ice and exotic forms of water are still with us; premium ice made a resurgence in Japan during the 1980s, when fine old single malt whiskey was considered best paired with naturally blue ice cubes freshly harvested from Alaskan glaciers.

The journey of ice in the nineteenth century shows how the economy adapts extreme capabilities to deliver value. The ice journey uses an enormous amount of energy and resources, converting them into value. The rest of this book explores mechanisms like these, showing how the economy works as an adaptive system that takes in low value inputs and processes them with energy and knowledge into higher value forms.

Fundamentally, the economy is adaptive, and this creative and destructive process of adaptive evolution is the best-known and most effective mechanism for creating societal wealth and human well-being. This book explores a number of questions surrounding this idea of economic evolution. For instance, how does this process create value? And how can one make money out of it? Understanding this mystery can help capital allocators, investors, and managers stay ahead of capital-destroying forces while contributing profitably to the thriving stages of value and knowledge creation for us all.

Ecology as a Model for Economy

Life and the economy follow a similar adaptive process. According to ecologists Daniel R. Brooks and E. O. Wiley, life has:[1]

1. Increasing self-organization
2. Increasing entropy that is irreversible
3. Increasing specialization

These are traits of economic systems as well.
Some other aspects of life and ecosystems:

- Ecosystems strive to grow and capture all available resources.
- Ecosystems compete with other ecosystems at their boundaries.

Evolutionary change is expressed over time as phylogeny. Each species (actor) or evolved form has embodied within it the survival information and knowledge from past successful structures and behaviors.

Economies, again, also go through these adaptive processes.

Linking nature and economy is well-trodden intellectual ground. Charles Darwin's *On the Origin of Species* was published in 1859,[2] and by 1873 Walter Bagehot, editor of *The Economist*, had published *Physics and Politics*, linking political economy with Darwin's theories. It was generally well received:

> "Physics and Politics" has been written to show that the noble field of political thought and activity is not necessarily the chaos it is generally supposed, but that it involves great natural laws, which it is the destiny of science to trace out and formulate, just as it has done with other branches of knowledge which have been made scientific by modern inquiry.[3]

In 1890, Alfred Marshall, founder of the economics department at Cambridge University, again linked biology and economics in his *Principles of Economics*. He argued, among other things, that "like trees in the forest, there would be large and small firms but sooner or later age tells on them all."[4] In the 1930s, Friedrich Hayek stressed the importance of the evolutionary processes of creative birth and destruction in economics.

Linking the economy and nature's process can also lead to misunderstandings, however. Marx had a negative and incorrect perception of competition as a wealth and value destroyer. Marx's linear and mechanical view of economic history was deeply flawed. He understood history to be on a human-guided, predictable trajectory, contradictory to nature's more discursive path. Karl Popper effectively critiqued Marx in his book *The Poverty of Historicism*. Popper pointed to the unpredictable shifts seen in both the economy and nature, between utter chaos and fully mechanical determinism.

In the 1950s, Joseph Schumpeter redefined competition in positive evolutionary terms with the concept of "creative destruction," highlighting the adaptive selective process as socially and therefore economically value creating, rather than value destroying, in the long term. From the 1930s to 1950s, Ludwig von Mises supported arguments for open non-interventionist economics, and emphasized the value of the consumer price feedback signaling mechanism. Today, evolutionary economic thinking is found in various universities and think tanks such as the Santa Fe Institute. In addition, economic thinkers like Reiner Kümmel[5] and Robert U. Ayres[6] have pushed the boundaries of economic thinking into the field of evolutionary dynamics.

Not all twentieth century economists embraced the evolutionary model of economy. Keynes and other economists ignored, dismissed, or seriously misunderstood growth, innovation, value, and adaptive economic processes. Economists' mathematic models treated the economy like a linear or simple probabilistic machine. They focused on point solutions and mechanistic equilibrium models, using linear capital and labor flows suspended in false clouds of implausible assumptions and caveats. But adaptive system growth, by definition, is adaptive and can't be linear mechanistic. According to Ayres, Keynes disregarded growth as neither an important or enduring phenomenon. Keynes, working in 1930, expected growth to come to an end within two to three generations, and the economy to plateau. He referred to this imagined state of equilibrium as "bliss."[7]

Ultimately, Keynes's historical determinist state of "bliss" proved as deeply flawed as Marx's dreams of the equilibrium-perfected state associated with the utopian proletariat. Both these mechanical theories still have adherents, however, and can be dangerous if pursued aggressively using monetary or political force. The only economic systems found today that are truly at or close to equilibrium are nearly dead economies. A cow that achieves equilibrium is called a steak, and the economy closest to achieving equilibrium today is probably North Korea circa 2013.

According to Ayres, Keynes's models were relatively static, and—sadly similar to today's economic models—use simple linear inputs and outputs. Keynes wrongly believed in homothetic growth—growth without structural change. Keynes was wrong on a lot of things due to this flawed assumption of a fixed, finite economic structure. The homothetic model approach is the opposite of an evolving open system like the economy.

In the 1920s, Frank Knight—most well known for his economic work differentiating risk from uncertainty—was closer to a dynamic model of the economy, looking for a series of accelerators and multipliers to explain the varying rates of change across an economic system over time. As we shall see, evolutionary systems flow, change, and adapt structurally in order to increase their capability to create, maintain, and grow economic value.

Variations of Keynes's linear savings-led input models and static structures from 1928 are still abused today. Many economists would rather apply bad models than admit to having none at all, and so like pre-Copernican astronomers they add epicycles to fantastic mechanistic universes. At best this reflects ineptitude, and at worst intellectual fraud, which can do actual harm when governments and central banks rely on these models to justify policies affecting millions of people.

Mainstream economic models deal with structural adaptive change, wealth (expected value), and innovation poorly—although there are useful exceptions to this, such as experience curves, which are examined later. Mainstream macroeconomics focuses on static equilibrium or steady states. By contrast, the nature of value approach seeks to generally explain why and how economies grow and adapt. Like ecology, the nature of value approach focuses on generic processes and trends versus precise deterministic prediction.

In order to understand this growth perspective, it's important to understand that life and value aren't *things*; they're *processes*. Take a flower, for instance. We can think of it as a thing in itself, but we can also consider it as a process that has been optimized to create more flowers. The flower is itself alive, but it also spreads life over time and space. Life "flows" from the soil, to the flower, to the bees that suck its nectar; life also flows from one flower to the next that grows from its seeds. Flowers thus adapt to increase not only life but the flow of life.

Value, in the form of products and services, is much the same. The flower evolves to increase its ecological viability, and thus encourage the spread of flowers and the flow of life. A valued product or service adapts using innovative knowledge, and in doing so increases its economic viability and encourages the creation of more applied value creation. The continual and increasingly efficient creation of a product allows more and more value to flow through the economy. One of the key ideas of this book is that we should look not just at life and at value as static entities, but at life and value as continuous flows through a system that adapts for greater and greater flow capacities.[8]

Adaptive Flow Creates Complexity and Efficiency

Adaptive, selective processes work the same in economy and ecology. In both cases the process is more nuanced and interesting than naturalist Herbert Spencer's 1864 catch phrase "survival of the fittest," which he used to refer to both biological and economic processes, and which for our purposes is quite telling. (The phrase was first adopted and used by Darwin in the fifth edition of *On the Origin of Species* in 1869.)

Darwin had three conditions necessary for what he referred to as "adaptation by natural selection:"

There must be a struggle for existence so that not all individuals survive.

There must be variation such that some types are more likely to survive than others.

The variation must be heritable so that the advantage can be passed on.

The three preceding rules hold for economically valued goods and services.

We shall see that species and niches in economies and ecologies don't have exactly predictable trajectories. Ecologies and economies optimize themselves for conditions and possibilities at given moments in time. There is no fixed equilibrium point for an economy or ecology; rather there is constant adaptation that attempts to increase the flow of life and value.

Just as the economy and the ecological domains undergo continuous adaptation, they also grow increasingly complex. Both systems, in fact, can be described as "complex adaptive systems"—a concept visited throughout this book and one that informs much of the discussion about these two domains. As systems adapt, their very structures change in order to allow for a continually increasing flow of life or value, respectively. One flower species evolves into three; a first generation iPod evolves into an iPod Nano, iPod Shuffle, and iPod Touch. These structural flow splits are called "bifurcations." Bifurcating systems become more complex while gaining the capacity for increased throughput (the quantity of raw material or information that moves through a system) and efficiency.

Figure 2.2 shows a simple bifurcation, or spread of variation in form, over time. The diagram starts from an original organism or value-creating form on the left, and begins to split as time goes on.

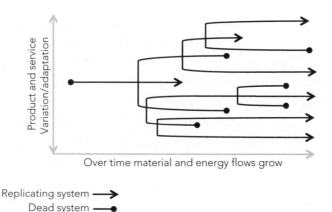

FIGURE 2.2 Bifurcation Flows
Bifurcation of form allows for increased flow efficiency.

Arrows indicate value-producing, economically viable forms going forward; dots indicate extinctions due to failed adaptations.

Adaptive change doesn't follow straight lines or occur at a steady pace. For years, there was a debate among biologists about whether ecological systems adapted gradually or in fits and starts. The debate was mostly resolved as the late evolutionary biologist Stephen Jay Gould determined that the process of life and its resulting ecologies follow an unpredictable "punctuated equilibrium" process of evolving change. In punctuated equilibrium, not much happens for long periods, and then suddenly everything changes before stabilizing once more. Economies and industries show punctuated equilibrium behaviors in their rates of adaptive structural change.

Adaptive change isn't always positive, in terms of increasing the flow of value or life through a system. There are periods of decline, regression, and falling back. For instance—252 million years ago, a mass extinction called the Great Dying occurred. Ninety-six percent of marine species went extinct, along with 70 percent of all terrestrial vertebrates. The exact causes are unknown, but speculation includes a meteor, which may have landed in the ocean. In economies, widespread declines in value throughput measured as GDP contractions or recessions accelerate organizational extinction rates. Economic value flow contractions vary in size and cause, just like large extinctions and ecological collapses.

Although these kinds of temporary fallbacks do occur, over the long term ecology and economy grow more life flow measured as living biomass and their capacity for value flow increases. For instance, according to the late scholar of historical economics Angus Maddison, the annual GDP flow facilitated by one person in 1 A.D. is estimated at $460 in constant 1990 U.S. dollars.[9] Humanity's flow of value and the rate of growth have increased significantly over the last 2,000 years, as indicated in figures 2.3 and 2.4.

The struggle for life and economic survival isn't that different. Imagine two rams fighting for territory in the Rocky Mountains. The butting of horns makes a furious sound as they compete for dominance. The rams' genes are a determining factor in the size of their horns. The capability for growing large horns (among other

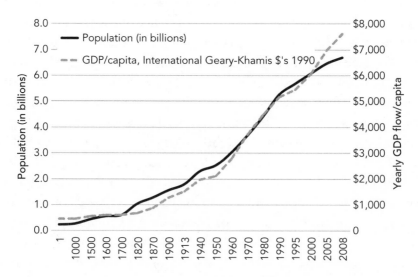

FIGURE 2.3 Global Population and GDP Per Capita, 1–2008 A.D.
Source: Angus Maddison

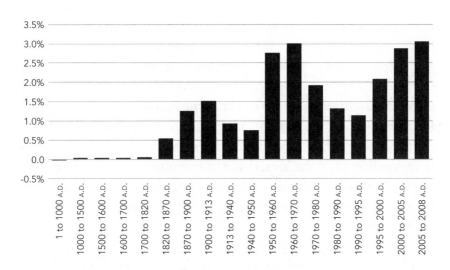

FIGURE 2.4 Annualized Global GDP Growth, 1–2008 A.D.
Source: Angus Maddison

capabilities) enables the ram to win fights, ultimately securing reproductive access to females via territorial dominance. Successful reproductive sex acts as a feedback loop—since rams with large horns
are more likely to reproduce, more rams with large horns will be
born. This amplification of genes can eventually lead to larger horns
among the ram species that populate the ecological landscape.

Across an open plain, miles away, a man smiles as he looks
forward to purchasing a new Dodge Ram truck. The Ram truck's
branding, engine technologies, and marketing capabilities are all
innovations expressed by the manufacturer. The brand promotes a
sense of masculinity, authenticity, and power to the potential male
truck purchaser. The cash value exchanged for the truck purchase
allows for more Ram truck advertising to replicate and keep the
macho Ram truck brand innovation alive. Just as reproductive sex
amplifies genes and their expressed traits, perpetuating the iterative cycle of life, shopping and purchasing are the acts required
for innovations to capture resources and reproduce the flow of an

innovation's expressed capability. This economic process of selective value informational feedback amplifies successful innovations.

Biological or economic reproduction alone doesn't guarantee successful forward propagation. Reproduction merely captures resources and the potential to begin the amplification cycle. Likewise, resource consumption doesn't guarantee an innovation's propagation, but merely signals the innovation's success at producing value for a customer. The cash value from a sale may be put back into reproducing and expressing more of an innovation, but doesn't guarantee future value creation success.

Understanding the Networked Panarchy

In complex adaptive systems whether physical, ecological or economic in nature, all things are networked and connected. This is obvious, but also so overwhelming that it is often forgotten. The image of a butterfly's wings flapping in Japan leading to a typhoon in Australia is a popular metaphor in chaos theory literature. The romantic notion of a single organism's impact on the future is poignantly accurate and simultaneously useless. Looking at complex systems in fine grain detail is like chasing butterflies to predict typhoons. Likewise, knowing the location of every painted dot in the pointillist painter Georges Seurat's painting of an afternoon picnic on the island of La Grande Jatte won't explain the context, mood, or beauty of the painting.

Vision comes from a sense of distance and synthesis of how points combine to create a flowing narrative. Just as with Seurat's painting, adaptive systems like the economy are better understood in broad contexts and as narrative processes rather than in overwhelmingly reductionist detail.[10] In ecology, some practitioners estimate that only three to six key variables are needed to track the basic drivers of a system. This may be true for adaptive economic systems as well. Some key economic variables explored in later chapters, dealing with pricing power and competitive differentiation, will attempt to explain longer-term economic survival traits.

Complex adaptive systems exist as linked networks of elements organized into feedback loops and hierarchies. A term from ecology that helps capture the "big picture" of this complex network connectedness is "panarchy." A panarchy is a network of connected adaptive hierarchical systems.

Panarchies are everywhere. Your body is a panarchy, ranging from your smallest to largest systems: intracellular mitochondria found within your 200+ types of cells form tissues, which arrange themselves into functioning organs, which in turn support your entire body's goal of staying alive to reproduce its genes. Each hierarchical level is a system set among a panarchy of connected networks.

Panarchies of nested hierarchies can be visualized as stacked pyramids or nested circles. The economic panarchy is analogous to the ecological panarchy, as seen in figure 2.5. Each ecological layer

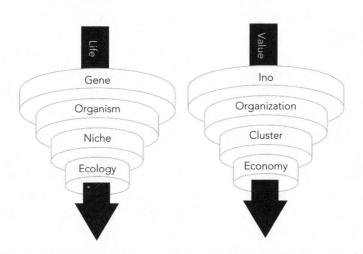

FIGURE 2.5 Ecological and Economic Panarchy Process
Each layer in the ecological and economic network acts as a macroprocessesor, selecting survivors and weeding out those incapable of propagation. Over time, this leads to the adaptation of life and of value.

corresponds functionally with a parallel economic layer. Comparing selected flows through value- and life-creating panarchies can help us understand the economy and value-creating processes.

The information captured within an innovation can be broken into units called "inos." Inos are the economic analog to biology's genes. Inos, expressed as capabilities and behaviors by organizations, cascade down into the economy, just like genes expressed by organisms cascade down into the ecology. Each layer—and the relationship between layers—is explained in later chapters, from top to bottom, so don't worry too much about the mechanism now. The thing to remember is that panarchies are wonderful adaptive, flowing feedback networks composed of a number of levels.

Adaptive changes and knowledge cascade down the panarchy, either rejected as nonviable or selected and amplified by the layer below. This filtering macroprocess is adaptive selective feedback, the heart of evolution's process. The value and life generated in aggregate provides the material for creating and sustaining fresh inos and genes. As material and energy flow through it, a panarchy structurally adapts, creating more complexity and increasing the capacity for life and value flow.

Panarchy's networked hierarchies overlap across time and space in terms of interaction, structural knowledge shared,[11] resources, and energy flows. Figures 2.6A and B show the nested relationships with ecology and economy. (Note that the time and space axes in the charts that follow are logarithmic, not linear.)

Panarchies help us link the big and small adaptive pictures. In studying economies, it's not worthwhile to look at each individual actor's choice or the impact of every individual innovation that pops up. At the top level of the economy, it is difficult to predict the short-term fits and starts of an economy's flow measured as real GDP. However, looking at the interaction among all these pieces and some of the patterns displayed at every level can help us better understand the workings of the economic system, and how economic and organizational growth happens.

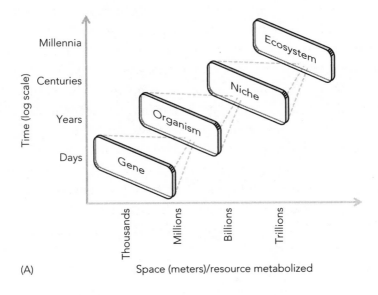

(A)

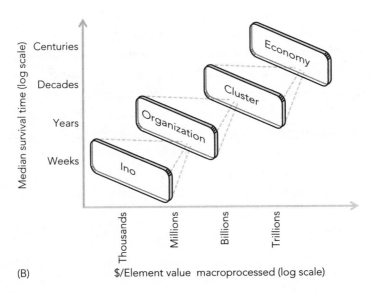

(B)

FIGURE 2.6 (A) Ecology's Panarchy Network; (B) Evolution's Economic Panarchy of Network Links and Elements

This growth creates remarkable opportunities for individuals. Understanding how the adaptive panarchy works has important ramifications for investors. For value investors, the focus is on the organizations' ability to sustainably capture excess value, in the form of profits, as it flows through a competitive cluster (market). Efficiently allocating capital to organizations means understanding the middle economic layers: the cluster and the organization. The ino's layer is typically too volatile and risky for most allocators and is more suited to venture capital. The top layers of aggregate economy and beyond are affected by government debt, monetary policy, and sociopolitical drivers beyond the scope of this book.

Summary

Evolution's complex system of life (ecology) is analogous to the continual flow of the adaptive economy. Understanding one adaptive system—or panarchy—helps us understand the other. As material knowledge and energy flow through it, a panarchy's structure changes, bifurcating into more complex forms and allowing for greater and more efficient throughput of material and energy. Adaptive systems don't lend themselves to reductionist thinking, but by looking at general patterns and rules, we can start to understand some of their traits, behaviors, and goals.

CHAPTER THREE

The Theory of Value

THIS CHAPTER IS THEORETICAL and less directly applicable to investing. It examines the underlying macroprocesses forming both the economy and ecology. Those wishing to skip the theoretical underpinnings of nature of value investing may skip this section. For others, it may help give a deeper and more substantial understanding of value.

In order to truly grasp the power of evolution's process and its relationship to economic value, it's important to first set straight a few common misperceptions about evolution. First, evolution is often incorrectly summed up as "survival of the fittest." It's not quite as simple as this. Rather, evolution is a complex, energy-driven process that can be distilled into three steps: adaptive change of form, selective feedback, and amplification of selected form. Second, evolution is not just a biological phenomenon. It actually occurs across many domains: the geophysical, the ecological, the economic, and others. This chapter will examine the three steps in the process of evolution, and show how evolution takes place both in the ecological and the economic domains.

Evolution, at its core, is fundamentally an energy-driven change process. As early as 1886, the Austrian physicist Ludwig Boltzmann—father of statistical heat entropy mechanics—suggested that the energy from the Sun drives all living processes. Boltzmann postulated a Darwinian-style competition for sunlight energy, which was then converted into biochemical energy that fueled life forms. As mathematician and biostatistician Alfred J. Lotka put it:

It has been pointed out by Boltzmann that the fundamental object of contention in the life-struggle, in the evolution of the organic world, is available energy. In accord with this observation is the principle that, in the struggle for existence, the advantage must go to those organisms whose energy-capturing devices are most efficient in directing available energy into channels favorable to the preservation of the species.[1]

Evolution, in other words, favors the energy efficient. We'll start our exploration by looking at this first principle—energy—before moving on to derived outcomes.

Energy

Things change when energy flows through them. This simple flow mechanism has some profound repercussions, and is the key driver of evolution's process. Evolution is really nothing more than a story of energy flows and the structural adaptation that takes place to encourage further effective flow.

Energy flows due to gradients. A gradient is the gap between high and low energy potential. Burn a match and you have taken highly structured potential chemical energy—the match—and converted it to lower grade heat and light energy—the flame. As this example suggests, energy flows "downhill," from a higher quality to lower quality, with energy quality defined as the maximum amount of potential work extractable from a form of energy. Physicists call this change from high to low potential a "gradient." This continual deterioration in energy quality is due to the fact that each time energy changes form, some of it is lost as unrecoverable heat known as "entropy." Heat or entropy is considered lower quality because, statistically speaking, it is increasingly disordered, dissipated, and generally unrecoverable to perform useful work.

Energy gradients act as if under constant pressures to reduce themselves to lower potential states. A high-energy hot kettle cools down to room temperature, releasing heat into the room as entropy during the cooling process. Over time, the cooling kettle resolves the energy gradient between kettle and room to an equilibrium temperature. Another example: A ball on the edge of a cliff has a high potential energy. As the ball falls, it transfers potential energy into kinetic energy and dissipates some heat (in the form of friction) as entropy while lowering its potential energy state. Yet another example: Water falling or flowing downhill reduces its gradient, losing its gravitational potential energy and dissipating entropy along the way. The waterfall drop height represents the energy gradient. As we shall see, high- and low-value gradients work in a similar fashion. One final example: Gasoline is a form of highly ordered potential energy stored as hydrocarbon chemical potential. Burned gasoline is reduced from a high potential state down a gradient to a lower potential state of energy. Gasoline burned in a combustion engine is converted from high grade chemical potential energy into kinetic (motion energy) and low grade entropy (heat).

In seeking to reduce energy gradients, systems tend towards equilibrium. Equilibrium is the state in which all things are equally balanced or resolved. Energy equilibrium is the state that a closed system pursues as it dissipates its energy. The water in the hot kettle eventually reaches equilibrium when it gets to room temperature. The push towards equilibrium, or gradient reduction, drives all change. Life and economics are all about how open systems receiving constant energy inputs adapt to resolve disequilibrium more efficiently over time.

The Effect of Energy on Physical Systems

Physical systems adapt, changing over time as energy flows through them. These changes follow the same pattern—they allow energy flowing through the system to dissipate more quickly. The quicker energy is dissipated, the more quickly energy flows through a system overall. Some examples of basic physical systems help illustrate this point.

A sandbox tilted downward with a trickling water hose at its high end is an adaptive system of energy and material flow. Over time a tiny stream will slowly emerge, carved out of the sand by the running water as it exits at the lower side. Over time the stream carves a deeper channel, taking more turns and twists, becoming more complex, and carrying more water for a longer period of time. The water flowing downhill creates this structure in the sand as it seeks a lower potential energy state at the bottom of the tilted box. The system physically adapts a pattern that gives it a greater capacity for storing and dissipating the water's potential energy. Full-scale river systems mature the same way, carving out large, varying paths over thousands of years. Geologically young rivers flow straight and fast, whereas older rivers adapt to have more turns and twists. The changing shape of the river represents the patterned "knowledge" embedded in it from thousands of years of resolving gradient flows, with the prior shape providing the guide for how to "capture" more of the flowing water's potential energy and dissipate more energy into the surrounding system.

Thus, as energy flows through things, it changes their structure and capabilities to dissipate energy faster. Energy doesn't flow through things in straight lines, infinitely. Things adapt structurally in order to dissipate flow more efficiently. Dissipation creates entropy.

The stream's adapting path and searching pattern in the sandbox is not exactly predictable, but it does have easily generalizable mathematical flow rate and branching properties. One general theory for explaining the physical forms created by energy flow is called "Constructal theory." This theory explains how and why seemingly random living and inanimate systems adapt to have certain efficient structures when measured over time and flow. Put forth by distinguished mechanical engineering professor Adrian Bejan, Constructal theory states that "For a finite-size system to persist in time, to functionally live, it must adapt in such a way that it provides easier access to the imposed currents that flow through it."[2] Bejan's theory has three tenets:

Life is flow: All flow systems are live systems, the animate and the inanimate.
Design generation and evolution is a phenomenon of physics.
Designs have the universal tendency to evolve in a certain direction in time.

We will not go into Constructal theory in detail, but we will return to some of these core ideas throughout the book. Indeed, the very premise of this book—that it can be useful to think of the economy and ecology in parallel—is based on the idea that the economy and ecology exhibit similar evolutionary patterns.

One key idea to take away from Constructal theory is that all things can be considered dissipative structures—that is, all forms evolve for energy to flow through at increasing levels of efficiency. We will see that the study of evolution across economic and ecological domains is actually the study of dissipative structures adapting over time and through selective processes.

Measuring Φ_m

Every system or structure can be compared by measuring its capacity to dissipate energy in order to resolve a gradient. Physicists measure energy in units called ergs.[3] A system's energy dissipation capacity can be measured in ergs/gram/second. Harvard astrophysicist Eric J. Chaisson calls this metric Φ_m, pronounced "phi-m." Chaisson's research has found that higher Φ_m energy dissipation capacities are associated with more mature adapted structures and systems. Increased Φ_m capacities emerge over time as energy flows form complex physically linked networks with discrete levels, structures, and hierarchies. It should come as no surprise that complex panarchies like the economy and ecology have high Φ_m capacities, as we'll discuss a little later in this chapter.

I'll use one of Chaisson's examples to explore Φ_m—our very own Sun. The Sun's interior generates nuclear energy at a rate of 4×10^{33} ergs/second at its core. This brings the core to an estimated temperature of 15 million degrees C internally. The sun's dense mass (almost 2×10^{30} kilograms) means that an excited particle travelling outward from the core at the speed of light collides with so many neighboring particles that it takes millions of years to flow from the center to the Sun's surface 690,000 kilometers away. An uninterrupted straight path would take less than three seconds. When particles finally arrive at the Sun's surface, their temperature is a relatively cool 5,500°C.

Given the Sun's mass and the time required for energy to flow through it, Chaisson's Φ_m for the Sun is 2 (ergs/second/gram). This is a relatively low rate; life, as we shall see, has selectively adapted to become many orders of magnitude more effective at energy dissipation—and the economy goes beyond even that.

The Sun's particles physically adapt faster dissipation pathways and patterns over time, like drops of rain forming streams and rivers with higher flow capacities. As the Sun structurally adapts, it will become a red giant, with a radius expanding beyond the earth's

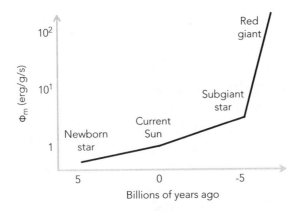

FIGURE 3.1 The Sun's Φ_m Adapts Over Time
The Sun's energy dissipating capacity, or Φ_m, adapts for greater flow over time.
Source: Eric J. Chaisson, *Cosmic Evolution: The Rise of Complexity in Nature.*
Harvard University Press, 2002.

current orbiting distance. No need for immediate alarm—this process is estimated to take another five billion years. The chart in figure 3.1 from Eric J. Chaisson's book *Cosmic Evolution* shows a star's throughput capacities over its lifetime. The vertical axis is energy dissipation Φ_m and the horizontal axis shows the star's age in billions of years. As you can see, although not yet a red giant, our older, structurally adapted Sun has a higher Φ_m capacity than its earlier self. Just as the river evolves channels that enable more capacity and flow over time, the Sun adapts structurally to support increased energy throughput per unit of mass over time.

Evolution: Flowing Change

The process creating these increasingly dissipative energy structures over time is called "evolution." Evolution, generally speaking, involves three processes: selection, adaptation, and survival knowledge (selected information) amplification. These processes occur in physical, biological, economic, and posteconomic domains. Selection occurs among competing forces. Adaptation is the change or pattern variation that occurs in a system as a result of selection. Amplification is the increasing rate of occurrence of a pattern or form over time and space.

Selection is the result of choice. Every state of a system has multiple potentials or outcomes, and selection is the process of one path, pattern, form, or outcome chosen over another. As we shall see, selection generally chooses systems that have the highest Φ_m factor. The selective process determines which patterns and forms are sustained and which will decay over time.

Adaptation, then, is the change in form that survives the selection process. Existing adapted stream pattern, species, or products are likely to persist for longer than extreme mutant varieties of new patterns or forms. Slight adaptations are typically more robust than old patterns, which occur over the course of many selection cycles and in the long term lead to greater efficiency. Adaptation may appear locally random but actually follows broad patterns of increasing Φ_m over selection cycles. Evolution can be considered a form of "information processing," in that it adapts and transforms highly ordered energy potentials into disordered entropy patterns faster by macroprocessing, selecting for the forms that enable better Φ_m capacities.

Adaptations amplify and spread over time, branching out to explore new forms for capturing and dissipating energy more effectively. Occasionally multiple successful adaptations emerge and exist simultaneously, spread over physical space. These splits, as discussed briefly in chapter 2, are called "bifurcations." With each new replicating bifurcation, the complexity of the overall system increases. The increasing structural or patterned complexity within a system reflects increased selected information or knowledge embedded in the system. Nobel Laureate Ilya Prigogine found that as a system is pushed further from energy equilibrium (or, in other words, as the energy gradient increases), the system's structure goes through sudden transitions or bifurcations.[4] Successful bifurcation continues to take place until a less articulated state, such as turbulence, sets in. This allows for occasional spurts in the evolutionary process.

Amplification is the third step of the evolutionary process. Amplification occurs via replication or reproduction of a selected form. The forms that most successfully dissipate energy are most likely to survive, and thus to be replicated. As the components of a system adapt increasing Φ_m capacities, the entire system achieves increased aggregate Φ_m capacities.

Evolution's process is the same across physical, ecological, and economic domains. Evolution's process of selection, adaptation, and knowledge amplification leads to increasing Φ_m capacities—and one of the most impressive Φ_m capacities is held by DNA-based life structures. Biological organisms can dissipate energy faster than any of the nonlife examples mentioned previously. Life uses the knowledge stored in DNA to express increasingly efficient forms for dissipating energy, cumulatively pushing evolution's Φ_m boundary forward.

Adaptive, bifurcating structural complexity is easy to see expressed in life forms. Take, for instance, the evolution of increasingly specialized cell types. As Eric D. Schneider and Dorion Sagan explain in their book *Into the Cool*, "570 million years ago there were 2 cell types, 500 million years ago it was 75, four hundred million years ago 125 and in humans there are now an estimated 220 structurally differentiated cell types. . . . [This] pattern of structural bifurcation is typical for systems in which more energy pathways are established as gradient breakdowns lead to new stable routes and pathways."[5] Billions of years ago, the single cell structures most effective at harvesting and converting chemical or solar energy reproduced more single cells. These dominant growing cells, such as bacteria, then harvested and ultimately dissipated energy ever more efficiently. Eventually, bacteria and the other single cell organisms combined to create the greatest mechanism for biological adaptation ever seen:

the process of information and trait sharing that is sexual reproduction. Sex enables the transfer and exchange of adapted survival
knowledge patterns between two cells or two organisms. Eukaryotic cells were the first to reproduce sexually, and became far more
efficient at playing evolution's game of adaptation, selection, and
knowledge amplification to harvest and dissipate energy faster.

From eukaryotic cells came the first basic plant forms. Plants
compete to capture high grade (low entropy) sunlight energy to
reproduce effectively, with the selective pressure for material and
energy resources creating a network of organisms that are increasingly efficient at dissipating energy. Figure 3.2 shows how plants
adapted an astounding capacity of 10,000 Φ_m over time. As Kevin
Kelly wrote in his book *What Technology Wants*,[6] a sunflower as
a system dissipates its incoming energy 5,000 times more effectively than our Sun with its mere 2 Φ_m capacity.

Schneider and Sagan provide a great example of this capacity at the ecosystem level in *Into the Cool*. Although the Amazon jungle is warmer at the surface of the earth, high altitude

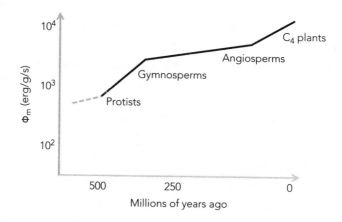

FIGURE 3.2 Plants' Φ_m Ascended Quickly
Plants quickly adapted more efficient energy consuming and dissipating capabilities.
Source: Eric J. Chaisson, *Cosmic Evolution: The Rise of Complexity in Nature*.
Harvard University Press, 2002.

temperature readings show that when measured from the upper atmosphere, the Amazon is actually cooler than the Artic. Why? The Amazon's complex ecosystem structure absorbs, retains, and dissipates the incoming solar energy very efficiently. The Arctic, on the other hand, reflects a lot of energy back into the atmosphere. Measured as a whole system for processing and dissipating energy, the Amazon's rich ecological network consumes, metabolizes, and dissipates solar energy far more efficiently than the barren Arctic.

Keeping up evolution's macroprocessing trend finds animals are even more effective than plants at dissipating energy. Carnivorous animals eat the structured, low entropy chemical energy stored in plants and herbivorous animals. The Φ_m capacities selected for in animals over time are shown in figure 3.3. Animals dissipate structured energy by metabolizing and dissipating the high quality biochemical energy stored in plants and other animals.[7]

Competitive selective pressure acted on animals, selecting for those organisms capable of more effectively metabolizing and dissipating

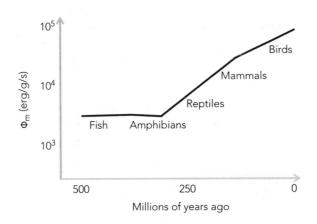

FIGURE 3.3 Animals' Φ_m Ascended Quickly
Animals' Φ_m capabilities became 10 times greater than that of plants.
Source: Eric J. Chaisson, *Cosmic Evolution: The Rise of Complexity in Nature.* Harvard University Press, 2002.

energy. The animals that reproduced most successfully were those with the adapted capabilities to capture and dissipate energy in their given niches.[8] A powerful adapted animal capability was neural cells, which gave individual animals the capability to interact, respond, harvest, and thus metabolize energy from their environment at Φ_m levels as no previous forms of life had done before.

Later nerves aggregated into brains allowing for group behaviors like hunting in packs, knowledge sharing via calling out danger, or signaling for mates at great distances. Neural cells unleashed a flood of adaptive behavioral capabilities. Physical capabilities are a slow method of adaptive change when compared with the adaptive plasticity of even the smallest neural ganglion or brain. Neurons allow physical capabilities to rapidly adapt new patterns of expressed responses and actions. These neurons empowered individual or group capabilities are behavioral traits.

Neural-based behavioral adaptation accelerated everything, and the most effective animal user of these new tools for storing successful patterns of knowledge to drive adaptive capability was the early human. Humans expressed radical new adaptive methods of applying neurons to survive and thrive via the capability to create and store patterned knowledge in the form of ideas and patterns of shared complex languages. Ideas shared orally with language are rather fuzzy; humans soon fixed language into exacting and efficient written symbols. The exactness of written language enabled the next developments of abstracted knowledge, such as science and mathematics. Before science and mathematics, but spurred on by language and knowledge-sharing advances, another evolving past ecological network domain was born: the economy.

Economy

Linking the ecosystem and the economy together in the proper context of evolution's process can help us better understand how the economy functions. The human economy operates within the ecosystem. If there were no bacteria, plants, animals, or people, there would be no economy. The economy is an evolving network of material, energy, knowledge, and linked value flows operating as an extended branch of the ecological network. We can think of the economy as one of the next steps in evolution emerging from the knowledge, beliefs, and behaviors of the human species.

Prehistoric individuals used simple tools and cultural patterns (shared symbolic language and behavior) for hunting and gathering. This culture and technology allowed organized groups to consume and control huge amounts of energy relative to other species. It is pure conjecture, but it can be argued that proto-language use fueled the birth of economy in the form of group relationships, using sophisticated reciprocity and the ability to communicate ideas of fairness, equality, and—importantly—relative value.

Just as energy gradients are seen as the driver of the ecological system, perceived value gradients can be seen as the driver of the economic system. We can think of people as having value gradients that exist in the form of goals, wants, and needs. These value gradients are resolved by trade as the economy delivers goods and services, fulfilling a desired consumer experience.

Early economic dominance was likely tied to biochemical energy capture in the form of food and burnable fuels for warmth. These energy gradient needs correspond to the very lowest level of Maslow's hierarchy, as detailed in chapter 2. Over time, we evolved more efficient ways of creating value. For instance, we farmed because it was likely more effective at creating value than hunting and gathering. As our society evolved further, microeconomic bands of individuals adapted into macroeconomic agricultural societies with increasingly specialized knowledge, skills, and roles. As society advanced, so did the qualitative nature of our value gradients, climbing Maslow's hierarchy. Food and warmth alone were no longer enough. Our ability to resolve higher Maslow values was reflected in the diversity and complexity of new economic outputs. The trading of valued goods and services became a way of swapping accumulated knowledge, materials, and captured/expended energy. At its core, economic trade is a knowledge-based network driven toward maximizing value. The networks of consumers and consumed value flows define an economy.

Larger groups or economic units tend to be more efficient at certain things. With the development of kingdoms and larger politically definable structures like nation-states, value flows increased. The most common way of measuring value flows is via the gross domestic product (GDP),[9] and it's no surprise that the growth of larger socioeconomic states is highly correlated with increasing GDP (value flows). Figure 3.4 displays estimates of accelerating economic growth in terms of annual global GDP flow growth over the last 2,000 years.

Economic value flow and intensive energy utilization and dissipation are correlated. As with life's adaptive systems, economic success involves greater and more efficient energy consumption. As

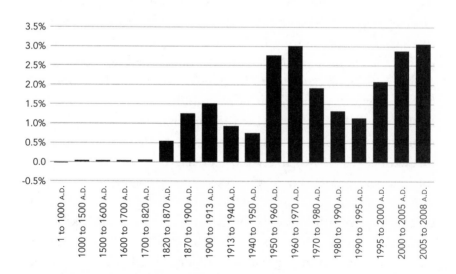

FIGURE 3.4 Annual GDP Growth, 1–2008 A.D.
Source: Angus Maddison

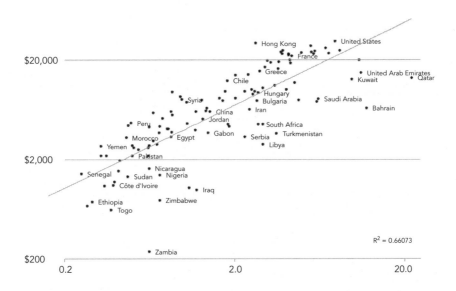

FIGURE 3.5 Annual Per Capita GDP vs. MTOE (Energy)
Source: 2006 OECD (Metric Tons of Oil Equivalent), World Bank adjusted to 1990 GDK $'s w/power law curve fit.

figure 3.5 shows, the annual per capita GDP correlates strongly with annual per capita MTOE (Metric Tonnes of Oil Equivalent) energy consumption per economy (country). The story is clear: Energy consumption is highly correlated with value creation and consumption, which drives value flow throughout the economic network.

So how does the evolutionary process operate within the economy? As with the ecology, selection, amplification, and adaptation still apply. If genes are the predominant unit of information used by the ecology, then we can consider inos—short for the unit of information associated with innovations—to be their informational economic equivalent, as discussed in chapter 2.

Information can be stored in a variety of media. Genes, for instance, can be created from scratch and synthesized as DNA using data stored in a computer memory. Inos can be stored in people's heads, blueprints, patents, or any medium that provides a path to a final, value-delivering expressed structure or form.

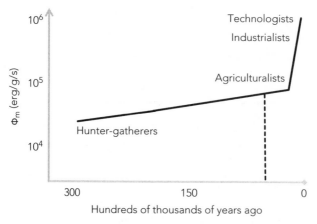

FIGURE 3.6 Economic Φ_m Network Adapted Rapidly
Economic systems adapted to achieve ever greater Φ_m capacities.
Source: Eric J. Chaisson, *Cosmic Evolution: The Rise of Complexity in Nature*.
Harvard University Press, 2002.

Inos, and the cultural knowledge they represent, help individuals and groups reduce and resolve value gradients as they satisfy their wants and needs. Those inos that facilitate the flow of value most efficiently "win," and get amplified throughout the economy.

Larger economic networks of inos are even more effective at capturing and metabolizing energy into value and knowledge. Chaisson's graph (fig. 3.6) shows the story of how economic systems adapted to control and dissipate more energy.

Like ecologies, economies are large macroprocessing networks that adapt increasing metabolic efficiencies for delivering value and capturing energy. Ecologies contain networks of metabolizing organisms; economies contain networks of metabolizing organizations. Both are organized adaptive network structures with increasing metabolic densities. Like most adaptive structures, efficiency either increases or the system dies altogether. Figure 3.7 shows the efficiency of energy consumption relative

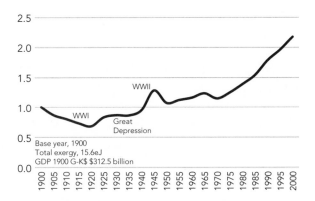

FIGURE 3.7 Exergy Efficiency, 1900–2000
U.S. energy efficiency per dollar of GDP, 1900–2000; normalized to 1.00 in 1900.
Source: Robert U. Ayers and Benjamin Warr, *The Economic Growth Engine: How Energy and Work Drive Material Prosperity*. Edward Elgar.

to value creation in the U.S. economy; as this graph makes clear, the economy adapts as it matures to become a more effective metabolizer of energy and resources.

As figure 3.7 makes clear, it now takes us less energy than ever before to deliver a $1 unit of GDP value. The trend of increasing energy consumption and higher Φ_m values over time is evolution's hallmark across physical, ecological, and economic domains. The economy adapts to increase both dissipative efficiency and flow capacity, just like evolution's other adapting systems do.

As measured by energy throughput, the economy is now evolution's most complex, rapidly evolving structure for dissipating energy ever known. Like the ecology, the economy organizes all addressable energy and knowledge into new forms, with ever-growing dissipative capacities. Value gradients are merely the means to this end. Just as evolution pressured life to adapt more efficient dissipative energy forms, evolution has pushed the economy to evolve many forms of energy dissipation even faster. From microchips to jet engines, the economy has continued the evolutionary process of exponentially increasing its

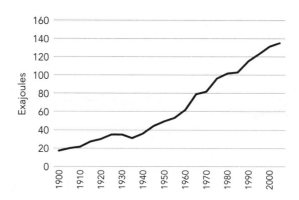

FIGURE 3.8 Total U.S. Energy Consumption, 1900–2004
U.S. total energy consumption (exajoules), 1900–2004.
Source: Robert U. Ayers and Benjamin Warr, *The Economic Growth Engine: How Energy and Work Drive Material Prosperity*. Edward Elgar.

efficiency in capturing and dissipating energy, while at the same time consuming *more* energy as the system expands and the knowledge that it holds grows.[10]

Indeed, economic network adaptation has seen significant increases in global energy utilization. Figure 3.8 highlights the 750 percent growth in U.S. energy consumption from 1900 to 2004—in that time, population grew just 380 percent.

The pattern of increasing energy consumption correlates with increasing GDP (value flow). Even as the population grows, in aggregate humanity has become wealthier, as shown in figure 3.9.

This march of adaptive economic progress brings up a question—what is the next adaptive move? Evolution has pushed beyond DNA-based ecology to ino-based economy, the most effective energy dissipater ever seen. What are the posteconomic structures for energy dissipation? Embedded in the question of evolution posteconomy lies the potential for structures, knowledge, and goals distinct from the climb up Maslow's hierarchy—an intriguing idea called the symbology but beyond

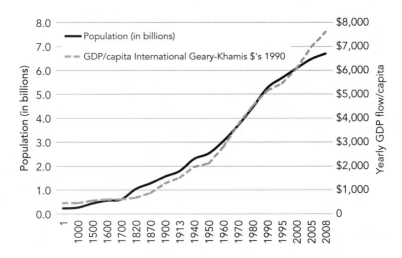

FIGURE 3.9 Global Population and GDP Per Capita, 1–2008 A.D.
Source: Angus Maddison

the scope of this book. (An addendum and discussion forum covering the topic of evolution's posteconomic present—and future—is available at http://www.thenatureofvalue.com.) So, let's take this new understanding of the economy and get practical by exploring how to allocate or invest money into organizations to grow value.

PART II

Inos

CHAPTER FOUR

Knowledge and Innovation

APPLIED KNOWLEDGE CREATES the economic value we experience. Adapted knowledge—innovation—creates the new forms of value that drive economic growth. Adaptation, competitive selection, and replicated knowledge are all the result of evolution at work in the ecology and economy.

In his book *The Selfish Gene*, biologist Richard Dawkins gave people a new way to think about DNA—the knowledge carrier of the biological realm. Genes, Dawkins wrote, can be thought of as selfish. The gene's one aim is to replicate itself, with various organisms acting as mere vehicles to fulfill the gene's objective of replication. The selfish gene rhetorical device helps explain the flow and amplification of successful genetic information throughout the ecological network. Applying the metaphor to economics means replacing "life" with "value," and replacing the biological unit of information, the gene, with its economic equivalent: the ino.

The ino is an informational unit of innovation that has the potential for aiding in value creation. The ino is a piece of economic information, much like the gene is a unit of life information, or the bit is a unit of computational information. The gene, ino, and bit all enable the expression of various capabilities in the domains or contexts within which they function. A life form has physical and behavioral capabilities, determined by its genes, and these traits allow it to compete for resources, capture energy, and replicate. An economic form has capabilities determined by its inos, and these enable it to capture resources, create value, and replicate its inos. Inos, expressed as organizational capabilities, determine how firms convert energy and resources into potential value. Inos' propagation depends on the effectiveness of their value-producing capabilities.

Understanding the ino's role as the original informational unit facilitating value expression is a starting point for understanding the nature of value. The root of every organizational change, large and small, is in the inos. A branding strategy, a product, a business practice, even a slogan—all of these emerge from inos. Of course, understanding the detailed mechanics of inos or genes is not required to appreciate the strength and capabilities of an organization or organism. However, it is good to keep in mind that the changes seen at the macro level are a result of the selective adaptation of these fundamental units.

Genes and Inos

In life's adaptive process, genes are the physical units of information that give organisms the potential to express physical capabilities and behaviors. Genes only survive by delivering capabilities and behaviors that allow an organism to replicate and amplify its genes. Genes that don't deliver winning capabilities don't survive. Genes are the patterns of stored knowledge and incidental changes that accrue from prior selective survival and replication.

Inos work like genes, accruing knowledge plus incremental changes that are expressed as an organization's capabilities. Value-delivering inos reproduce like genes, working through selective, adaptive, and amplifying processes. Inos are combined and swapped to create organizational capabilities and behaviors in the same way that genes combine to create variations on functional organs or limbs for the capability of motion.

Most fundamentally, inos give organizations the potential to deliver value. An ino's impact and survival is measured by how it helps an organization's value-creating and value-delivering capabilities. While most inos are basically benign, occasionally inos can impact whole industries or economies, such as the transistor or the advent of refrigeration. The organizations that most efficiently deliver greater customer value will, by virtue of their success, amplify or replicate their inos and the associated economic survival knowledge. In simpler terms—a successful value-creating ino gets to replicate and amplify itself. An unsuccessful ino, like an unsuccessful gene, is a pattern of decaying information that disappears into the entropic fog. When customers purchase better mousetraps, more of the better mousetraps are made, propagating the inos required for making better mousetraps.[1]

Figure 4.1 illustrates the parallel processes of inos and genes. The components of living organisms and economic organizations are different, but their processes are similar.

However, just because an animal has a certain gene doesn't mean it gains the full possible advantageous capability of the information that gene holds. Genes aren't like computer software; they aren't hard coded, and they aren't expressed identically in every organism. Rather, genes are said to have a potential for expression. Genes express themselves in a probabilistic fashion, and the extent to which they'll promote a certain capability depends on their environmental context and other variables. It's not just because of its genes that an antelope is

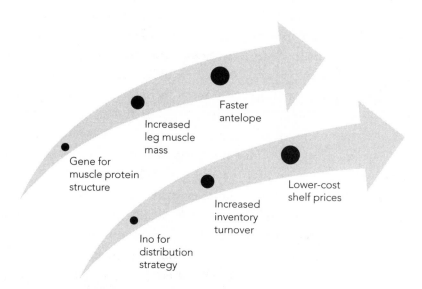

FIGURE 4.1 Genes and Inos Information Units in Different Media
An organism's genes or an organization's inos are the knowledge required to enable their replication.

fast; the antelope's capability for great speed is the outcome of genes, body, and environment working together over many generational cycles of selection. Each organism is a trial run of the gene's effectiveness at expressing and replicating itself, to prove the value of its accumulated survival knowledge. An organism is a collection of genes that together express a solution to resolve the problem of species, organism, and pattern survival. Organizations' inos, likewise, express themselves as potential solutions to the problem of economic survival. The expressed capabilities that act as potential "solutions" for an organism or organization can be thought of as ongoing physical attempts at solving a network optimization problem involving materials, energy, and information in the context of the economy. Thus, the act of living or creating value is a form of macroprocessing these potential solutions. Each oak tree creates tens of thousands of potential solutions to the shifting problem of life—in the form of acorns. On average, one acorn per tree will survive macroprocessing, successfully solving the problem of how to replicate the knowledge associated with surviving and thus creating another oak tree within ecology's network.

To reproduce successfully, an antelope must avoid being lunch for someone else, such as the cheetah. Those antelopes possessing genes for strong muscles and high capacity lungs survive and dominate over many life cycles, creating more fast antelopes and populating an ecology with antelope genes. Not every animal with those genes successfully reproduces, if other environmental factors keep them from doing so. This means that for a specific organism, many useful genes are never expressed successfully. Your genetic potential could make you strong and smart, but if environmental conditions lead to malnourishment during critical stages of childhood development, your strength or intelligence will not reach its full genetic potential. These capabilities or traits would be expressed in a diminished form.

The full expression of inos, too, is dependent on their environmental context. Many inos fail in one economic niche only to succeed in another. For instance, Xerox had the inos for revolutionary value-creating products such as the laser printer, computer mouse, and Ethernet. The great research discoveries at Xerox never expressed their full value delivery potential due to Xerox's organizational and structurally limiting environment. Apple computer ended up successfully expressing Xerox's inos in the first Macintosh computer and Apple LaserWriter printer.

In the same way, new value-creating economic inos may or may not succeed in creating significant value for their originators. The impact of an ino depends on the context and environment in which it is expressed. An ino for using 5 percent less printing ink has more value-producing importance to a specialty printer than a bank. Genes work in the same way. A gene for 2 percent lighter bones may not be reproductively important to a walrus, but could be vital for a bird migrating thousands of miles. Inos, like genes, can only be assessed in the broader context of the advantageous capabilities they create for organizations.

Most new inos are expressed as minor—often unnoticed—changes. But sometimes even these minor changes have big impacts. Apple obsesses over countless details in product design—taking, for instance, three years to develop the iPhone. This design focus leads to great word of mouth marketing, which reduces Apple's marketing budget. In 2011, Apple spent $1.1 billion marketing the iPhone and iPad while generating $67.3 billion in revenues from them.[2] That means 1.63 percent of sales revenue was spent on marketing.

To put Apple's marketing capability edge in perspective: According to a 2009 survey by Marketing Sherpa, large organizations spend up to 6 percent of their revenue on marketing.[3] Apple's inos for design and customer experience leads to fatter profit margins.

Inos and genes are, at their core, simply information. The better the information solves the problem of life or value creation, the more successful the gene or ino. We can think of knowledge as the accumulated flow of information with an increased propensity to replicate across the economy over time. The survival knowledge gets embedded in the physical forms and structures of organizations and organisms.

Of course, it's not always clear if a given ino will create value or not. Innovation is everywhere, but new inos that survive to carry value-creating knowledge are rare. If an industrial baker starts baking bread at 350°F instead of 375°, that 25° change may or may not have big value repercussions for the baker. The baker may save energy, or she may make raw, unsalable bread. If she ends up saving energy, that ino becomes knowledge that allows the baker to create more long-term value and potentially economically dominate a part of the economic network.

Accumulated knowledge and the selective process are essential to adaptive original change. Walmart's low cost edge is the result of competitive pressure and cost-reducing knowledge accumulated over millions of customer purchase cycles and competitive selection iterations. Every trait of Walmart has been created or impacted by earlier successfully selected inos. Walmart's accumulated knowledge, combined with resources such as people, energy, and capital, created Walmart today.

So from where do new inos and capabilities come? Although it may be tempting to think that all value-creating capabilities are completely original, they are actually quite rare—just as genetic mutations that enhance a species survival are extremely uncommon. In ecology, a common form of incremental genetic variation is sexual reproduction, when genetic crossover comingles all the genes between sexes. The rule for adaptive biological systems seems to be slow incremental improvement, with only occasional radical leaps forward; the same is true for the economy. In a study of 7.7 million patents from 1900 to 2005, researchers found that only 0.65 percent of patents could be categorized as originations—technologies not previously in existence. Truly novel combinations, defined as technologies combined in new ways, represented 0.87 percent of all patented inventions. These two most novel categories of invention are rare. Fully 98 percent of the patents studied were recombinations or refinements of earlier inventions (prior accumulated knowledge). In the economy, mutant inos are rare. More often, big ino-enabled chunks of functional knowledge and capabilities are borrowed, shared, and mixed.[4]

Most value-creating knowledge diffuses across economies to be shared by many organizations. One example of this is the open shelf model of food shopping, which was once considered a new and novel innovation. The use of open store shelves in a supermarket was first seen in 1916 at the U.S.-based Piggly Wiggly store. Before 1916, people would go into shops and ask clerks behind a counter to select items for them, similar to visiting a pharmacy or deli counter today. The innovation of an open shelf grocery store quickly caught on for its speed, efficiency, and cost savings. Tesco grocery in the United Kingdom successfully adopted the open store innovation in 1951. Tesco has a history of rapidly adopting value-creating knowledge, and this has served it well; with 440,000 employees, it is the third largest retailer in the world. An example of an innovation that became a standard organizational capability is double entry accounting—a sixteenth century successful ino that is still going strong. Free wireless Internet in coffee shops is a recent example of a minor retail innovation becoming a standard retail capability.

Ino selection leads to knowledge accumulation, which changes companies' structures over time—if they are flexible enough to adapt. In 1975, Apple started manufacturing computers with plywood cases. Nokia started in 1867 as a Finnish lumber company. Neither one started with a competitive capability for mobile phones; instead, both firms adapted mobile phone capabilities that were successfully selected by consumers for a period. These are exceptional examples of successful radical adaptations.

Shared or industry standard inos give limited competitive advantage to a particular business. Some organizations have exclusive inos, such as an original patent or brand, and this leads to a competitive advantage. Inos survive for as long as a host organization expressing them survives. After organizational death, inos decay into randomness unless they have been inherited in other organizations.

Although it is survival knowledge in the form of inos that drives value creation in organizations, focusing on minute units of knowledge or specific expressed capabilities isn't necessarily helpful. This is because specific inos only count relative to their sustainable contribution to an organization's value-creating success. Studying the exact genes of an animal or plant isn't necessarily required to understand what makes it a successful survivor in its niche.

The late physicist and specialist in self-organized critical systems Per Bak—whose specialty was sandpiles—had this to say about focusing on all the small components in complex self-organizing critical systems:

In the critical state, the sand pile is the functional unit, not the single grains of sand. No reductionist approach makes sense. The local units exist in their actual form, characterized for instance by the local slope, only because they are part of the whole. Studying grains of sand under the microscope doesn't give a clue as to what is going on in the whole sandpile. Nothing in the individual grains of sand suggests the emergent properties of the pile.[5]

The atomistic components of a large system, in other words, are less interesting than their aggregate behaviors. These aggregate behaviors can be unpredictable yet still exhibit general patterns of behavior. For instance, occasionally inos combine or cascade into one another, creating chain reactions of knowledge amplification and diffusion through an economy. The inos for the just-in-time (JIT) manufacturing process are an example of this. The JIT process amplified the value of whole supply chains as organizations adapted it, creating value across entire economies. The sandpile graphic (fig. 4.2) represents an ino

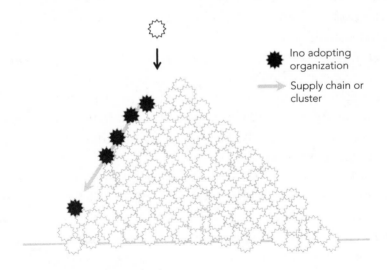

Ino adopting organization

Supply chain or cluster

FIGURE 4.2 Inos Cascade Through the Economy
Innovation diffusion cascades through the economic network's links.

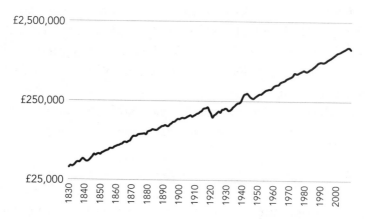

FIGURE 4.3 UK GDP, 1830–2012
UK value flow GDP in £ millions
Source: Hills, Sally, Ryland Thomas, and Nicholas Dimsdale. "The UK recession in context—what do three centuries of data tell us?" *Quarterly Bulletin*, Bank of England, Q4 2010.

spreading or diffusing knowledge through the economy. Inos trickle into firms constantly, like grains of sand falling onto a pile. Most inos don't affect the pile much. But occasionally a big avalanche occurs.

Cumulatively, feedback has a bias toward the accumulation of knowledge (winning inos) for greater value delivery and flow. Economy-wide knowledge contributes to increased value flow capacity in GDP/capita, which ultimately leads to progressively increasing GDP, as seen with the GDP of the United Kingdom in figure 4.3.

Because the aggregate patterns are so much more meaningful than their component parts, it's useful to focus on the bigger picture. We acknowledge the ino as a facilitating mechanism, but our focus on value is not served by overly reductionist analysis of each ino's expressed outcome. This would be similar to tracking the history of every acorn falling from an oak tree. Our focus will be on the next level up the panarchy from inos—the capabilities formed by expressed inos.

New Capabilities Lead to New Offerings

Inos combine to express new capabilities, and these new capabilities create new forms and behaviors in life and value. In economy, these newly expressed capabilities show up as adaptive explosions or radiations of products and services.

Organizational capabilities live or die in competitive environments shaped by customer choice. Like flowers using different chemical smells and colors to compete for the value of a bee's pollination services, organizations compete for customer value selection with products and services. Economic selection occurs at the point of purchase.

The competitive and selective feedback process is the engine of economic adaptation. Winning organizational capabilities and knowledge are amplified, whereas nonselected forms disappear into the corporate fossil record. Adaptation of new inos (and their associated expressed capabilities) is how the economy explores what is possible. Selection prunes the network's ever-growing possibility paths, revealing the winning solutions.

Adaptation over iterative cycles leads to complexity and a diversity of forms and functions. One of the most famous graphics of adaptive biological knowledge is Charles Darwin's finches (fig. 4.4). Selective pressure pushed each finch species beak to adapt, and over many reproductive cycles, to become more efficient at eating specific food types found on various islands. Each new species represented a bifurcation from the ancestral finch, developing a specialized set of genes that increased their reproductive success.

We see this adaptive bifurcating process unfold in the economy as well. Adding value to the most basic human function of sitting

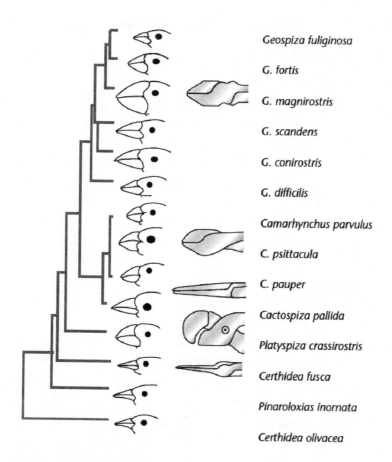

FIGURE 4.4 Darwin's Finches
Phylogram of Darwin's finches based on microsatellite length variation. Birds are drawn at approximately actual size. Horizontal branch lengths represent genetic distance. The beak shapes of Darwin's finches are compared to different types of pliers. *Source*: Redrawn from Petran et al. (1999) and Bowman (1961). Source: Michaela Hau and Martin Wikelski. 2001. "Darwin's Finches," *Encyclopedia of Life Sciences*. Nature Publishing Group.

leads to a multitude of adapted design and organizational capabilities, creating multiple forms of the chair (fig. 4.5). There is even a book celebrating this proliferation of forms called *The Taxonomy of Chairs*. Each chair that's produced reflects an organization's knowledge of design and manufacturing capabilities, and

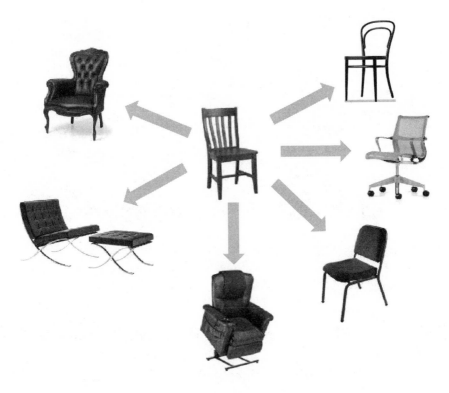

FIGURE 4.5 Taxonomy of Chairs

the most successful organizations are those that have adapted to be the most efficient at creating and capturing customer value in the form of chair purchases.

These same bifurcating structures, caused when inos enable new capabilities and forms, also occur in more sophisticated products such as airplanes. Each aircraft seen in figure 4.6 was produced in an attempt to harvest economic value by ino's serving a unique customer need or economic network niche. Many of these economic forms are extinct, although some of their inos survived as the knowledge inherited by future generations of aircraft manufacturing organizations.

Adaptive bifurcation is also seen within firms, as products adaptively radiate through distribution channels. Starting as a single product in 1866, Coca-Cola sold nine drinks per day in its first year.

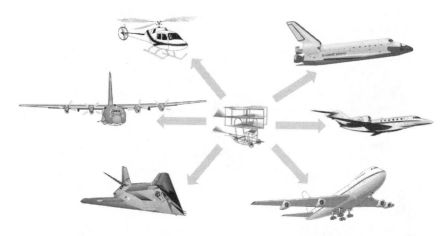

FIGURE 4.6 Taxonomy of Aircraft
Aircraft taxonomy: value-capturing knowledge adaptively radiates into more complex and effective forms.

By 2012, it had more than 3,500 brands, with 1.7 billion 8-oz. servings of Coca-Cola consumed globally each day. Coke's value-creating brand and product ino adaptations form a vast network with a diverse geographic reach. Coke's value-creating capabilities have spread globally like a wildly prolific species populating a new niche. Procter & Gamble, Nestlé, and PepsiCo behave the same way, using their knowledge of global brand and distribution channels to offer portfolios of new products.

The competitive process of selection, combined with exponential growth or amplification, leads to adaptation for efficiency and fitness. In life, increased flows and adaptation create a bifurcation into different expressed physical forms and behaviors, as mentioned in chapter 2 and seen in figure 2.2.

As more throughput flows through an adaptive system, the system itself accumulates knowledge and splits or bifurcates into new forms, becoming increasingly structurally and/or behaviorally complex—as with Darwin's finches.[6] The theory of how bifurcation unfolds as a function of processed throughput is known as Constructal theory, as introduced in chapter 3. According to its creator, Adrian Bejan, Constructal theory relates a system's throughput rate and the system's form mathematically. The Constructal law reads:

> For a finite-size system to persist in time (to live), it must evolve in such a way that it provides easier access to the imposed currents that flow through it.[7]

For example, the U.S. highway road infrastructure network built in the 1910s couldn't handle the volume of road traffic by the 1950s. In 1956, a new form of highway network, The Dwight D. Eisenhower National System of Interstate and Defense Highways, familiarly known as the interstate highway system and modeled on Germany's autobahn, allowed for increased economic flow capacity.[8]

Occasionally, a change in capability creates a rapid explosion in species variety, as a species splits and expresses radically new capabilities and those in turn create and explore new ecological niches. In ecology, the most well-known genetic explosion in life form variety was the Cambrian explosion 580 million years ago. Seemingly from nowhere, bizarre new species and forms began showing up in life's network, with mammals arriving only 65 million years ago. Occasionally, a collection of inos and knowledge does the same thing. The nineteenth century Industrial Revolution is an example of innovation leading to an explosion in new forms of value creation. The rapidly adapting ino knowledge—expressed as steam engines, cheaper steel, electric motors, and telegraphs—transformed economic networks and the world in an explosive informational macroprocess, and continues to unfold to this day.

Summary

We have seen how inos, expressed as capabilities, are selected for their value-creating potential, and successful inos accumulate as knowledge. Over time these capabilities take on myriad forms as organizations pursue economic survival through value delivery.

Accumulated knowledge and inos change as organizational capabilities adapt over many sales cycles and inos diffuse into the economic network to deliver value-adding goods and services.

The most effective inos, like the most efficient genes, replicate and amplify themselves in an attempt to capture customer and corporate value. Inos are everywhere, exerting a constant competitive pressure to deliver more value. In the right context, this selective pressure expresses itself as value creation and capture for the host organization and society. In the next section, we look more deeply at the capabilities that give companies sustainable, value-creating advantages. Understanding the nature of sustainable, unique capabilities is of particular interest to the value investor.

CHAPTER FIVE

How Innovative Capabilities Enable Value Creation

UNIQUE CAPABILITIES that can provide a competitive advantage and a propensity for reproductive success are the only ones that count for organisms or organizations. A lobster may grow an extra eye, which is certainly unique but may not provide an advantage in the gene replication game. By the same token, a furniture store may decide to open a drive-through window for ordering, but it probably won't help the chances for replicating the store's accumulated inos. Thus not all inos become sustainable knowledge; those inos that don't increase their propensity for information survival and replication don't add value to an organization's accumulated knowledge. By the fact that new capabilities consume resources, they may actually be detrimental to existing knowledge and its fight against decay. On the other hand, uniquely advantageous capabilities, such as a cheaper distribution system or unique product performance, give a value-capturing edge versus the competition. Companies are shaped and defined by unique competitive advantages.

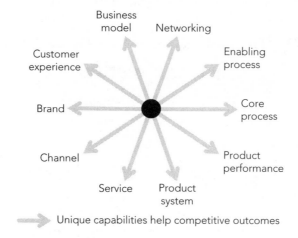

FIGURE 5.1 Ten Types of Innovation Capability

Charting advantageous capabilities is a good way to show how a company creates extra value. The innovation strategy firm The Doblin Group has identified ten categories of business innovation capabilities.[1] By quantifying 3,000 innovations from thirty years of data across various industries, Doblin built a large quantified database of innovations and their value-creating impacts. Doblin research indicates that companies with multiple unique capabilities acting in concert across categories or types are the key to sustainable value creation. The ten capability types are mapped in figure 5.1.

To explore these, let's imagine how a lemonade stand business could use these ten capability types to deliver and differentiate its products and services. These examples are rather whimsical but show how even simple capabilities may differentiate a business so that it earns higher margins, creating and capturing more value for customers and shareholders.

1. Business model innovation—innovation in how a business makes money: Big M lemonade sells discounted lemonade through coupons for five gallon family sized jugs of

lemonade. They also allow customers to pay with PayPal or Bitcoin.

2. Networking innovation—joining other businesses for mutual benefit: Ned's lemonade stand is vertically integrated with an orchard and sells lemons to other vendors wholesale.

3. Enabling process—innovation in how a business supports its own core processes and workers: Elva's Lemonade distinguishes itself by being sold by Elva, who runs it as a cooperative. Her customers are certain "her" lemonade tastes better than big brands.

4. Core process—innovation in a business's core offerings: Crazy Pete's has a machine that can juice and mix faster and cheaper than anyone else's. He juices for noncompetitors.

5. Product performance—innovation in the design of core offerings: Paul's Power Lemonade has fiber added, which is a big hit with the older crowd and sells for a premium.

6. Product system—linking multiple products: Sallie's Educational Lemonade System is a kit (lemons, sugar, and booklet) that teaches kids how to run a lemonade business in their neighborhoods.

7. Service—providing value beyond the product itself: Le Chateau du Citron charges a premium for each glass of hand-crafted lemonade, served on silver trays.

8. Channel—innovation in getting offerings to the market: Charlie's Squeeze-o-rama delivers lemonade direct to the customer's door. Charlie's also sells its lemonade at lemonade parties hosted by groups of friends.

9. Brand—innovation in communicating offerings: WYFLI Lemonade runs a marketing campaign around its WYFLI (Well! Your Friends Like It) positioning. It's a hit with younger audiences seeking recognition for drinking what's cool. WYFLI is served in big Day-Glo cups, so the other kids can see who is drinking it.

10. Customer experience—innovation in how customers feel interacting with a business: Organic Citron imports Organic European lemons and aims to evoke its customers' memories or dreams of lemonade consumed in exotic locations by featuring glasses with pictures of lemon tree orchards, Rome, and Paris on the side.

The ten types of innovation capability represent how companies conceive, finance, produce, process, distribute, position, sell, and get paid. The connection between product offerings and capabilities can be visualized as an innovation iceberg (fig. 5.2). Most people only consciously consider the visible product attributes. This isn't accidental; many firms hide or protect their knowledge edge as trade secrets.

As mentioned, the Doblin innovation group indicates that multiple advantaged capabilities improve long-term value creation.

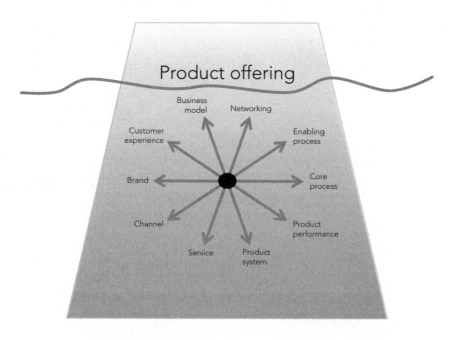

FIGURE 5.2 Innovation Iceberg

In his book *Ten Types of Innovation*, Larry Keeley of Doblin Group shows that organizations that express five or more types of unique innovative capability outperformed the S&P 500 by 100 percent over the 2007–2011 period.[2] Multiple unique capabilities diversify risk, so when one unique capability is adapted by competitors to become an industry norm, margin erosion is hopefully minimized. A product or service with many unique value-adding capabilities may create a sustained competitive advantage.

Charting an organization's unique capabilities helps the investor understand the firm's potential for value creation. The more unique, value-creating capabilities a firm has, the higher and more sustainable the margins are likely to be. Figures 5.3 and 5.4 plot the unique capabilities of two firms—General Motors in 2012, and Walmart in the 1970s to 1980s. Although these plots can be helpful in getting a big-picture understanding of an organization, it's important to keep in mind that these diagrams—called capability footprints—are crude estimates of unique capabilities that change over time. Key offerings and capabilities need to be examined in some detail.

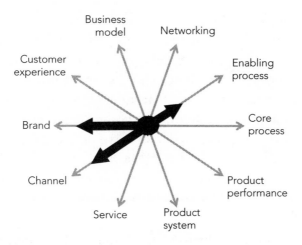

FIGURE 5.3 GM 2012 Unique Capability Footprint

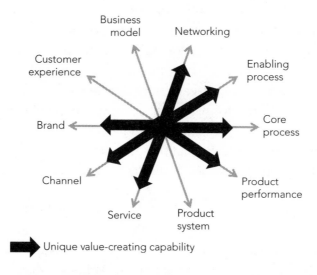

FIGURE 5.4 Walmart Footprint, 1970–1980s
Walmart's unique innovation capability footprint from 1970–1980s propelled Walmart's stellar growth.

General Motors (GM) was a force to be reckoned with years ago, but as this crude plot shows, GM's current unique capabilities may be limited. General Motors has a unique historical brand portfolio, allowing it to extract margins from some repeat clients. However, many of its other capabilities are not unique and thus don't contribute to excess sustained returns on capital. General Motors's recent bankruptcy and bailout reflect its diminished state.

Walmart, on the other hand, accumulated knowledge and inos that led to unique capabilities, which in turn allowed for amazing value creation and growth for both customers and shareholders in the 1970s and 1980s. Walmart possessed an impressive array of unique capabilities, and each new one amplified Walmart's value-creating capability. More specifically:

1. Networking: Walmart's merchandise flow allowed for uniquely strong negotiating power and relationships with

fast-moving consumer goods (FMCG) producers, leading to cost reductions and operational efficiencies.

2. Enabling process: The volumes and flows through Walmart's stores allowed for enhanced efficiencies across the organization.

3. Core processes: Walmart's distribution, logistics, and information capture, all integrated with suppliers, was unparalleled. They now run the world's second largest private logistics operation, behind only the U.S. military.

4. Product performance: The product performance, as measured by price and the ease of one-stop shopping, was unparalleled at the time.

5. Channel: Walmart had a geographic advantage in the retail channels it chose to compete against, namely, small town main street retailers.

6. Brand: The brand emphasized consistently low prices, which was unique relative to main street retailers that stressed service, selection, and familiarity.

7. Customer experience: Walmart customer experience— huge warehouses with merchandise piled high—were new experiences at the time. Walmart allowed for a unique single visit slightly out of town that replaced multiple store visits in the center of town. It focused on "friendly" people to create a personal atmosphere to compete with local small town stores.

8. Service: Walmart offered low service relative to local retailers. This conscious unique capability choice of minimal service effectively weeded out the customers who required high service while allowing for lower prices and higher margins.

These capability footprints show what can be called an organization's "morphology." In biology, morphology is the form an organism's capabilities take—four legs, a set of wings, scales,

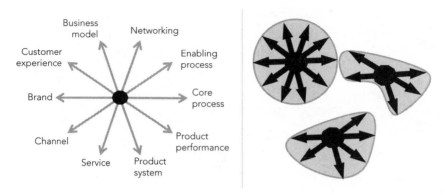

FIGURE 5.5 Organization Morphology
Unique competitive capabilities define organizational morphology (shape and behavior).

and so on. Cats and dogs are both mammals, but their form and behaviors are very different; they have different morphologies. Businesses morphologies are also determined by their capabilities and competitive behaviors. Morphologies are the result of accumulated knowledge, behaviors, and environmental factors that interact over many product and consumption cycles (fig. 5.5). Seven-Eleven convenience stores evolved a different morphology from Walmart stores, which are different from regular grocery stores. The basic retail components are all there; they are just expressed in different scales and forms.

Understanding the unique capabilities and morphology of an organization helps the allocator define a firm's potential for value creation.

Experience Curves

When you're first learning to ride a bike, the feeling is new and the experience is difficult. But the more you try, the easier it gets. You learn by doing.

The process of producing goods and services works the same way. The more one does it, the easier it gets. Knowledge accumulates as firms and economies learn to do things more efficiently.

This praxis—or learning by doing—creates knowledge-based efficiency that shows up as a downward curved cost line driven by value flow through an economic system. The slope of the line indicates the rate of decline in production cost. Organization and economic networks adapt efficiencies, becoming more structurally complex, creating greater varieties of products and services. They also become more efficient at delivering customer value and managing both material and value throughput. This increased value-delivering efficiency effect is called the experience curve.

Advantageous capabilities drive the cost-reducing efficiencies of experience curves. The following are some well-known examples of innovation capabilities that contribute to experience curve effects. Most are information or knowledge driven.

- Improved equipment use: As total production increases, manufacturing equipment is more fully exploited, lowering unit costs. At volume, purchase of more productive equipment can be justified.
- Resource optimization: As a company acquires experience, it can alter its mix of inputs, becoming more efficient and resilient.
- Labor praxis (learning by doing): Workers and managers get better by learning, experimenting, and making mistakes.
- Network building and use-cost reductions (network effects): As products enter widespread use, consumers use them more efficiently. One e-mail account in the world had limited value, but if everyone has one, they build an efficient communication network. Cars and roads worked the same way.
- Product form redesign: Manufacturers and consumers improve value delivery with adaptive designs.

- Shared experiences: Experience curve effects are reinforced as more products share common activities or resources. An efficiency learned from one product gets applied to other products. It's easy to use an iPad if you have used an iPhone.
- Standardization, specialization, and method improvements: As processes, parts, and products are standardized, efficiency increases.
- Technology-driven knowledge: Automated production introduces efficiencies as new technologies are implemented and people learn how to use them.

Improving inos as economic inputs show up everywhere, but their individual impacts are mostly small and difficult to measure or see. Inos are like individual atoms, impossible to easily track by the investor or allocator. They show up in aggregate as cost reduction outputs. As mentioned in chapter 4, it is better to measure inos' impacts in large bunches. Experience curves become an important tool for measuring an organization's value delivery performance because they are trajectories of required improvement. Experience curves measure the effect of random inos accumulating as knowledge over long-term volumes of value flows. These curves reflect evolution's ascending drive for flow efficiency and growth, and come to define the efficiencies required for survival.[3]

The experience curve effect was discovered and quantified in 1936 at Wright Patterson Airforce Base while studying airplane manufacturing.[4] It was found that each doubling of throughput in airplane production volume drove efficiency gains of 10 to 15 percent. The more units being made or flowing through the system, the cheaper they each were to produce, due to accumulated knowledge and efficiency effects. The airplane experience curve effect occurred regardless of production scale; it was a function of aggregate unit value flow.

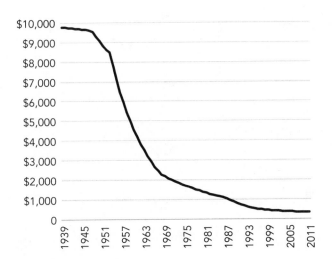

FIGURE 5.6 TV Cost Declined Over Time
The cost of a television declined as knowledge was applied to grow value.
Graph interpolated using data from: http://www.theawl.com/2011/ 11/how-much-more-do-televisions-cost-today.

Generally, then, experience curves mean that each doubling in the number of widgets leads to each widget's cost declining X percent. Long-term historical unit volume data are difficult to collect so unit cost is often plotted over time to show experience curve effects. Figure 5.6 shows the cost of television production as an example.

Over time, televisions are produced on average 4.85 percent more efficiently per year. In some industries, the experience curve is even more accelerated. Moore's law, commonly expressed in time rather than unit flow, is a well-known experience curve rule in the computer industry. It stipulates efficiency gains of 100 percent every 18 months. Although Moore's law is impressive, gene sequencing efficiencies are even more notable, accelerating at more than 1,000 percent annually. Figure 5.7 highlights the capability impacts of Moore's law across time and technologies.

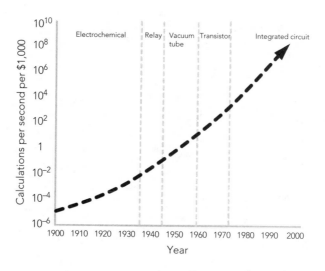

FIGURE 5.7 Moore's Law Over Time and Forms
Moore's law: adaptive capability expressing value and increasing Φ_m over time.
Note that this is a semi-logarithmic plot.
Source: Based on Ray Kurzweil's fifth paradigm chart.

Experience curves show the powerful forces creating and destroying once-viable knowledge and capabilities. If a single firm can capture all these new advantages, it may achieve a long-term adaptive edge for value capture.

Experience curve effects don't always create a single corporate winner. In most industries, the experience curve puts competitors on a forced efficiency march, requiring ever-lower prices or higher quality in their competitive offerings. This forces competitors to redefine markets with increased volume; otherwise, firms die. The experience curve effect is particularly important for the allocator to take into account, as it can make competition for survival so fierce that most competitors lose rapidly.

In most cases, even as individual firms fail, society wins, benefiting from increasingly efficient value flows and the creation of new products. The value and efficiency gains caused by experience curves are remarkable; table 5.1 highlights some of these gains.

Table 5.1
Work Hours Required to Purchase Various Items, 1895 vs. 1997

	1895	2000	Productivity Multiple
Horatio Alger books (6 volumes)	21	0.6	3,500%
One-speed bicycle	260	7.2	3,611%
Cushioned office chair	24	2	1,200%
100-piece dinner set	44	3.6	1,220%
Cane rocking chair	8	1.6	500%
Gold locket	28	6	467%
Encyclopedia Britannica	140	33.8	4.100%
Steinway piano	2,400	1,108	220%
12 oranges	2	0.1	1,900%
1 pound of ground beef	0.8	0.2	300%
1 gallon of milk	2	0.25	700%

Source: Bradford J. DeLong. *Cornucopia: Increasing Wealth in the Twentieth Century.*

The costs of knowledge-intensive technology goods, driven by Moore's law, fall even faster than those in table 5.1. The amount of knowledge and economic value creation is exciting, but as mentioned before, these innovative forces are also incredibly dangerous for the allocator as they can make it difficult to select a long-term winner in a fast-moving industry. Industries with short, fast capability cycles are often unstable for organizational and shareholder value capture. This is the paradox of innovation; the better the economic network gets at creating knowledge and value, the harder it gets for individual firms to sustainably capture value.

Sustainable unique capabilities are the key to corporate value creation—just as unique innovation from competitors is the key to destroying corporate value. As industries grow, some businesses may be positioned to capture the value through scale-activated capacities such as bulk purchasing, more efficient distribution, or more marketing dollars. These advantages can become virtuous feedback loops, where faster macroprocessing of value flow leads to greater advantage. Costco and Walmart, for instance, used these efficiency capabilities to fuel their growth. These value-creating positive feedback loops are called "lollapaloozas" by Charlie Munger. These are explored in depth elsewhere in this chapter.

Increased competition and value flow accelerates experience curve effects. The more competition is present, the more organizations seek advantages and unique capabilities. This desire for value creation drives bifurcation, and can be a matter of organizational life or death. If the efficiency curve is driven by upstream suppliers, there may be limited competitive advantage for any downstream player. Lower supply costs may increase margin pressure on everyone, forcing the consolidation of competitors. The PC business experienced consolidation in the 1990s–2000s as price points moved from thousands to hundreds of dollars. The available dollars-per-unit profit shrank proportionately.

Allocating to markets with stable volumes and low price sensitivity is like playing musical chairs. The music goes faster as everyone runs around passing more value to customers, while over time smaller generic competitors keep disappearing. To survive, smaller companies must focus on specialized niche offerings or exit the market.

In ecology, as the weak die, there is more food or available energy resource left for the survivors. Experience curve effects that are uniquely tied to one firm mean that a winner tends to win even more. As weaker competitors exit, the customer's choice set shrinks. This means stronger negotiating positions and better margins for survivors as they capture more market share and compete with fewer firms. Experience curve effects that are driven by one or a few firms are very interesting from an investing standpoint, and allocators should be on the lookout for the opportunities offered by firms like this.

Allocating in the Face of Negative Optionality

Innovation, as suggested, is both a giver and a destroyer of value. The entrepreneur—and society—sees innovation as a positive option that can potentially deliver new forms of value. But innovation expressed outside one's own firm is a negative option viewed from the firm's perspective. A competitor's positive option can kill other firms. This negative optionality is unpredictable and extremely difficult to avoid. The allocator must guess the scope and scale of negative options that may be created by others. Firms with well-known fat margins can become negative option magnets, attracting entrepreneurs.

Businesses that rely on a single unique capability for market share or margins are highly vulnerable to negative optionality (we explore businesses like this in chapter 6, in the discussion of "hero products"). Many technology firms fall into this category, and thus are weak candidates for sustainable value creation and capital allocation. Paradoxically, many of these firms are mispriced at high earnings multiples.

Negative options look like radical innovation to existing competitors. James M. Utterback, an MIT professor of innovation, has done in-depth innovation research and said the following about radical innovation and corporate death.

> A product's life could end quite suddenly with the appearance of a radical new competing product that invades and quickly conquers the market. Not many firms have the dexterity to retool their capabilities in order to survive successive waves of innovation. Over the life of a product, few of the firms that enter the market to produce the product survive. Firms holding the largest market share in one generation of a product or process seldom appear in the vanguard of competition in the next.[5]

Lurking within rapidly adapting sectors is the allocator's nightmare; sudden organizational and value death. Negative optionality and adaptive ino pressure play a huge role in the microprocessor sector. Just as biologists study fruit flies because of their short life spans, microprocessors are in an extremely fast adaptive sector, which can demonstrate in years lessons that would take decades of study in slower adaptive cycle sectors.

In a highly technical sector, one might assume that an entrepreneurial firm with sophisticated technology, a large knowledge base, piles of cash, and a focus on research and development (ino exploration) would become dominant in product development and innovation. But, as a study by Rebecca Henderson and Kim Clark that examined five generations of microprocessor-related technology has shown, no firm that led in one generation of products figured prominently in the next. As they explained it, innovations in such sectors "destroy the usefulness of the architectural knowledge of established firms, and since architectural knowledge tends to become embedded in the structure and information-processing procedures of established organizations, this destruction is difficult for firms to recognize and hard to correct."[6] Motorola, Nokia, and BlackBerry are examples of failed architectural leaps into the smart phone space.

This means that, surprisingly, no technology leader managed to hold onto the lead in the next iteration. For an investor in the technology sector, the leading firm must provide incredibly high returns on equity due to the short value-creating life span. Innovation-led companies are often severely overpriced, with little regard for the forces of negative optionality that lead to short life spans. Looking at the big picture over time makes this obvious. Focusing on today's single "lottery ticket" firm ignores the silent negative options held by others.

Why call this a lottery ticket? In highly uncertain environments, capital plus a huge uncertainty premium must return to the investor rapidly, within one or two product cycles. Such capital allocations aren't investments. They are bets, with a small chance of success. These popular bets are too uncertain and often too highly priced for serious investing consideration.[7]

Many growth- and technology-focused investors unknowingly invest in lottery tickets. The gambler in the search engine cluster in early 1998 would likely have invested in large dominant firms like Yahoo! or Ask Jeeves. Both were marginalized by Google, which didn't even exist until late 1998. Fast cycle, lottery ticket investing is best left to others.

History is filled with famous lottery ticket betters. The author Mark Twain was an early venture capitalist. He correctly saw the potential of the early typewriter, and invested in it. The typewriter flourished as a smash hit product for over a century, but the particular firm Twain bet on didn't last long. Twain lost so much money he was forced to go on a global speaking tour to recoup his losses.

Investors should beware, as well, of firms that are pushing innovation simply for the sake of innovation. This is usually nothing more than costly activity, driven by fear, masquerading as productivity. Bad innovation like this happens all the time, and is endemic at firms where analysts, boards of directors, and shareholders insist on "pushing the envelope" and keeping up with R&D initiatives regardless of the return on invested capital (ROIC). Activity like this may push share prices up in the short term, but it does not create value.

Some innovation races have negative impacts on entire GDPs, when capital resources spent on competition spiral out of control relative to value. Competition can produce remarkable value, but blindly aggressive competition and allocating resources to chase pipe dreams or social positioning goods can be value destructive for competitors and investors. In the worst-case scenarios, this can impact the economy as a whole, such was seen in mortgage banking innovation and consumer real estate from 2003 to 2007. In such situations, the human, capital, and material resources wasted on competing and short-term "winning" have major social impacts such as recessions, GDP contractions, and long-term unemployment.

Summary

We have seen how inos and accumulated knowledge enable new organizational capabilities, just like genes enable new biological capabilities. These capabilities let firms compete to survive and capture value by offering customers more value relative to competing choices. As goods and services flow through organizations and the economy, the competition for value-creating capabilities typically leads to increasing efficiencies and net positive outcomes for society as a whole.

Experience curve effects deliver increasing value-delivery efficiency using accumulated knowledge that is associated with adaptive cycles. Organizations that can sustainably capture excess value without succumbing to negative optionality are good for capital allocation.

CHAPTER SIX

Allocating to Firms with a Unique Capability Mix

A FIRM'S MIX OF CAPABILITIES determines its survival chances in the economic wilds. Companies focused on one unique capability or product are vulnerable to negative option forces. Firms possessing many categories of unique capabilities have a greater chance to grow and thrive.

For the capital allocator studying an organization or project, the first thing to look for is survival potential, and the second is the organization's ability to thrive. This can be distilled to a handy maxim: First, don't lose value-creating capabilities, and second, make those capabilities grow. New technology and innovation is exciting, as it is the future and evolution's path of progress. However, the desire to purchase a ticket to tomorrow can make one forget about the twisting unpredictable journey. One trap many investors fall into is the beautiful lie of the hero product that will deliver sustained value and wealth.

Hero products aren't always products; they are organizations or projects based around a single all-powerful capability. Going to market with a single unique capability out of the ten Doblin capabilities is equivalent to betting on a new mousetrap being the best one ever to be built. The hero product approach works until the slightly better mousetrap innovation comes along to charm the customer's ever-roving eye.

Firms need many types of unique value-adding capability. The more types of unique capabilities a firm's goods and services offer, the longer it may dominate competitors. To use a biological metaphor, it is one thing to be the fastest frog in the pond. It's another to be the fastest, healthiest, best-looking, strongest, most fertile, and most metabolically efficient frog in the pond. Ideally, a firm should have long-term advantages in each of the ten innovation capability categories, with each capability impossible to replicate by competitors for the foreseeable future.

If an industry is filled solely with hero products, the best decision the allocator can make is to stay away from that industry altogether. As a former hedge fund analyst, I researched hundreds of firms and technologies across the renewable energy sector in 2007. I found no companies worthy of investment. Here is a small part of the story I can share.

The photovoltaic (PV) solar cell industry from 2000 to 2010 was filled with hero companies. Solar cell customers focused exclusively on a single capability metric: dollars per watt of electricity produced. The cheaper a cell generates watts, the better. Shares from PV companies were sold to investors based on their unique and particular approach to solar cell technology that reduced cost per watt of electricity generated. These heroic capabilities included thin film, lower silicon usage, cheaper or more exotic materials, and other innovations that each cut the cost of producing solar electricity. The PV solar cell industry became a siren song for many entrepreneurs and investors. Companies were drawn in by the promise of fantastic global growth. Of course, the expectation of huge volume and revenue growth was widely shared, meaning that each solar cell entrant would reduce the potential prize and possibility of winning for other entrants. Each firm basked in the

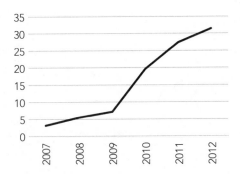

FIGURE 6.1 Installed Solar PV Market in Gigawatts
Source: National Renewable Energy Labs (NREL)

glow of its own brilliant capabilities, while other entrants' negative optionality was mostly ignored.

First the good news: Many of the new ino-expressed technologies worked as promised. The perceived prize of a multi-gigawatt (GW), multi-billion dollar global market became real. In the early 2000s, the solar industry projected fantastic growth rates of more than 50 percent a year for years to come, and this proved correct. The amazing volume growth is shown in figure 6.1. A gigawatt is 1 billion watts of solar power—equivalent to a large coal plant. Volume growth in watt capacity flow grew 800 percent over five years, as shown in the figure.

Next, the bad news for individual investors: Many of these technologies worked as promised. Each organization struggled to maintain hero status by becoming the cheapest provider. Each heroic role was short-lived due to experience curve forces that reduced the minimum viable solar cell electricity production cost. When the race started in the 1950s, costs were measured in the thousands of dollars per watt. Even in the 1970s costs were still in the hundreds of dollars per watt. By 2012 the costs were down to nearly $1 per watt. Evolution's adaptive selective forces had accumulated the knowledge and capabilities to produce ever cheaper solar electricity (fig. 6.2). The selection pressure

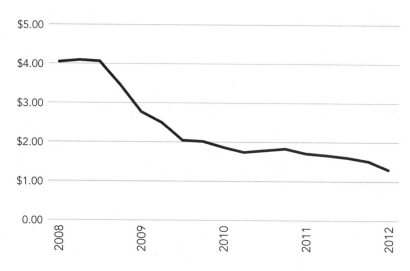

FIGURE 6.2 U.S. Solar Panel Average Price ($/watt)

intensified, allowing only larger international survivors. The mix and rate of capabilities, speed, capital, and raw technical talent was awe inspiring—but although many heroic technologies performed as promised, the investors were mostly wrong.

As this case demonstrates, great technology and monstrous market growth do not always equate to sustainable value creation. A few companies made money from the solar gold rush, but in aggregate most fell among the rocks. The value of a company is based first on its ability to deliver excess value, and second on the duration of that value-delivering ability. Many solar cell companies didn't survive long.

Single-capability firms' lifetimes can often be measured in technology cycles. If a firm misses a cycle, customers move on. Some examples of hero capability products include the Motorola Razor phone, Zune MP3 player, Blu-ray players, and now TiVo. The "safe" solar index investor whose story is told in figure 6.3 lost out, as did many who bet on single-capability heroes. Who won this race for cheap solar power value creation? The answer

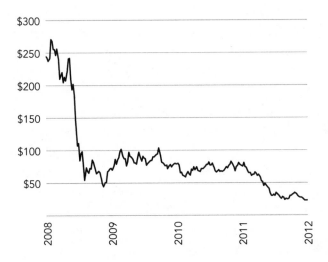

FIGURE 6.3 Global Solar Energy Index Exchange Traded Fund (ETF) Symbol [Ticker Symbol of the Fund (TANFT)]

is simple. We did. Society now has the accumulated knowledge and capability to deliver incredibly cheap solar electricity that gets cheaper by the day. In many parts of the world, solar electricity is a cheaper or better alternative for energy.

How can the capital allocator win these competitions? Again, the answer is simple. Go on vacation. Stay away from hyped hero product firms and sectors. Single-capability value-generating processes are not smart value allocation bets; they are venture capital bets. A single-capability bet is too uncertain and filled with negative optionality. Step away from the siren song. Chain yourself to the mast if you must and put wax in your ears to avoid the serenade of CNBC, venture capitalists (VCs), and brokers or analysts with hot tips on amazing growth opportunities.

Multiple unique capabilities are more likely to be enduring value creators. It is tougher for evolution's adaptive inos to erode multiple advantages. Some multi-capability strategies are called "ecosystem strategies," in which webs of capabilities, relationships, and offerings provide multiple competitive advantages.

Many large technology and fast-moving consumer goods (FMCG) firms use ecosystem strategies to create unique competitive capability sets, fostering many relationships with each customer rather than betting on one-off hero products. Ecosystem strategies use multiple points of customer value delivery and perception, linked into a network of reinforcing capabilities. Technology giants such as Amazon, Google, Apple, Facebook, and others use ecosystem strategies. Fast-moving consumer goods giants like P&G and Unilever leverage brand and distribution ecosystems to leverage customer physical and mental touch points. Specialty firms often wrap incredibly high rates of service and interaction around a product to create similar effects.[1]

As in life, all organizational capabilities have an expiration date for when they become economically unviable. The life spans of technically led firms are especially uncertain. In technically led markets, cheaper, better, faster offerings may come from anywhere at any time, threatening returns on capital. In 2012, some argued that Apple had found the magical fountain of endless value-creating innovation. This is the technologist's version of "this time is different." This thesis may be correct for a few product cycle iterations. Most likely, however, is that Apple has found an interesting fountain of strategic design thinking. This guides Apple in applying technical, design, and service innovations to its ecosystem of hardware and services in the right form at the right time. Apple's products and message also generate tremendous emotions of love and loyalty. Product love and learned behavioral lock-in are strong brand advantages, leading to high margins. However, few firms retain technical dominance and fanatic customer loyalty over time.

Apple possessed a strong unique capability footprint from 2003 to 2013 with its "i" line of products. Each leg on the plot (fig. 6.4) is a unique competitive capability. Note that this figure doesn't include duration (lifetime) estimates for the capabilities.

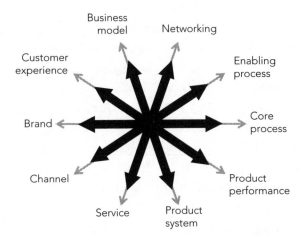

FIGURE 6.4 Apple's Unique Capability Footprint, 2003–2012
Apple's capability footprint changes rapidly due to the fast cycle clusters they compete in. It is unknown if 2013–2022 will repeat the last period's wildly successful footprint.

As of 2013, Apple's resurgence is ten years old in the history of a thirty-six-year-old company. It is quite challenging to project the next five to eight years for Apple. The investor must be coldly calculating about the source and durability of competitive advantage. Unless you fully understand the sustainable capability set within Apple's strategy, this currently exciting firm is likely not an acceptable long-term (five to fifteen years) capital allocation.

Assessing Advantageous Capacities for the Allocator

Unique capabilities expire as the knowledge stored in inos diffuses among competitors becoming standardized, rejected, or replaced by better knowledge and capabilities. The capital allocator or manager needs to assess the duration and value-creating potential of a capability, and only allocate resources to those with high long-term returns on capital (ROC) payoff potential. The high death rate of the new and novel is how adaptive evolution works through the competitive process. According to a study of millions of U.S. businesses started in 1994, 64.2 percent fail within a ten-year time window. This failure rate would be even higher if success were measured using a reasonable risk adjusted rate of return on capital.

Frozen yogurt in the 1980s, videocassette rental outlets, e-commerce, early stage biotech, fruit juices in the 1990s—all became billion dollar markets, and had billions of dollars thrown at them by smart people. Some people and firms made fortunes, but most did not. Many highly attractive markets can be net destroyers of capital as the resources poured into pursuing the opportunity may be greater than the market prize itself. Like lottery ticket purchasers, many managers, entrepreneurs, and investors believe they own the winning ticket.

Even long-lived "winners" in the technology race eventually fade and expire if they rely on old capabilities or narrow strategies. For decades, Kodak, Xerox, and Polaroid believed in their superior technology, seemingly unassailable competitive positions, and innovation capability. Xerox survived by moving into services, to avoid being solely product led. Kodak, on the other hand, was so focused on cameras and film that they failed to realize they were enablers of personal image–based experiences. As a result, the company died after 123 years in business,[2] because most people today get personal images delivered via phones and Facebook.

Having the best product doesn't matter. Efficiently delivering the best perceived user experience is what determines survival. When considering product-led firms, the salient question to ask isn't when, but rather how fast can evolution's inos deliver a better experience?

Understanding innovation, adaptability, and exclusivity is essential for the capital allocator because it determines both who creates value and the sustainability of returns on capital.

Competitor behavior can be irrational and affect short-term profitability for quarters or even years. Bogus competitor noise can temporarily suppress a firm's or cluster of competitors' margins as firms try to capture market share. A firm with a defensible unique set of capabilities will find that these competitive events prove temporary and that most operating margins will revert to normal. The thoughtful manager distinguishes ino noise from real threats to a defensible value creation process.

The manager needs to identify the nature of an innovator's threat and respond by replicating it or ignoring it as a capital-destroying fad. If the innovation provides a sustained advantage for a competitor, it may shrink the market to such a degree that the logical position is for the allocator to exit and allocate capital to more productive uses.

This loss of competitive capability happened to the original Berkshire Hathaway textile mills. The mills lost pricing power and finally the ability to price competitively in the textile markets. Even as Berkshire's managers sought capital to invest in cost-saving innovations, Warren Buffet, as allocator, correctly starved the firm of capital investment in new technology rather than throw good money after bad.

Summary

Accumulated knowledge and inos express themselves among the ten categories of organizational capabilities. Capabilities are used by organizations to explore economic possibility spaces while competing to add value. Customer perception determines the value of capabilities and the surviving accumulated knowledge. Capabilities with long expected life spans are highly desirable for investors.

Having fantastic innovation or possessing a single powerful capability doesn't guarantee a firm's success. Hero products and markets are dangerous because fierce adaptive competition shortens the value-creating life span of unique capabilities. Competitive forces and experience curves are how value gets transferred from an information ino into accumulated knowledge that delivers material economic progress for society.

Competitive forces and capabilities do battle in clusters of competition. Clusters are the niches in economic networks. They are the next level of system above organizations in the economic panarchy, and the focus of the next chapter.

PART III

Clusters

CHAPTER SEVEN

Birth and Growth of Clusters

IN ORDER TO RESPONSIBLY allocate capital, the investor must understand how a business beats or avoids competition over the long term. The competition that a firm faces determines how much excess value it captures as profit, with profit effectiveness measured as the best return on allocated working capital (ROC). The firm's competitive space is called the cluster.

The competitive cluster for a good or service is equivalent to the niche in an ecosystem. A niche is the multi-variable space in which an organism functions, and includes its network of links to food, resources, relationships, and physical environment. Network niches are more complicated than eat or be eaten; they encompass the organism's entire symbiotic web of relationships. The niche for a bird or butterfly, for instance, may span thousands of miles over a season and includes all the things the organism consumes for energy and all of the other organisms it interacts with. The niche for a frog may include the living network of things found in a pond and the detritus it feeds upon.

In a small pond, many types of frog may compete for survival. This makes the "space" of the niche a competitive one, as each type of frog uses its own strategies and capabilities to best eke out a way to survive. Some frog species may evolve capabilities to swim faster, stay warmer, reproduce more, or eat "exotic" foods, all in an effort to expand their addressable resources and, ultimately, to survive and reproduce.

In economic clusters, competitors battle for the scarce resource of customer value flow. Just as the conditions in the pond determine which frogs will survive, the nature of the cluster determines which organizations can flourish. Clusters thus act as macroprocessing machines, providing selective feedback—choosing which inos are fed resources and amplifying the presence of those inos in the economy. Feedback in the form of selective pressure is a critical component to all complex adaptive systems. Feedback selectively amplifies organizations if they are value creating and eliminates them if they are not. Clusters process and select for firms that most efficiently create customer value, just as a niche selects for and processes organisms that most efficiently sustain life and reproduce.

The act of purchasing value creates the money (informational) flow required for organizational survival. As customers make a purchase, the selling firm receives cash from the customer, which gets turned back into more value for the firm and shareholders. Surviving and growing customer value creates shareholder value in the form of long-term stable high returns on equity (ROE), realized by the investor as increases in real book value or dividends paid. The more Chia pets that are bought, the more Chia pets that get made. The Chia pet inos capture value for the organization, and this excess value is expressed as more Chia pets. Increased Chia pet value in the economy also causes bifurcations that explore possible variations on the original ino, such as creating Elvis Chia pets.[1]

In evolution's biological domain, life captures all addressable resources by adapting new capabilities to occupy new niches. In evolution's economic domain, as the original expressed ino and its variations create more value, the economy grows. This process, of adapting forms becoming more complex and either being eliminated or amplified, is a universal theme found across evolution's domains.

Successful capabilities are amplified by an organization, leading to exponential growth crowding out competitors and their inos. For instance, since the 1960s many small restaurants have shut down as customers have chosen McDonald's. Rightly or wrongly, a high customer value perception of McDonald's, relative to its competitors, leads to a more efficient delivery of perceived value into the economy as McDonald's flourishes, growing volumes, efficiencies, and outlets across the economic landscape.

Ecological niches themselves have a life cycle. The niche emerges in the ecological network, changes, and eventually disappears, often replaced by new specialized niches with new network links and actors. Economic clusters share this cycle pattern with ecology, the difference being that economic adaptive cycles turn over orders of magnitude faster than ecologies to process energy and information faster. Accelerating adaptive selection—in other words, faster macroprocessing—is a broad trend across evolution's physical, biological, and economic domains. Some economic clusters last briefly, like seasonal or fad markets, whereas others may last for decades or longer. As value investors, we are interested in long-lasting clusters, as short-lived clusters are rarely priced at a bargain, in terms of the extractable profit relative to expected viable life cycle.

Defining Cluster Boundaries

Cluster boundaries are defined by customer choice set. Nothing more, nothing less. For instance, how many brands of gum can you name off the top of your head? Three? Four? The set of brands you can think of defines your likely choice set. This choice set is your likely purchase set as well. There may be more choices available, but they don't come to mind as viable, so they don't count as part of the competitive cluster. If you really look at a shelf of gum and consider all the options, you will realize how you typically narrow the possible choices to a familiar handful.

The space of the cluster is shown in figure 7.1. The black circles are the customer's perception of choice. The white circles represent choices that may be on the shelf but don't enter the perceived choice set, and so aren't in the competitive cluster. If you haven't ever chewed Tutti-Frutti gum, it isn't likely to jump into your choice set, even if it's sitting right in front of you. How customers define choice sets is a do-or-die contest for organizations. Your perception of relative value as a consumer determines company survival.

FIGURE 7.1 Clusters: Defined by Customer Choice Set

The market of products may be enormous from the economist's or market researcher's perspective, but for a real consumer the list of choices is necessarily short, quick, and constrained. Many economic models imagine people rationally optimizing among all available options. This is wildly unrealistic. Most likely, the last time you went into a store looking for laundry soap, toothpaste, or ketchup you chose among two to four brands you used before (this is known as "consumer choice blindness").

Defining cluster boundaries and competitive choice is critical for the capital allocator's analysis. Simply defining competitive spaces by industry participants widely misses the mark. When defining a cluster, include viable substitute offerings among the choice set. In some cases, the customer choice set can include offerings from more than one industry. Airplanes and passenger railroads don't compete much in the United States, but in Europe they compete for some mid-distance commuter travel. So allocators in that instance would need to recognize that both trains and planes can be part of the same competitive cluster. In the United States, freight customers for short haul railroads may look to truckers as an alternative choice for some transport needs. The cheapest means of moving people and shipping boxes count more for the customer than the category of transportation mode. Defining clusters is simple. Just remember: the customer's perception is always right.

Competition dynamics determine value's flow and where excess profits may be captured and collected by the organization. A useful rule from competitive ecology is the rule of competitive exclusion known as Gause's law. Gause's law states that two species cannot coexist competing for the same resources if all other ecological factors are constant. If one species has even the slightest advantage over another species, the advantaged species eventually dominates. The loser exits the niche or changes strategy, adapting new competitive capabilities. The equivalent competitive economic law would state that two competing organizations can't coexist competing for the same customer base over consumption cycles if all other factors are constant. One competitor dominates, while the other must adapt a different strategy or exit the cluster.

Many investors compare similar companies' metrics at a point in time to arrive at a valuation. Company X is worth three times cash flow so company Y should be worth three times cash flow. But this method of using comparables by comparing one firm's operating or price multiples to another's multiples is flawed, because it woefully ignores the source and unfolding competition between X and Y and their capability differentials. Thinking about how Gause's law of dominant competitors works, it becomes obvious that comparable valuations are often naïvely misused due to the requirement for mutually exclusive strategies for long-term survival. A firm that eventually dominates a cluster may not have relevant comparable metrics. For instance, the investors using a comparable approach to value Walmart and Kmart likely did themselves few favors early on. Walmart incorrectly looked too expensive and Kmart too cheap. Comparables fail to take into account the waxing and waning margins and factors that occur as one firm's capabilities squeeze another's out of a cluster or force strategy and capability shifts on other firms. It's vitally important that allocators think in terms of customer-defined competitive clusters, because that's the key to hunting out sustainable value in the economy.

Cluster Origins and Adaptation

Large functioning adaptive systems follow a general rule of thumb. Whether biological or economic, all large systems started out as small functioning systems before evolving and growing into a larger complex network of links and flows. Large working adaptive complex systems never suddenly arrive wholly formed; rather, they represent the result of a multicycle, selective, adaptive macroprocess of flows. Every large economic cluster seen today started as a small set of limited capabilities created by opportunistic firms or entrepreneurs.

A good way to think about clusters is as "adjacent possibility spaces." Adjacent possibility spaces are the potential growth and survival spaces[2] that an adaptive system explores at its network edges to adapt, expand, and control more resources. The adjacent possibility spaces concept was put forward by theoretical biologist and Santa Fe Institute Fellow Stuart Kaufman, who explained how biology explores and creates possibilities for more life. Kaufman, in one example, explained how a fish species adapts a swim bladder that may in turn create a space, becoming the origin for a potential symbiotic parasite to live within.

In economies, new large clusters create economic possibility spaces, analogous to Kaufman's example of a biological possibility space. The interstate highway system created in the United States in the 1960s, for instance, was a huge infrastructure network that became the origin for the growth of many automotive lifestyle–derived clusters including truck stops, McDonald's, and new hotel chains like Howard Johnson's. Inos seek out any possible excess value-delivery mechanism or resource-capturing method required to exist, and so as new stable clusters are formed, inos will immediately begin to adapt new capabilities to harvest excess energy and evolve symbiotically. Thus, economic possibility spaces fill up with increasingly diverse forms seeking to extract value by competing in new ways with new capabilities. Economic or ecological adjacent possibility spaces are contingent on so many things that their emergence and form are impossible to predict in advance, as are the originating adaptive subsystem capabilities. For example, that tiny bottle of five-hour energy found almost everywhere originally lived within a small niche on gas station counters. The allocator should be on the lookout for any burgeoning possibility spaces, because they may provide the environment for rich value capture.

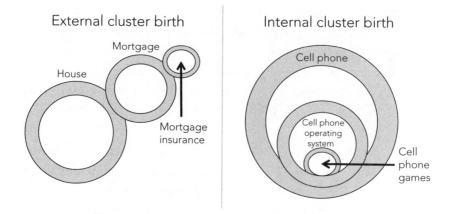

FIGURE 7.2 Clusters Adapt and Emerge Externally or Internally from Existing Clusters in the Network

Every innovative adaptive revolution bears within it the seeds of future revolutions, spinning out possibilities ad infinitum. This seemingly endless evolutionary birthing process typically takes one of two forms: internal or external (fig. 7.2).

Internal cluster births emerge from possible opportunity spaces within a cluster that are symbiotically reliant on the larger cluster. This exclusive symbiosis becomes the possibility space for a new viable capability. An external cluster, on the other hand, depends on many clusters or on an external resource. We will examine the internal cluster birth first.

Internal Cluster Birth

In ecology, each new species can provide a viable niche for other new species. A single species becomes the possibility space, or host, for a symbiotic or opportunistic parasitic species. The relationship may involve living outside the host but being fully dependent on the host. This is a closed system, in which one species adapts to rely exclusively on another for survival. Thus, the cluster emerges internally, within an existing form.

The remora, for instance, is a cleaner fish that eats dead skin and ectoparasites off of whale sharks. The remora cannot exist, in its current form, without the whale shark's ectoparasites. Over many generations, symbiotic relationships can evolve where both species coadapt and become fully exclusive codependents (a situation that could be termed external symbiogenesis). For example, the average human has an entire "forest" of bacteria within his or her gut, and an estimated ten times as many bacteria cells as somatic (human) cells in his or her body.[3] The small size and mass of the bacteriological cells means they are dwarfed when measured by weight, but their symbiogenetic capability contributions are vital for our bodies' survival.

Clusters become economic possibility spaces almost anywhere that inos can gain a toehold. Any niche or economic space, no matter how small or obtuse, can become stable enough that inos will explore a way to capture resources and extract more value from it. Examples are shown in figure 7.3, comparing ecological and economically exclusive ino spaces.

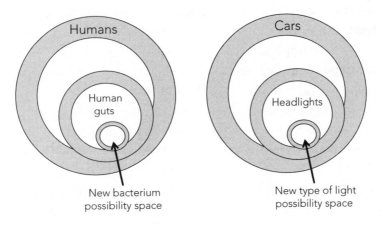

FIGURE 7.3 Macroprocessing Is Evolution Exploring Possibility Spaces Inside the Network's Niches and Clusters

In the economy, Facebook's ecosystem strategy allows firms access onto its "platform" via application programming interfaces which can host third-party applications. This strategy created a mostly internal cluster space for symbiotic software applications to live within. The social gaming company Zynga, for instance, created the Farmville game, which runs inside Facebook from the user's perspective. In 2012, Farmville had 80 million players raising virtual crops and animals. The relationship is mutually beneficial; Facebook's platform and API (application programming interface) gets content, keeping users engaged inside its site, and Zynga gets revenue. Facebook's open API created an internal possibility space. Smaller firms are highly dependent on the whims and survival of the host firm in such ecosystems. Advertising also works by symbiotic relationships, creeping into increasingly esoteric and microscopic attention spaces.

External Cluster Birth

In an external cluster birth, the products from one firm become a platform for sub-innovations from another. These sub-innovations can become nested, making space for ever more esoteric sub-innovations and consequently improving product quality and complexity while increasing value flow. The car as an adaptive complex system has subsystems creating external adjacent possibility spaces and clusters. In their book *Figments of Reality,* mathematician Ian Stewart and biologist Jack Cohen discuss how early cars were modeled on horse carriages and were open to the elements. Cars adapted glass windshields to block wind and rain as inos explored the car's adjacent, value-adding possibility spaces. Because the adapted windshields collected bugs and debris during dry conditions, they required cleaning. This possibility space led to the creation of artificial rain in the form of windshield washer fluid. Extreme cold made windshield wiper fluid freeze, which drove the need to adapt specialized low-temperature nonfreezing additives for the windshield washer fluid. These new possibility spaces were external—once developed, windshield washers were put not only on cars but on a whole variety of transportation vehicles. Each economic artifact creates possibility spaces for inos to explore new value-creating capability spaces as the entire car value delivery network gets more capable and informationally knowledge dense, evolving into a complex nested hierarchy of subsystems. An example of an external possibility space in biology is the coral that forms the Great Barrier Reef ecosystem. The coral creates an ecosystem network with countless external opportunity spaces or possible niches for other species to explore and fill in.

To sum up, clusters are born among other networked clusters in symbiotic or parasitic relationships. In an external cluster birth, a new company uses many products as an open platform to evolve from. In an internal cluster birth, the cluster is dependent on a single value-adding product or firm for survival in a symbiotic relationship. The established older clusters create the possibility space for new clusters. In this way, evolution's economic macro processing of flowing value and survival knowledge becomes self-accelerating or autocatalytic—just like life.

Newly evolved subclusters may create feedback loops, accelerating the original cluster's development. Businesses try to harness this dynamic using "ecosystem" strategies, symbiotically enabling others' capabilities in an effort to enhance their own value-delivering capabilities. Over time clusters link up to form value chains, as one cluster's output becomes another's input (as shown in fig. 7.4). These value chains are important to consider during times of economic upheaval—such as extreme inflation or deflation—as the links in the value chain can be rattled by these types of events. These will be discussed further in chapter 14.

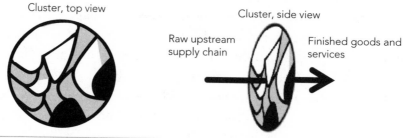

Value chain flow = GPP (gross produced product)

FIGURE 7.4 Economic Macroprocessing
As value in (energy, information, and form) flows through the network of links and clusters, it is converted from low-value raw inputs to higher-value goods and services.

Competitive Balance and Instability

Fred and Sue sell lemonade on a strip of beach, and every morning they need to pick the best place to set up their stands. Fred and Sue have identical products; the only difference is the distance beach goers must walk in order to get their lemonade. The walking distance is a form or dimension of added cost from the customer's perspective. Where should competitors locate themselves to optimize their return?

This economic optimization problem was solved by Thomas Schelling. One optimum location is for the vendors to locate themselves next to each other, allowing for an equal split of beach goers with neither seller having an incentive to move. Another would be for the vendors to locate themselves the same distance, in opposite directions, from some central point, which again would allow for an equal division of the market.

This type of product positioning works for other problems—not just when considering location. For instance, what type of lemonade should the two vendors make to optimize their value capture in the competitive space? If half of the customers in a cluster place a higher value on sweeter lemonade and the other half prefer sour lemonade, the vendors have two choices. They could produce nearly identical lemonade, which is equivalent to locating their stands right next to each other. Or, one could sell a sweet lemonade while the other sells a sour version. This is equivalent to locating stands on the opposite sides of a physical space, assuming that sweet and sour are equally favored along the flavor dimension continuum. Complex products make tradeoffs among consumer choice dimensions to capture and define their territorial space or cluster boundary relative to competitor offerings (fig. 7.5).

In young, growing clusters, organizations develop an array of capabilities to explore a wide variety of possible value capture

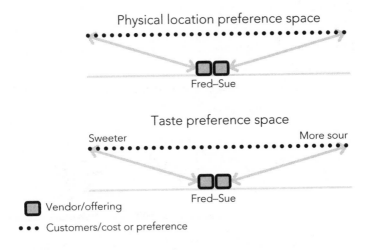

FIGURE 7.5 Schelling Beach and Flavor Solution Spaces

strategies to optimize returns from the multidimensional cluster of customer demands. These strategies may work early on in picking up the "easy" customers rapidly. However, as the cluster matures and organizations create more bifurcated offerings, competitors will start bumping into each other as offerings overlap. At this point, the customer's ability to separate an offering or differentiate the experience as unique becomes more challenging and margins suffer.

As clusters mature, strategic positions of products stabilize. The differences become quite slight, such as with Coke and Pepsi. Coke appeals to traditionalists and Pepsi aspires for youth. The flavor and branding are subtle but distinctively trying to distance themselves from each other in order to avoid overlap and direct competition, which would harm both of them and reduce the range of perceived value experiences available to consumers.

Competitive cluster diagrams show the relationship of competitors among clusters in various stages of development. These simplified diagrams can be useful when considering the competitive spaces between offerings. Figure 7.6 shows the cluster life cycle process and how the open, addressable, high-margin competitive space shrinks as the cluster matures.

Diagram rules:

1. Dotted circles are the potential addressable market of customers.
2. Gray shapes are competitor product positioning.

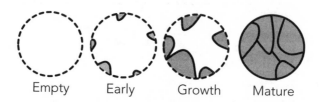

Empty   Early   Growth   Mature

FIGURE 7.6 Cluster and Growth Maturation

3. White spaces in a cluster are open addressable market revenue potential. A circle entirely filled with gray competitors has 100 percent of its market addressed by a choice of product. This is a mature market. The addressable market is the carrying capacity of the market.[4]

4. A cluster may be easy to enter or may have high barriers to entry. A dotted circle is easy for new competitors to enter. A solid circle is difficult for new competitors to enter.

Early clusters typically take one of two forms—fast follower or open field. A fast-follower cluster is characterized by participants that piggyback on one another's simple strategies to get ahead. An open field cluster has a number of competitors using distinctly unique capabilities, strategies, and behaviors (fig. 7.7).

The search engine cluster is a good example of a fast-follower, short-cycle cluster. The cluster on the right in figure 7.7 illustrates this, with the hindsight of Google's success. Although the search market is now understood to be larger and complex, in 1999 search was viewed as a mature commodity technology, with Yahoo!, AltaVista, Lycos, and other firms in the cluster. Search was a service that ran on portal web pages littered with banner ads and scraps of content. The consensus thinking in the late 1990s was that better search results were a commodity, giving minimal

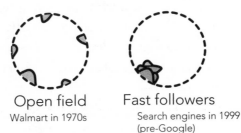

Open field
Walmart in 1970s

Fast followers
Search engines in 1999
(pre-Google)

FIGURE 7.7 Early Stage Clusters: Dispersed vs. Clumped Strategies

advantage to the predominant web portal firm using them. This single-capability–led cluster highlights the risk of allocation to product- or technology-led clusters with low barriers to entry and rapid adaptation. Even dominant technology firms or seemingly mature clusters may disappear in a single product cycle due to the entrepreneur in the garage next door.

The "open field" cluster, on the other hand, is a cluster with one or two firms that lack direct competitors or that have competitors with vastly different strategies. In the 1970s, Walmart's cluster was geographically open to copycat competitors either nationally or internationally, but instead was filled in with Walmart's own later growth. This was largely because Walmart's competitors, the small town "mom & pop" retailers, weren't used to fast change. Walmart's focus on low prices and fast inventory turnover, and the powerful experience curve effects that maximized value through-put, were overwhelming. Walmart was an extreme revenue and price shock predator devouring Main Street's friendly, domesticated stores. This open field cluster contrasts with fast-follower markets, in which similar incremental approaches mean a "clear" long-term competitive advantage or margin boundary isn't as obvious.

Fast-follower clusters, as the name indicates, adapt quickly. Each economic cluster has its own cycle pace and rhythm. Every time a product is selected for purchase and the cash is fed back into producing more of the product or service, a cash flow cycle has occurred. The speed of these cycles depends on the rate of change in primary capabilities, pace of technical innovation, experience curve–related throughput growth, and competitive forces. Key capability adaptation cycles vary in length from weeks to decades, depending on the cluster and capability. Semiconductors and Internet software clusters, for instance, iterate faster than railroads and aircraft manufacturers. The faster a key cluster capability adapts, the higher the risk for those firms whose margins rely on that key capability. Product-led firms in fast-moving electronic hardware-only businesses are like this. In stable value-creating clusters, on the other hand, key competitive capability cycles are long, whereas the cash flow and sales cycles are fast and short. It's best to bet on firms in slow-cycle clusters, and to look for the firms within these clusters that have faster relative adaptation rates. A fast-adapting firm may capture experience curve benefits while also recording higher ROEs than competitors.

Growth clusters are fast, exciting, and value creating for the economy. That doesn't necessarily make them good allocator bets. New clusters can grow rapidly, attracting a lot of excitement as the aggregate cluster's revenue swells. Many confuse the cluster's revenue growth with individual organizational value capture. Fast clusters with short capability cycles often have firms with unstable ROIC margins, because new disruptive firms and capabilities show up all the time. Fast destructive disruption occurred a lot in the early Internet days. Rapid growth in the tech world made it look as though most tech companies were safe bets as they overtook non-tech traditional clusters. But many found that when the dotcom bubble burst, they had confused new cluster growth with a specific company's potential for value creation. Many fast-adapting Internet firms could kill each other just as quickly as they could kill traditional "dinosaur" business models.

When a race has faster participants, it doesn't make it any easier to pick the winner. The paradigm[5] of relative cluster competitive dynamics doesn't change, only the participants' absolute capabilities do. Picking the winner from a race filled with mostly ninety-year-old runners is easier if one of the competitors is in his or her twenties. Picking a winner is all about sustainable relative advantage.

Confusing cluster scale (revenue), experience curve effects and value-creating processes can lead to disappointment. During the dotcom boom, it was hoped that volumes of "sticky eyeballs" (page views) and registered users would "automagically" create shareholder value. People were so enamored watching the near vertical growth of these useless metrics that they forgot to assess the firm's capability for sustainably generating excess cash flow.

Looking at these firms as clusters adapting in rapid cycles with unstable consumer choice would have shown most of these firms to be one competitive click away from oblivion.

Growth firms are often grossly overpriced due to ignorance of the hidden negative optionality of innovation. These firms' share prices may suffer severe price declines as growth stalls or markets mature as competition compresses or eliminates the dreamed-of profit margins. Many growth firms never create value and disappear rapidly once the fuel of cheap equity or debt financing disappears. For every Facebook, there will be tens of thousands of small social website projects quietly put to rest after a few months or years. Economies and societies experience huge benefits with innovations like Facebook or cheap solar cells, at the marginal cost of the loser's exploration efforts. Fortunately, the selection feedback mechanism amplifies the winner's value-delivering capabilities across the network, producing net gains for us all.

Early cluster stage innovation companies often trade at higher multiples under flawed growth reward expectations. This lottery ticket paradox ignores the threats of fast, competitive innovation. This disparity between economic hope and adaptive competitive reality can be a costly gap for the allocator. For instance, a fast-cycle firm with a median adaptive capability life cycle of three years needs to earn and retain a 33 percent ROE just to break even. This implies a required PE ratio of 3:1 on a go-forward basis. New technology firms are almost always priced as lottery tickets, beyond any reasonable level for the value investor. An IPO for a three-year, short-cycle technology firm priced at a 12:1 forward PE ratio is easily 400 percent overpriced.

Truly sustainable value-creating processes often repeat for many iterations, having the same or similar customers returning excess ROC to the firm year after year. Costco is an example of a virtuous repeating cycle. Pets.com is on the other end of the spectrum—the increasing number of registered one-off users and visitors didn't turn out to be very value creating. If only there'd been more dogs with credit cards on the Internet! Pets.com is a good example of how a new strategy that looks extremely successful and valuable at first can prove ineffectual over time. As clusters mature, high margins and ROE diminish rapidly. Allocators should seek long capability-cycle processes with fast, efficient cash flow turnover cycles. Expanding on the biological metaphor, bet on a slow, stable niche and a stable, quick-learning species within that niche that survives and thrives relative to others.

The Cluster's Macroprocessing Life Cycle

The birth, growth, and unfolding maturity of clusters is interesting, but the important question is: what are competitive clusters actually doing, and how do they do it?

Competition in clusters acts like a selective macroprocessing force, optimizing the economic knowledge and value delivery of organizations and pushing their flow across the economic network. Without clusters or competition, organizations could monopolistically capture and retain the bulk of value flow for themselves with minimal adaptation. Clusters diffuse excess marginal value from organizations to customers into the broader economy. The cluster's selection pressure determines a firm's potential for excess value capture (profit). The diagram following shows the relationships among costs, value-adding capabilities, prices, and margin squeeze of customers and competitors found in a cluster (fig. 7.8). The more unique capabilities a firm has, the further it can push its relative price points and the more profit it can generate. A firm with only one or two unique capabilities, or with capabilities that are on the verge of being adopted by competitors, cannot generate as much profit.

Cluster carrying capacity—that is, how much value flow a cluster can support—and the competitive pressures determine a competitor's marginal quality of life. For instance, say that an island filled with banana trees is a niche with the carrying capacity to

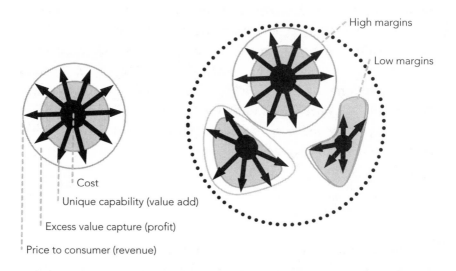

FIGURE 7.8 Customers' and Competitors' Pressures Squeeze Cluster Profit Margins

support one hundred monkeys. Everything is fine on the island as long as there are fewer than one hundred monkeys competing to eat bananas. But if two hundred monkeys show up, all of the monkeys may starve or be so stressed and weak that they become vulnerable to opportunistic disease or predators.

A mature cluster filled to capacity with competitors, with each firm's offerings viewed as the same commodity by customers, is like a stressed and overpopulated island offering barely marginal survival. As clusters and products mature, they become commodified, pushing margins down. Commodities have minimal profit margins, as by definition they have few differentiable traits other than price. Knowledge sharing in the form of competitive ino diffusion drives capability commodification, leading to low or no margins for competitors.

The carrying capacity for an economic cluster is determined by addressable consumer demand for a given quality level. In commodity clusters, ROC margins are volatile, small, and sometimes negative, because there may be no dominant strategy for earning advantageous margins. Maturing clusters lack stable, differentiated competitor capabilities and have declining profit margins. However, allocating to a maturing cluster can be lucrative if one has a reasonable guess as to the sustainable winning firm. Each purchase or product cycle may have a winner and loser. Over time the fortunes of winners and losers can diverge wildly as cumulative advantages accrue and become overwhelming, as in Gause's exclusion principle mentioned earlier.

The purchase and capability-amplifying process works over cycles, a bit like compounding interest. During the early stage the advantage seems slight, but even a slight competitive pressure or adaptive advantage dominates everything, given enough time. Over many cycles, competitive advantage compounds exponentially, reshaping the network niche leading to winner-take-most outcomes. Like Gause's law of ecological competition, a slight initial value delivery advantage of 51 percent versus 49 percent works the same way, as winning firms use their excess cash flow to amplify their winning capabilities through things like better marketing, distribution, or materials sourcing. Winners can make many times more returns, ending up with a 100 percent versus 0 percent advantage like Coke versus its earliest cohort of long deceased competitors. High relative returns on operating capital often indicate dominant capabilities. Higher ROC relative to competitors is a sign of a firm's fitness. Higher returns won't guarantee or prolong the life cycle of a cluster but may indicate longer life for a competitor within that cluster.

A few product cycles may be all it takes to start separating winners from losers. When two lemonade stands are situated side by side, it's not difficult to imagine one of the lemonade vendors having a 1 percent advantage of some type, such as buying lemons in bulk. The more efficient vendor can lower her price, increasing her market share, which will then enable her to buy more cheap lemons in bulk or expand another capability such as offering new flavors. Her increased throughput may further accelerate her experience curve effects or other lemonade-selling advantages.

This positive feedback loop is the "rich get richer" effect. The vendor's advantage and profits may grow with every purchase or cash flow cycle, while the competitor's relative capability to compete shrinks. Thus, what appeared as an almost random fluctuation in the initial competive landscape leads to a somewhat predictable end state as the "rich get richer" positive feedback loop kicks in. This type of dominating structural accretion feedback process works across evolution's physical, ecological and economic domains.

Value Flowing Through Clusters

Clusters are mechanisms for transferring ino-enabled capabilities into consumer value. Clusters force competitors to offer more value to customers. Regulated capitalism enables this. The cluster itself acts like a selfish superorganism seeking out the best value-creating innovations to capture the information, energy, and material resources required to serve its customers and grow.

Many innovations come to be adopted by most or all competitors, such as double entry accounting or cash registers. This process of adaptive innovation transfer and sharing among organizations is called innovation diffusion. The earliest adopter of an ino may gain an advantage, but over time, as diffusion occurs, the early adopter's excess margin is competed away as the ino diffuses into the economic network among competitors.

Figure 7.9 shows how this value capture spike travels through a cluster over time. There is a brief initial spike as an early adopter gets a higher return on capital, but the ROC reverts back to its historical mean as the relative advantage diffuses among competitors and margins erode. When all competitors adopt a capability, most of the ino's value flows to the consumer. This diffusion and competition mechanism is the invisible hand that selectively pushes value into the economy via consumers' selection pressure. Most clusters act as value conveyer belts, pushing knowledge-created value from competitors out to consumers in the economic network.

FIGURE 7.9 Ino Margin Shock and Mean Reverting Cluster Margins
Innovation diffusion over time forces value flow to customers: (1) initial normal returns on capital; (2) hype spike: initial adopter has high margins due to exclusive capability; (3) diffusion phase: competitors adapt by adopting the ino; (4) normal returns on capital return as competitive pressure erodes margins.

Many firms and CEOs claim to target 15 percent annual earnings growth. Fifteen percent growth is extremely difficult to sustain. The chart in figure 7.10 is taken from a 2001 *Fortune* magazine article challenging the 15 percent earnings growth targeted by many firms. Using Value Line data, *Fortune* studied 150

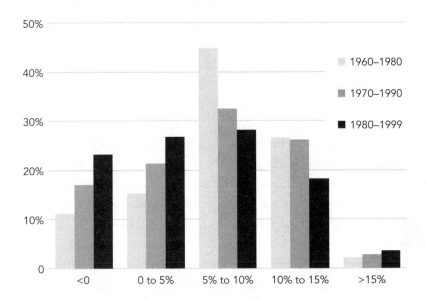

FIGURE 7.10 Twenty-Year Earnings Growth Rate
Source: Carol J. Loomis. 2011. "The 15% Growth Delusion." *Fortune Magazine*. Time Inc., a Time Warner Company.

of the largest firms over three 20-year periods in order to study their earnings growth. As one can see, only about 1 in 30 firms can grow annual earnings 15 percent over twenty years. Many clusters are filled with organizations eking out low margins fighting for survival, all the while capturing no or minimal value for shareholders.

Firms within a cluster can grow in a few different ways.

1. Grow capacity with increased throughput rates (grow annual revenues)
2. Bifurcate offering capabilities between firms (increase profit margins)
3. Increase turnover cycles rates of inventory or cash flow cycles for operating efficiencies (reduce costs)

The allocator's challenge is to find firms that are following one of these growth strategies in a way that will lead it to a long-term value advantage—not just a short-term, inflated share price. Again, the speed of cycles is an extremely important concept to take into account when considering this. The Internet era of 1996–2000 was a blink in economic history but saw incredibly fast capability-cycle speeds and excitement. Although significant knowledge and economic value was created, it flowed mainly to customers and society rather than to shareholders. Watching Procter & Gamble roll out a cheaper packaging technology for Tide laundry detergent may not quicken the heart, but over the years it may fatten the wallet. As this example demonstrates, picking the right cluster is just as important as picking the right firm—clusters with fast cycles can be almost impossible to allocate to effectively.

Of course, firms' capabilities have different cycle lengths. Apple is a good demonstration of this. Although its hardware capabilities cycle through quickly, Apple counteracts this by having a slower-moving ecosystem of relationships around the Mac OS and iOS consumer experience and the associated applications. Apple hopes this leads to repeat hardware and service purchases, with their hardware serving as a gateway to familiar experiences people love.

As this Apple example makes clear, organizations require multiple capabilities to survive and thrive. Staying at the forefront of a single key capability or innovation wave is impossible over the long run. It is best to have many categories of capability differentiation with slow-moving cycles, like beer and chewing gum, which rely more on brand, production, packaging, and scale of distribution capabilities that have slow adaptive cycles.

Summary

Clusters are shaped and defined by customers. Clusters emerge and grow from the economic possibility spaces of existing clusters in the network. During the growth phase of a fast cluster, winning and losing firms are difficult—if not impossible—to predict. Competitive pressure forces firms to continually adapt new advantageous capabilities, and keeps excess value flowing to the consumer.

Cluster life cycles can be measured and tracked using product and service adaptive cycle times. For most allocators the birth and early stages of a cluster are too risky or priced too high (yield too low) to make sense for allocation. Clusters with slower life cycles can be easier to allocate to than those with very quick life cycles.

CHAPTER EIGHT

Cluster Convergence, Maturation, and Death

AFTER A MATURE FOREST BURNS DOWN, and nothing remains but charred topsoil, there is a standard growth pattern and cycle for the way species repopulate the forest. The first returning species are fast-growing grasses and shrubs. These opportunistic fast growth species provide low groundcover. Next, small softwoods start to fill in, also growing quickly and providing some shade canopy. Finally, the slow-growing hardwood trees begin to reappear, offering significant canopies over decades or centuries.

At each phase of development, different organisms are best suited for the network of available ecological resources. Grasses thrive in the bright light and can withstand harsh, unsheltered conditions, but when hardwoods have grown in, these grasses don't get enough light to thrive. Hardwood saplings aren't as hardy and quick growing as shrubs, but once there is some groundcover, they can grow to great heights, achieving long life spans. Life's early stage strategies don't make sense as the ecological network matures, and later stage strategies don't take hold until the local conditions are right. By the same token, economic clusters offer different value-capturing opportunities relative to their life stage.

Just as with the growth of a forest, clusters and economies have a natural pattern to their development and life cycle stages. Early opportunistic offerings based on multiple simple capabilities and strategies develop first. Over time, one set of capabilities starts to dominate, and the cluster converges into a few large mature offerings backed by these dominant robust processes and capabilities. Many later-stage offerings aren't viable until a market evolves and matures. Early opportunistic entrepreneurial firms are necessary for cluster growth but won't all adapt to survive as mature cluster participants.

The rate of change in cluster capabilities often seems to follow Gould's punctuated equilibrium model, as described in chapter 2. There are short periods of rapid innovation flourishes, followed by long, relatively quiet intervals. Web browsers exploded on the scene in 1994, and now in 2014 perform broadly the same way from a user perspective. Qualitative browser features have been added and adopted, but the rate of change after the initial Netscape Navigator and Internet Explorer days has been incremental, as far as most users can tell. Firefox, Opera, Safari, and Chrome put minor spikes in innovation, but the basic browser design experience appears stable and slightly better to the average customer.

During the growth stages of newly created economic clusters, it is difficult to determine who, if anyone, is going to capture an advantage. It may be easier to spot the strongest capabilities rather than the strongest firms. As clusters mature, the cluster consolidates to a few dominant participant capabilities and strategies.

And as clusters mature, product innovation decreases, and process and service innovations may become increasingly used to differentiate offerings. The success of Domino's pizza in the 1980s was less about great pizza (a mature product) and more about the streamlining of delivery service, quality guarantees, and branding. This theme—of capability bifurcation emerging around a product, using non-product capabilities—is a common one. As products become commodified, service, branding, and other categories from the ten types of innovation capabilities presented in chapter 5 take on increasingly important differentiating roles. These capabilities explore and expand the cluster value, adding possibility spaces at the economic network's edges.

Dominant Design and Enabling Architectures

Over purchase cycles, capabilities are pared down by the competitive selection process and a favored set of offerings emerges as the preferred and dominant form. These remaining forms and capabilities are called the "dominant design." The dominant design emerges to define the cluster offering, with minor variations radiating outwardly from it. Figure 8.1 shows early variance in product capability and form, followed by successful and unsuccessful adaption converging toward the dominant design among various offerings.

The concept of the dominant design and the process of dominant design emergence are described well by Utterback in his book *Mastering the Dynamics of Innovation*. The dominant design in a cluster defines the minimum level of efficiency and set of capabilities required to capture resources and survive in the cluster. As the inos and capabilities required to deliver the dominant design diffuse and become available to everyone, costs and margins converge to lower levels, reflecting competitive pressures measurable as experience curve effects. The dominant design represents the required set of combined capabilities, and not necessarily the most advanced form of each single capability. For instance, the DC-3 aircraft was

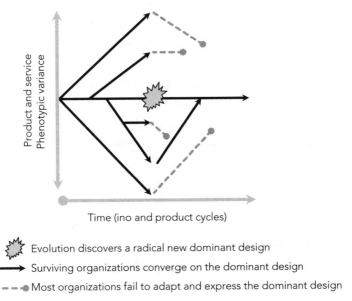

FIGURE 8.1 Selection Forces Dominant Design and Capability Convergence

not the fastest, longest range, or largest aircraft of its era. However, its balanced combination of capability tradeoffs was a big winner. The combination, and some of the DC-3's design, survived from the 1930s to today. If the dominant design is exclusive to one firm, the other firms will be forced to exit or bifurcate into new clusters while the original firm attains monopoly margins. The 747 jet, for instance, was a dominant design for Boeing for decades, forcing consolidation in related large-body aircraft clusters while maintaining dominance in its cluster. As clusters mature, research indicates the cluster's rate of evolution slows. Utterback's research findings indicated that "as a few firms came to dominate the industry with superior product technology and productivity, both experimentation and progress would be expected to slow. The renewal or broadening of competition would be required for rapid progress to recur."[1]

Convergence to a small core capability or product feature set can be done pre-emptively by a participant in the cluster. For instance, the design philosophy used by Apple is to offer "the least, best feature set" for its products. This design philosophy reduces both complexity of manufacturing and user confusion, and leads to the production of elegant and simple experiences. The original iPod could have been a horrible gadget with twenty buttons; instead, it was a streamlined and highly constrained device (with a set of related services to boot) that has continued to adapt, dominating the portable music player field. Its capabilities then diffused to the iPhone. Good product and service design follows designer Steve Krug's "Don't make me think"[2] rule; the iPod is a great example of a product following this maxim. To see where Apple went wrong, consider the Apple ROKR phone from 2005. The ROKR was the bastard lovechild of Apple and Motorola, and failed utterly as a phone and MP3 player combo.

The dominant design and the knowledge it reflects is often so widely diffused and adopted that it quickly starts to seem obvious and is no longer recognized as innovative, just like a nearly button-free smart phone. Few people today would ask if a car had the capabilities of an electric starter, horn, or windshield wipers. These dominant design features are expected requirements of a car. Being able to deliver these features in a car represents the minimum survival capabilities required for an auto manufacturer. The process of converging to the successful dominant design among firms determines success or failure. Figure 8.2 shows how the minimum saleable feature set of the automobile dominant design has adapted over time.

This diagram highlights how capability and product offering consolidation occurs as volumes of value flow increase over time. Early in the evolution of automobiles, craftsmen assembled cars using the same techniques as carriage makers. Later, Henry Ford's manufacturing assembly line became the dominant ino in manufacturing capability. Firms that didn't adapt this new efficient capability died out. The remaining auto manufacturers converged on this capability, and it became a capability associated with the dominant design that manufacturers had to adopt to survive.[3]

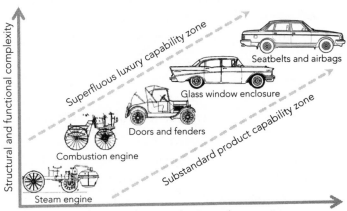

FIGURE 8.2 Automobile Dominant Design Selected and Adapted for Increasing Functional Complexity

All cars now share a familiar set of features that we could call their "architecture," with architecture defined as the patterns of capabilities or structures that shape and enable mature products. For this reason, successful capability sets like these can be called "enabling architectures." Only a few firms can typically evolve and maintain dominance of an enabling architecture capability. Controlling the architecture of a dominant design is powerful. In the book *The Gorilla Game*,[4] Intel's X86 architecture is given as an example of a controlling architectural form in the tech industry, allowing Intel to maintain dominance since the 8086 chip's release in 1978—even as the manufacturing capabilities enabling the architecture bifurcated into increasingly exotic forms. By controlling the interfaces used by the PC hardware ecosystem, Intel exerted incredible control. Microsoft's operating systems became the enabling architecture on the software side of the PC. Architecture can provide lucrative excess value capture for the firm controlling it.

Microsoft and Intel formed a symbiotic, dominating relationship that lasted decades. This dominance is fading fast as new computer architectures emerge on new devices, like tablets and smart phones, with new interfaces. Evolution creates new patterns for value creation, ultimately leaving economic artifacts and relics decaying in its wake.

Surviving Convergence as Clusters Mature

The early stage empty cluster is a wide open market space with few competitors. In the early stages of the cluster, organizations can use single-capability opportunistic strategies to deliver value. During the growth phase, entrants focus on capturing market share. As the cluster grows and matures, key innovations, capabilities, and strategies stabilize. Competitor offerings overlap, filling the addressable market space. Margins may compress and stabilize, with returns on capital reverting to normal levels. If the barriers to cluster entry are high, margins can remain higher as competitors retain value relative to customers. As a rule, the cluster's maturation stage involves slower growth in revenue. Mature clusters have fewer participants, and these remaining participants exhibit stable strategies focused on margin and relative market share expansion.

As clusters mature, it becomes increasingly difficult for small players to remain competitive due to increasing volumes of production flow required for competitive efficiency. The corner lemonade stand is less efficient than a lemonade factory, as measured by the cost per gallon of lemonade produced. As efficiency-increasing innovations diffuse through a cluster, the production volume required for each participant to survive increases. The cluster only supports one or two participants with the lowest costs and highest mature volumes of minimum production due to scale and experience curve effects, assuming the addressable market's unit volume is fixed. Smaller players literally get squeezed out. Figure 8.3 shows how cost efficiencies shrink the number of viable competitors in a stable-revenue cluster over time, as each seeks economies of scale. Only higher

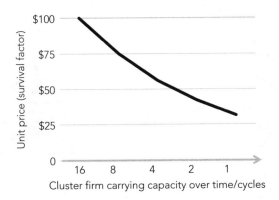

FIGURE 8.3 Declining Prices Reduce Competitors
Shrinking unit selling price over adaptive capability cycles shrinks competitor numbers (note that this assumes a simple fixed-unit cluster demand).

volume producers survive as learning curve effects raise the efficiency needed to compete. Investors aware of this experience curve effect should seek the most efficient operating firms, as measured by cost per unit of value delivered.

Figure 8.4 compares the dominant capability convergence diagram with a standard evolutionary bifurcation diagram. Organizations attempt to survive within an existing cluster by convergence or by creating new clusters. When the organization can't adapt into a viable form, it dies, becoming another fossil in evolution's economic strata.

For traditional allocators, early stage clusters are too risky or pricey prior to the emergence of a long cycle dominant design. The likely winning capability set is unknown until a dominant design emerges, ideally in a stable cluster with a limited number of competitors. After the dominant design emerges, significant value may accrue to the surviving firms, as they capture expanded operating margins and extra revenue growth due to extra market share and throughput. These survivors experience rapid returns on initial capital. The typical cluster life cycle example is shown in figure 8.5.

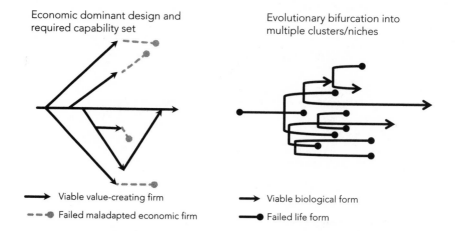

Economic dominant design and required capability set

Evolutionary bifurcation into multiple clusters/niches

→ Viable value-creating firm

--● Failed maladapted economic firm

→ Viable biological form

● Failed life form

FIGURE 8.4 Selection and Adaptation Process in Economic and Ecological Network Domains

Economic forms using inos adapt faster than life forms using genes.

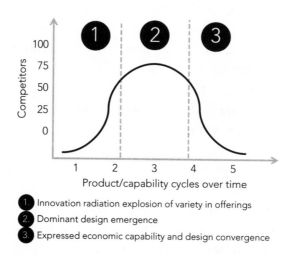

1. Innovation radiation explosion of variety in offerings
2. Dominant design emergence
3. Expressed economic capability and design convergence

FIGURE 8.5 Competitor Population Over the Emergence to Dominant Design Convergence Cycle

The cluster maturity cycles of auto manufacturers and U.S. television manufacturers are great examples of this flow toward maturity and efficiency. The innovation and cluster convergence macroprocessing follows a pattern of rapid proliferation of entrants and products followed by quick consolidation to a handful of participants who are capable of expressing the dominant design (figs. 8.6A and B).

Convergence doesn't have to mean limited customer choice. Under converging pressures, dominant value-delivering designs may radiate out and create new clusters. These new distinct clusters

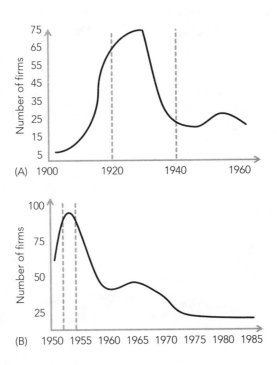

FIGURE 8.6 (A) Birth and Death of Competing U.S. Auto Manufacturers; (B) Firms in U.S. Television Industry

Stylized from: James M. Utterback. 1987. "Innovation and Industrial Evolution in Manufacturing Industries," in Bruce Guile and Harvey Brooks, eds., *Technology and Global Industry: Companies and Nations in the World Economy.* National Academy Press.

are birthed in the bifurcation process. Like Darwin's finches shown earlier in figure 4.4, each derivative form of the dominant design evolves to survive and serve its own unique cluster. This process of capability radiation is common to all of evolution's adaptive selective systems. The earlier illustrations of chair and aircraft taxonomies show how innovations and capabilities are expressed as different value-creating forms.

Like animal species, each firm has its own survival cycle, primarily driven by the intensity and rate of innovation change across the ten capability types. Even slow-changing, long-lived clusters fade away eventually or change into new forms entirely. Major local U.S. newspapers often lasted for fifty or one hundred years in their respective geographic clusters. On the other hand, technology firms with short product and innovation capability cycles flicker into existence only to fade away in a few seasons. As figure 8.7 shows, it may be more advantageous to own Coke for decades than to chase each hot new firm. The investor has a better chance of participating in the high ROC period of an organization's life

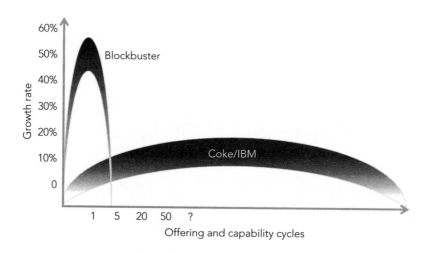

FIGURE 8.7 Many Unique Capabilities Prolong Life
Firms with many unique capabilities in slow-cycle clusters can create value over longer periods measured in absolute and relative time.

span by selecting a cluster with a long life expectancy with familiar competitors and stable strategies.

In figure 8.7, risk and uncertainty in the value creation process is greatest at the ambiguous start and end periods of the lifecycle arc. Because of this, beginning and ending periods are when the allocator, should she choose to participate, must demand extremely high yields. Markets often underestimate start-of-cycle uncertainty, mispricing these high-risk periods. Short-cycle, capability-based firms have smaller windows for value capture, requiring significantly higher yields.

Over time, the capabilities required to deliver products and services change—and even once-dominant firms can become ossified, unable to make these adaptive changes. Utterback's research in innovation found that most firms can't make the leap of dominance from one cluster product generation to the next. The inability of organizations to adapt is not conventional wisdom; firms appear malleable and capable of free will but are in fact similar to organisms in that most firms have a limited adaptive capacity relative to evolution's changing macroprocessing selection criteria. Witness cell phone manufacturers RIM and Nokia attempting to keep up with Apple in 2013—even though Nokia originally did this as it changed from being a local Finnish conglomerate that made rubber boots, among other things, into a global telecoms giant. The cash resources were there, but the organizational structure, beliefs, behaviors, and capabilities can't be easily changed. The inability to adapt eventually leads to organizational death as clusters change or collapse. The rate of evolution's economic macroprocessing and organizational selection seems to be accelerating as the average life span for a dominant organization shrinks, as represented by the chart of the S&P 500 life spans in figure 8.8.

Corporate death is mostly ignored in contemporary finance education, despite the fact that organizational life is brief and fleeting. As of 2012, one S&P 500 company gets replaced every two weeks. Traditional finance and valuation avoids the awkward

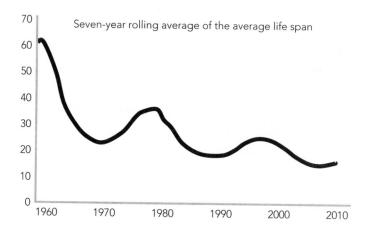

FIGURE 8.8 Adaptive Cycles Are Accelerating
Average organizational dominant periods on the S&P 500 are shrinking.
Source: Innosight/Richard N. Foster/Standard & Poor's.

death conversation by taking the easy way out, assuming earnings flow in a blissful straight line in perpetuity. From *The Nature of Value* investor's perspective, however, a firm's economic life is only as good as its current cluster and product cycle, so pick long cycles or relatively cheaply priced high-yielding short cycles. It is estimated that 75 percent of the 2012 S&P 500 will be replaced by 2027.[5] *The Nature of Value* investor's first question about a firm's earnings stream should be: when and how will it die?

As with the firm, the final life stage for a cluster is death. Death occurs when the products and services in a cluster are squeezed out of the network, replaced by offerings from competing clusters. Like the punctuated equilibrium from ecology, the entrance of economic death onto the stage may be shockingly sudden. Either way, be it sudden or long expected, firm and cluster death is a long-term vital part of all adaptive processes, in that death frees up resources for better-adapted and more efficient value-creating forms.

Death of economic clusters occurs in two ways. Either the cluster morphs, adapting a form so different from its original capability requirements that it is unrecognizable, or a new product or service destroys the ability for the cluster to add value, resulting in collapse. The decline of most major U.S. bookstores and their replacement by Amazon is an example of a sudden shock to the bookstore cluster, whereas changes in capabilities for airplane manufacturers have been of a more gradualist nature. The airplane manufacturer capability set of thirty years ago isn't economically viable today.

Even if the death of a firm or cluster seems inevitable, it can be difficult for management to accept and plan for this. CEOs and managements with dull or captive boards of directors are often encouraged or incentivized to spend every penny of shareholder capital to protect the firm's culture, jobs, and lifestyle. A typical organizational response to the cluster death process is to fight to the last penny even as it destroys shareholder equity, which is perversely considered more noble than quitting and handing back shareholder capital.

Managers are supposed to be first and foremost stewards of shareholders' value and capital. Many allocator/manager incentive schemes focus on protecting a soon-to-be-economically extinct firm and are not aligned with the trusted role of protecting shareholder value by maximizing long-term ROE. When there is no viable economic future for the firm it should be dismantled, replaced, or sold off so that the capital and resources can be allocated to viable value-creating firms.

In simple terms, the dying firms in a cluster destroy value. Dying firms and clusters must be let go of quickly. There are heroic exceptions to this rule, such as Apple's turnaround circa 1997 by Steve Jobs, but these kinds of radical, mutant turnarounds in the decay phase rarely work out.

When a firm or cluster enters terminal decline, shown by declining or even negative returns on capital (ROC), it is the manager's job to cease allocating capital to it. This is a challenge for many managers as their incentives, careers, and personal sense of worth may be tied to a single firm or cluster, rather than ROC. Change might be correctly perceived as career death for the individual or organization, so management becomes incapable of the required adaptation. Managers often burn shareholder capital loading up the balance sheet with debt to buy a few years of organizational and personal career life. This act destroys value for everyone. These situations end with evolution's inevitable chill of economic death.

One of the key roles of the capital investor or allocator is the ability to coolly stop capital allocations to dying firms and clusters.[6] Bad bureaucracies and misincentivized managers destroy value.

Summary

Birth, growth, and death are part of the nature of value at the company and cluster level. In aggregate, these processes behave similarly to those found across species and ecologies in nature. Throughout history, value has flowed through organizations and clusters into the economy, radiating out in flowerings of growth to be followed by eventual decay. This adaptive process creates more functional complexity and "progress" in the economy, increasing the capacity for value flow into society. The capital allocator needs to think in long-term cluster and corporate-capability lifecycles, selecting the periods and places in the flowing adaptive economic process where organizations can capture maximum value. In the next section we will examine the nature of clusters and why some are unstable, making them too uncertain for allocation.

CHAPTER NINE

Stable and Unstable Clusters

EACH CLUSTER MACROPROCESSES AS A SMALL living network with a unique pulse, of participants, suppliers, and customers coadapting; the cluster and network becoming more complex and efficient at transferring value into the economy. Allocating involves picking a cluster capable of supporting a great company. Even the strongest, most capable animal can't survive in the wrong environment or niche context. The ideal habitat is stable, providing the right context and resources for a firm to survive and thrive.

Stable clusters, like stable niches in ecology, are places where value flows without being interrupted by too much change. Clusters often converge towards stability as inos and capabilities form a stable web of strategies, and participants consolidate via mergers or exit. Just as capability convergence leads to dominant offering design, convergence of participants within the cluster leads to certain capabilities and strategies becoming stable and defensible.

Unstable clusters repeatedly destroy shareholder capital, as new competitors constantly enter, shifting the cluster's dominant strategies and required capability set. Firms in these clusters have little ability to sustainably differentiate offerings from competitors. No particular firm's strategy and capabilities win in ROC terms. Unstable clusters are easily spotted by characteristics like little to no repeat customer loyalty, no effective pricing power among competitors, and a minimal historical ROC.

Cluster stability is measured over product and offering cycles. As cycles turn over, stable clusters converge and undergo consolidation, providing the surviving firms with significant margin and profit advantages. All stability is a relative concept; as change dominates, meaning clusters, adapt a new, previously unrecognizable form, or die due to new strategies or capabilities. These new capabilities can come from inside the cluster or outside, from the economic network. For instance, the international long distance market, lucrative in the 1980s, was first upset by calling cards and then by Skype in the 2000s. The growth of Google's online search capability shocked the Yellow Pages telephone directory cluster.

Knowing the relationships among companies in a cluster is as important as—if not more important than—knowing the status of a single company. The extra work of thinking about a firm's chances in a cluster context for a few cycles is required to understand its chances for survival and value creation.

Table 9.1 highlights differences between stable and unstable clusters.

Table 9.1
Traits of Stable vs. Unstable Clusters

Trait	Stable	Unstable
Key innovation cycle	Long/minimal change	Short/large change
Customer cycle	Recurring/long	Volatile/short
Strategies displayed	Stable	Volatile
Market share	Stable	Volatile
Cluster competitors	Known familiar	Volatile new entrants
Operating margins	Stable	Volatile
Cash flow	Stable	Volatile
Value-creating process	Stable	Volatile
Capital or value at risk	Normal	Extremely high

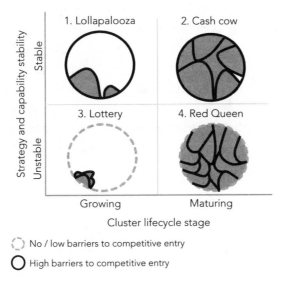

FIGURE 9.1 Cluster Stability vs. Cluster Lifecycle Stage

We can break both stable and unstable clusters into two broad categories based on revenue and on whether the cluster is in a growth or mature stage of its life (fig. 9.1).

1. The Lollapolooza cluster is the most coveted by investors. It is stable and growing with few, if any, serious competitors and high barriers to entry. The ability to grow revenues and margins in this situation can be remarkable.
2. The cash cow[1] cluster is dominated by stable strategies with participants offering high stable yields and limited growth. The closed circle indicates high barriers to entry.
3. The lottery cluster is characterized by fast follower growth and few barriers to entry, as shown by the dashed cluster boundary. These factors lead to high instability in capabilities, strategies, competitor mix, ROC margins, and of course near-term survival chances.

4. Red Queen cluster participants compete while being exposed to a continuous flood of new, capital-intensive capabilities and strategies. The Red Queen cluster is a stream of rapid innovations, producing great excitement. Most of the ino-created value flows through to customers.

You may use the checklist below to identify what kind of cluster you're looking at, and whether it may contain firms worthy of investment consideration.

The Cluster Checklist

1. Is the cluster stable or converging on a set of competitors and strategies?
2. Is it difficult for new entrants to force current participants to change strategies or lose pricing power?
3. Is the key capability iterative period longer than seven years?[2] Key capabilities are factors changing the cluster. They could be deregulation, innovation, interest rates, or any number of relevant factors.
4. Will the cluster survive more than ten years?
5. Have cluster participants shown longer term stable margins and strategies?

Thinking deeply about these questions can help you determine the type of cluster a firm exists within; the rest of this chapter goes into more detail about each cluster type.

Unstable Clusters

As seen previously, there are primarily two types of unstable clusters, categorized by their growth stage. The early stage unstable growth cluster, called a lottery cluster, has continuous new entrants and capabilities, and diffuses most of its value to consumers. The second type of unstable cluster is the Red Queen cluster. Red Queen clusters have no dominant strategy or required capability set. In Red Queen clusters, each participant is forced to constantly spend capital to adapt new strategies and capabilities but is unable to earn acceptable margins due to competitive pressure.

Lottery Clusters

Open unstable clusters, like the lottery cluster, are often hyped because they make excellent material for journalists' news stories and analyst "insights." New competitors drift in and out as products and tastes change or become outdated. These clusters are so competitive that it's almost impossible for firms to find a defensible position or a margin that yields reasonable sustained returns on capital. Despite this, capital will keep flowing in because of the lottery clusters' perceived juicy rewards—just like buying a lottery ticket. The cluster survives as long as fresh capital takes a chance at the big prize. The bar and restaurant markets in big cities are good examples of lottery clusters. Innovators pop up, hoping to strike it rich in these "hits"-based businesses.

The lure of innovative new growth markets and products is tempting. Amazon.com has been a huge success. Would you have picked it to succeed against the incumbent bookstores that had publishing relationships in the 1990s? What about all of the competing "e" online start-ups? If you bought into the Amazon IPO in 1997 at roughly $18 per share, by mid-2013, after stock splits, your shares would have returned over 17,000 percent. That's a lottery ticket high return, but that doesn't necessarily make it a good allocation. If Amazon was one of 170 Internet IPOs you bet on in 1997 and the others went bankrupt, your portfolio broke even. If you missed selecting Amazon among your picks, you suffered losses. This might sound extremely pessimistic, but looking at an Internet index later in chapter 15, I will show how this worked out. Never confuse a lucky idiosyncratic outcome with a systematic process for managing allocation risk and exposure. Process and method trump luck.

Focusing exclusively on winners and survivors is called survivorship bias. Survivorship bias creeps into lots of anecdotal post hoc investment analysis. Allocators must balance reward with the real risks and choice set available at a given time. From 1987 to 2002, 2 percent of technology IPOs accounted for 100 percent of IPO net wealth creation.[3] That indicates a 50:1 ratio of losers to winners in the technology IPO game during the Internet mania period. The odds of success when allocating to a cluster this volatile are low.

Allocating to lottery clusters is like gambling on a parimutuel horse race; the cumulative odds favor the house. This house-bias means that even clusters delivering "revolutionary" benefits to society can be a net loss for the investors, who fund the exploration of economic possibility spaces but rarely bet on the single winning horse. Allocating smartly isn't about picking a horse to win a long race; rather, it involves repeatedly finding a good race in which competing horses either don't show up, or the ones who do show up can barely walk. This doesn't sound sporting, but winning at capital allocation is about picking the right horse *and* the right race, not the excitement of a single day at the races. For the professional gambler, betting at the Kentucky Derby is probably less lucrative than going to an out-of-the-way track with a race that nobody cares about filled with a bunch of horses nobody pays much attention to. As an allocator, the race for value creation in the cluster shouldn't be glamorous; it needs to be easily won.

The lottery effect is alive in the stock market, dominating during periods of explosive innovation propelling debt or equity fueled price bubbles. Hope, not reason, fuels these investors' decisions. A hot cluster promising untold lottery riches is a centuries-old drama— the promises and outcomes are mostly the same; only the actors' names and innovations change. The end result for, say, the dotcom bubble in the 1990s was obvious to anyone who researched previous technology revolutions such as eighteenth-century railroads, radio in the 1920s, or television manufacturing in the 1950s. They are after all just repeat outcomes of evolution's selective adaptive process converging to a few dominant participants for a while, a macroprocess that evolution has repeated for millennia.

Many lottery cluster investors buy into the first-to-market myth. Being the first to own a ticket doesn't change the long-term odds of winning. Don't allocate to a businesses for which success depends on being first to market with a single novel capability. Rarely does first-to-market create a sustainable advantage; typically the early, adventuring firm finds that its early success acts as a flag, signaling and attracting stronger competitors who bring fresh new capabilities into the cluster.

The time between first and second to market is how quickly competitive margins disappear, especially in low barrier-to-entry clusters. The third and fourth to market simply pile on the margin compression misery for early entrants. Large pools of venture capital, private equity, new business initiatives, and merger and acquisition (M&A) activities around a "hot" competitive cluster are signals of competitor mix instability and future margin instability. If a strategy and capability can be replicated appearing to offer good returns on capital, it's safe to assume that someone will attempt to replicate the firm's capability set. Orkut, Friendster, and MySpace beat Facebook to market. These early social network winners are now twenty-first century digital ghost towns, relics of bygone days of technologists and venture capitalists mining for digital social gold.

Red Queen Clusters

The lottery cluster is a cluster with negative to marginal earnings and rapid revenue growth. The second type of unstable cluster—the Red Queen cluster—is mature with low or no revenue growth but poses a subtler innovation trap—it requires vigorous capital spending to keep up with competitive inos. As these inos are adopted by competitors, they deliver value to customers but not to allocators.

The name Red Queen is based on the story of the Red Queen's race, from Lewis Carroll's *Alice in Wonderland*, where all the participants run as fast as they can but never seem to progress forward. "It takes all the running you can do, to keep in the same place." It's a metaphor that's been useful in biology as well. In 1973, the evolutionary biologist Leigh Van Valen put forth the Red Queen hypothesis, stating: "For an evolutionary system, continuing development is needed just in order to maintain its fitness relative to the systems it is coevolving with."[4] Coevolution adaptation can be seen as an arms race between prey and predator(s) capabilities, or between a species and its symbiotic niche.

The common English peppered moth provides a classic study in Red Queen survival adaptation. The peppered moth lives in England between London and Manchester. In the eighteenth century the species was populated with 99.9 percent mottled white/gray color moths, with only 0.01 percent of the population being dark colored. The moth's light color let it blend in with native lichens growing on tree bark, to avoid bird predation. In the mid-nineteenth century, coal dust pollution from the industrial revolution mills killed the lichens, leaving the dark bark of the trees exposed. Peppered moths with darker coloring suddenly had an advantage, as they were able to better blend in with the soot-covered tree leaves and darker tree bark. By 1895, within a few moth generations, 98 percent of moths in Manchester were reported to be dark in color.[5] The peppered moth adapted a trait relative to an environmental shift, maintaining its species niche and population. This adaptation allowed the moth to survive but didn't necessarily improve its population or ecological representation measured in biomass terms from when it was mostly light colored in preindustrial England.

Coadaptation occurs among symbiotic or tightly coupled pred-ator prey species. A symbiotic coevolutionary relationship exists between many exotic orchids that have long flower channels required for pollination. These orchids and their flower channels have a direct relationship to a moth or pollinator species with an exact correspondingly shaped proboscis for pollination. The rela-tionship is like an evolving dance between a shape-shifting lock and key, coadapting symbiotically over plant and pollinator gen-erations. Neither species can advance or dominate relative to the niche's carrying capacity, but the coadapting symbiotic forms and shapes become increasingly exotic. This Red Queen dance creates complex exotic forms and structures while the relative species' population density per unit of ecosystem may remain fairly static.

So it is with Red Queen clusters. Innovation is constant—never giving any one firm a perpetual guaranteed competitive edge. As firms compete harder, attempting to stay in step with each other and with customer desires, the cluster competitive pressure squeezes margins, pushing value to the customer. Competitors face a game of perpetual operational and strategic destabilization. Ino value flows into and through the cluster, but little excess value is captured by any competitor in the cluster. Almost all knowledge value flows through to consumers.

The Red Queen process is expensive for shareholders. The capital for fueling the endless needed innovations repeatedly destroys ROC margins. Instead of leaving the race, most firms just fight harder, often spending capital on things like branding, distri-bution, or marketing. In the meantime, new innovations enter the cluster, diffusing among competitors leaving no sustainable mar-gin advantage for any specific firm. Firms that continue to fight this losing battle often do so because managers are prioritizing personal career over returns on capital and the honest protection of shareholder value.

As a new ino-powered capability enters a Red Queen cluster, early adopting organizations briefly capture higher margins before these margins revert to normal as remaining firms adopt the innovation. As discussed earlier, the process of margins spiking before reverting to the mean is an important lesson, as allocators need to distinguish temporary margin and earnings spikes from sustainable competitive advantages. Let's take a look at the rise and fall of an ino's value passing through a fictive firm, Bob's Lemonade, to see how this works at the cluster level.

The firm, Bob's Lemonade, hires a consultant who has just developed a "super squeezer" method for getting more juice out of each lemon. This new capability, after costs, saves Bob's firm an extra 1 percent (100 basis points) per sale, while holding the price steady at $1.00 per glass. This means an extra $0.01 in income. Given that Bob's lemonade business had a stable earnings margin of 4 percent of revenue prior to adopting the super squeezer capability, this new efficiency capability allows the firm to capture more value and grow earnings to 5 percent, a whopping 25 percent increase. When Bob reports these increased earnings publicly, analysts and investors go crazy for his stock. Originally priced at $100 a share, Bob's stock rises 25 percent to $125 a share, based on the new earnings. Brokers and the press make Bob's Lemonade a hot story stock among the staid lemonade business, encouraging many to buy in. Bob is heralded as an industry leader and visionary. Even the quantitative, efficient market types and momentum players pile in as the stock price moves up increasing economic price-based models that indicate significant value creation based on "statistical risk" and volatility measures.

But then, something happens. It always does in these stories. Bob's competitor, Lucky Linda's Lemon Emporium, also adopts the consultant's "super squeezer" innovation capability. Uh oh!

Lucky Linda's Lemon Emporium lowers its lemonade prices 1 percent to increase its market share in the cutthroat lemonade business. Linda figures she can grow sales by 10 percent with her cheaper price and still have a 4 percent net earnings margin. Her idea works, and Linda publicly reports earnings growth of 10 percent. Meanwhile, the other lemonade managers start to feel squeezed, with Bob's hot stock getting all the press attention and Linda eating into their market share with her lower prices.

It's at this point that the innovation diffusion process really kicks in. All CEOs in the lemonade cluster get pressured by their boards of directors to adapt and allocate capital to the new "super squeezer" capability. In order to keep market share and cover fixed operating costs, the competitors reduce lemonade prices 1 percent, delivering more value to the consumer in the network. With prices reduced 1 percent for all consumers, the super squeezer ino has triumphed at its game of replicating itself and delivering value into the economy, as everyone squeezes lemonade more efficiently. The super squeezer capability is now a required dominant organizational capability. But now the value isn't going to the firms—it's been pressured by the cluster to diffuse and flow downstream to consumers in the economy. And that's when the trouble starts for Linda and Bob.

Lucky Linda's market share returns to where it originally was. Lucky Linda's earnings and stock drop 10 percent, back to its original price. Shareholders in Linda's business are restless, hoping that the capital outlay for the squeezer capability and business process change was covered by the temporary rise in earnings. Meanwhile, Bob's new shareholders are really unhappy. In order to stay competitive and hold onto his customers to protect revenues, Bob was forced to drop his prices by 1 percent, like everyone else, to $0.99/glass. This returns his margins to roughly where they were, and reduces his revenue 1 percent below where he started, depressing his recently elevated earnings further. Bob's $125/share stock drops 20 percent, returning to $100. Shocked and confused analysts suddenly complain about Bob's volatile, unstable earnings and his shrinking revenue. The quantitative, Markowitz Efficient Frontier investors and momentum guys sell at a loss. Believers in modern portfolio theory who wrongly believe that stock price volatility fully represents risk[6] believe Bob's stock is riskier, arguing that his firm is worth less than its original $100 price due to increased volatility. Bob's CEO stock option plan is now below water, and the board wrongly starts a search for another visionary CEO to lift the stock price.

Research analysts looking at high flyers like Bob and Larry see that they have recently reported 20 percent and 10 percent earnings declines, respectively. The analysts are shocked and disappointed. These earnings contractions were unforeseen by analysts who didn't consider the Red Queen cluster's ino and value diffusion process. They blame management[7] for the dips in earnings. As a result, Bob's and Linda's firms are seen as dangerous investments. Analysts will move their recommendations on these stocks to "neutral" and start chasing the next hot story or sector. The journalists and pundits, looking at the 1 percent revenue shrinkage of the overall lemonade cluster, tell people to sell lemonade shares as the market appears to be in decline even as volumes hold steady.

The reality around all this stock market noise and journalist and analyst spilled ink is that evolution's economic process is humming along, with network accumulating knowledge and structural efficiency perfectly well. Bob's Lemonade has simply gone through a full innovation–diffusion cycle, which may have taken a year or two depending on the cycle speed. From a cluster point of view, the developer of the "super squeezer" sold each competitor a cost-saving innovation. The super squeezer value creation capability is now a required capability and dominant design among lemonade vendors, increasing the capability, complexity, and efficiency of the lemonade cluster to deliver value more efficiently into the economy.

The super squeezer Red Queen innovation flow and diffusion cycle story results in the economy (consumers) capturing value as lemonade became quantitatively 1 percent better—better, in this example, meaning cheaper. Hopefully the temporary extra value captured by early adopting firms like Bob's and Lucky Linda's allowed them to recover the costs and risks associated with adapting innovation early. The laggards, on the other hand, may not recoup the innovation's capital outlay costs, leaving the lagging firms to fall that much further behind in the ROC metrics and capability to create shareholder value. Smaller participants with lower margins and less operating capital may be unable to afford the new capability and be forced out of the cluster.

In many cases, however, the laggards have a sizeable advantage. Often an innovation or strategic process comes along that requires the competitor to do nothing but wait in order to minimize risk of failure. And this goes for the allocator as well. That's right—the most powerful allocator skill next to finding a stable cluster and sound competitive firm with a good strategy is the patience to do nothing while short-term noise and news unfolds, and the competitive ino and knowledge diffusion macro process takes its course. Most new capabilities put to work in the economy either fade as fads (nonhelpful mutations) or confer limited advantages as their benefits diffuse and become part of the required dominant design. Often, the art of capital management is choosing what not to do and when not to do it. A small minority of inos and capabilities may let a firm capture sustained value, escaping the Red Queen paradox.

Allocators win in the Red Queen cluster by staying away from it or by matching the capital allocation outlay to the time period in which there is a payoff. A one-year competitive advantage requires a greater than 100 percent ROC for breakeven to compensate for risk. The question to ask of an allocation to any organization's capability mix is, "How long can this be unique?" Allocating to a firm in a Red Queen cluster is like playing rock, paper, scissors with your investments; each strategy gives you an equal chance to win, but no strategy has the advantage in the short or long term unless you know your opponent's moves far in advance.

This is called a nontransitive game; nontransitive games are unstable relative to the strategy selected by the participant. In some versions of nontransitive games, knowing the first mover's strategy allows follow-on strategies to win. Red Queen clusters are like this; the game itself (cluster structure) doesn't allow for a winning dominant long-term value creation process, and seemingly anyone can win at any time. An open Red Queen cluster is even more risky than a traditional nontransitive game, as inos show up leading to almost limitless new temporary "winning" strategies or capabilities.[8]

Pre-emptive awareness of strategy and game dynamics isn't something found in nature. Winning strategies emerge through natural selection. In economics, the winning strategy or capability set can emerge from anywhere, like a random adaptation or mutation in nature, to surprise everyone. Winning stable strategies may only become apparent during the convergence or mature stages of the cluster. Nobody saw Google coming in 1998 and nobody knows its eventual usurper one or one hundred years from now.

Competitors in unstable clusters may have equal revenue "winnings" for long periods of time with minor differences and little to no sustained returns on equity. Large revenue clusters are often mistakenly viewed as lucrative by investors. Depending on the stability, these clusters can have negative rates of return that may persist for decades as existing or new firms throw capital at hot new strategies and counter strategies seeking to make it big, mistakenly paying for the right to survive and keep playing a losing game. Red Queen non-stable clusters with easily "seen" opportunities are the black holes of allocator capital. They destroy investor capital and value, spilling red ink over hopes and dreams.

A well-known big revenue Red Queen cluster is the American airline industry. American airline carriers, in total, have lost every dime ever invested into them when measured in aggregate. The cluster growth dynamics squeezed airlines, pushing value to flow upstream to aircraft manufacturers and downstream to passengers. Little value has been returned to airline shareholders in aggregate,[9] but the economy and, axiomatically, society have benefitted from the increased value flow-associated cheap and safer travel and transport.

Red Queen firms rationalize their "progress" by masquerading as growth firms. For the lone firm, progress in value creation capabilities is relative to the future capability state of the cluster. Growth hungry managers will use the balance sheet to raise debt money, to pursue lottery tickets and ignore the Red Queen reality. They will convince themselves and shareholders that they are pursuing growth strategies; too often, these will become value-destroying traps.

The growth trap occurs when managers become addicted to blindly allocating today's hard-earned capital, plowing it into clusters to chase revenue or market share growth. The trap is that these follow-on allocations may never deliver acceptable returns on capital, because the capability cycle is shorter than the payback cycle. This occurs when managers confuse their luck of operating a good business in a good cluster with their skill at identifying and allocating capital to other such situations. This can lead to one-hit CEOs and investor losses as allocators confuse a lucky jockey with a good horse in a good "easy to win" race.

Managers can become so addicted to growth, attention, and excitement via wrong incentive structures and shareholder expectations that they refuse to stop or reduce allocation and pursue cash harvesting strategies for fear of falling off of the overly hyped growth rocket ship. Sustained 15 percent returns on capital are often better than an uncertain 25 percent earnings growth. The 15 percent returns represent a high return on equity; the 25 percent earnings growth could represent an unlikely chance at a very high return on equity.

Many businesses justify upfront capital spending by using lifetime customer value analysis. Lifetime customer value models are based on spending money up front in marketing or other costs to create an ongoing customer cash flow relationship that pays off over time. Managers may engage in loss-leading activities in the hopes of securing customers or other structural competitive advantages going forward. This isn't always value destroying but needs to be scrutinized closely by the allocator. The sacrifice of today's ROC margins and treasure for tomorrow's economies of scale or scope is a risky bet.

At year-end 2010, Amazon had $1.9 billion in retained earnings paying no dividends after fifteen years of business and cumulative sales of more than $170 billion over that time period. This is less than 1 percent in retained earnings relative to sales. Amazon has plowed all of its earnings into capabilities and buying growth. For this Amazon was valued at $118 billion, 14 times the book value of $8.5 billion and 29 times cash flow from operating activities of roughly $4.0 billion in mid-2013.[10]

Amazon managers and investors have perpetually rolled forward the bet that the firm is correct in its allocation of free cash flow and capital to a collection of new value-creating and- capturing capabilities. Based on Amazon's market capitalization, investors appear to be hoping that these capabilities someday yield significant excess earnings that will accrete to the company's balance sheet or be paid as dividends rather than yet more low ROC revenue growing capabilities ad infinitum.

Amazon's management, like that of many growth companies, is throwing today's bird in the hand at tomorrow's three birds in the bush. Amazon is making a big, continuously rolled forward strategic bet. Based on Amazon's share price, shareholders don't see this as chasing Red Queens or lottery clusters. However, should Amazon stumble due to changes in the participants or dynamics of the clusters they compete in, the share price of Amazon and its collection of capabilities could significantly change. Shares priced for growth often fall significantly upon acknowledgement of limits to growth or failure to maintain the price implied growth trajectory and multiples. Eventually the rocket ship has to either land at its destination, yielding and retaining the high earnings, or plummet back to earth, burning up on re-entry. Unless the sources and capacity for sustained growth are understood, these investments can get ridiculously overpriced. Never confuse revenue growth with value capture; they are distinct but not mutually exclusive processes.

So, in summary—within Red Queen clusters, constant competitive instability erodes margins and returns on capital. These margins and ROC may become permanently low for all participants. The Red Queen cluster acts like a selfish entity, burning all competing organizational capital to apply the knowledge required for growing new capabilities. This macroprocessing drives the adaptation of ever more complex capabilities and technologies, for the cluster's own survival and increased value delivery. Value flows from ino to customer, bypassing shareholders.[11]

The lesson for allocators is to understand how innovation diffusion affects the flow and retention of value through a cluster over capability cycles and time. Great innovations don't always lead to great organizational or allocator outcomes. Constant ino creation embedded in products and enabling capabilities tends to transfer value to customers, increasing the rate of value flow through economies. Evolution's processes have no sympathy to any strategy or competitor—everyone must adapt the knowledge, structural complexity, and flow capacity to feed the economy's value-consuming demands.

Stable Clusters: The Allocator's Hunting Grounds

Stability occurs when dominant strategies are in place and a small group of one to five participants dominate by holding 50 to 90 percent of the cluster market share. In stable regimes, operating margins may also be high and stable, as potential competitors find the cost and risk of entry to be less attractive due to competitive threats. Many competitive processes adapt to leave few dominant winners. The distribution of value captured may approximate the 80:20 rule, with 80 percent of the value or excess returns on capital accruing to 20 percent of the participants.

A cluster's average return on capital hardly tells the full tale. The average return of public companies can be considered equivalent to a long-term index return. For instance, in the 80 to 20 percent rule, there are many times when the majority of smaller sized companies may be destroying capital as they struggle to stay in the race, while the few largest outliers on the tail of the distribution have ROCs significantly above the mean. Or, niche entrants may pursue the cluster, only to exit or be absorbed by larger players as bolt-on capability acquisitions. It's important that the allocator look deeper than just average industry returns on capital to understand the full picture of a cluster's composition—earnings share along with market share.

Cluster Pressure Forces the Convergence Phase

The cluster convergence process, leaving a few entrants remaining with a sustained competitive edge, is a common evolutionary path to network and cluster stability. Convergence by consolidation occurs as marginal competitors exit or are acquired by dominant firms possessing greater scales of efficiency in their production, distribution, finance, and marketing capabilities.

In nature, animals fight over territory and resources—such as a watering hole on the savanna. As the collective resource becomes more actively pursued and scarce, each species may exhibit signs of physical stress and weakness. Some species, if they are weakened significantly, may die out altogether, leaving only the strongest species remaining. This is the convergence phase. After the convergence phase has ended, those that survive and dominate will likely recover and get stronger once the less fit competitors have exited. When looked at from a product perspective, Gause's law of competitive exclusion seems to hold up at the level of the organization.

Examples of cluster convergence can be seen across many clusters in the United States. For instance, 300 bicycle manufacturers competed in 1890; by 1905, 12 bicycle manufacturers survived. Over 1,000 car manufacturers existed before 1920; by 1929 there were 44. 1,900 breweries competed in 1910; by 2010, three breweries in the United States accounted for 80 percent of beer sales. The capabilities of advertising, production, and distribution each lend themselves to large returns on scale, and so a few leaders were able to separate themselves from the pack, emerging faster by using their excess profits to expand their scale and marginal advantages in a virtuous amplifying feedback cycle—a Lollapalooza. In the United States there are now 1,500 craft brewers with marginal scale and niche products. Since 1984, the major craft brewer—Sam Adams—has attempted to challenge the three dominant players, and as a result sells $600 million worth of beer per year as of 2012 in a $98 billion U.S. market. Sam Adams's growth, while remarkable over time, is also a testament to the relative stability of the major players in the consolidated U.S. beer cluster.

For allocators, the advantage of a stable cluster is the ability to invest for the long term. This provides tax and transaction advantages, fueling significant impacts on the compounding effects of capital. Long-term allocations to stable value clusters are powerful.

Cash Cow Clusters

The cash cow cluster is an allocator's hunting ground. These clusters have stable strategies and a stable participant mix, with long stable product cycle periods and strong stable cash flow among a few dominant participants. Within a cash cow cluster, the allocator should be on the lookout for a firm that has zero or few competitors, with loyal customers happily repeating fairly high-margin purchasing behavior over and over again.

The fast-moving consumer goods (FMCG) sector is home to many cash cows, characterized by clusters with one or two dominating offerings. These are super brands as measured by consumer recognition and ROC. They shape and own their clusters. In the United States, Kiwi shoe polish, WD-40 lubricant, and Turtle Wax car wax are examples of super brands standing alone in consumer awareness, distribution, and pricing power for their clusters.[12]

See's Candy, an old favorite for discussion by value investors[13], is another example of a cash cow. See's Candy is a chocolate candy company and exists within a cluster that has few game-changing inos. See's focuses on this cluster, rather than expanding into new industries and products that may destroy shareholder capital. By and large See's sticks to its knitting and hands back a lot of cash to its owner, Berkshire Hathaway. The value-creating engine powering See's Candy may not grow revenues rapidly, but its more important ROC and ROE is terrific and has been operating for decades. See's Candy is the classic cash cow, and one that Warren Buffet has written about extensively.

Cash cows at the right price can make excellent long-term investments. Allocating to a cash cow means understanding, with confidence, the sources of its excess margin. Cash cows may appear expensive based on the book value of the firm's assets, because the innovations and strategies leading to excess margins and high ROC aren't highlighted explicitly on the balance sheet. This is why the investor must understand the sources of excess margin, and the likely duration and durability of those excess margins, in order to spot cash cows. In value investing terms, these excess margins are the results of capability sets forming economic moats. A moat is a useful concept and term created by Warren Buffet to define the unique properties a firm has that let it earn high margins sustainably. We will explore moats in detail in the next chapter.

Mature cash cow clusters can offer beautiful high and sleepy—by which I mean low volatility—margins. Firms with sleepy high operating margins that don't change are great when shares can be purchased at the right price. Even as share prices jump around, the long-term value creation process stays in place. All Coke drinkers aren't likely to wake up one day and start drinking tap water. As clusters stabilize, there's a tendency toward slower revenue growth, but there's also lower margin variability and a familiar competitor mix. Mature clusters often see extremely slow-cycle market share fights between a few dominant competitors for minor annual percentage point swings—like, for instance, the battle between Coke and Pepsi offerings.

Lollapalooza Clusters

The fourth and final category of cluster is that rare and special jewel known as the Lollapalooza. Charlie Munger uses the word Lollapalooza[14] to describe these fast-compounding, long-lived, value-creating organizations. Lollapaloozas are characterized by fast growth and an ability to scale revenue and ROC for a long time. They are driven by positive feedback loops that amplify competitive advantages. Lollapalooza clusters are growth clusters defined or dominated by a single firm. These single firm–dominated clusters are the kudzu of the investing world, growing incredibly fast and spreading pervasively for long periods. Walmart, Costco, The Home Depot, and other firms in Lollapalooza clusters grew exponentially.

In complex systems these self-growing behaviors are known as "autocatalytic," in which the outputs of the system flow feed back into inputs, acting as catalysts that accelerate growth. Charlie Munger's Lollapaloozas use fast-growing free cash flow to grow the scale of their growth operations by expanding the cluster and improving their operational effectiveness as measured by margins. This leads to wonderfully compounding high returns on invested capital. Figure 9.2 shows how positive feedback loops in life and value processes grow as "virtuous circles."

Lollapaloozas occur when a confluence of factors contribute to growth. Growth in earnings (excess value creation) comes from two distinct sources: unit growth and efficiency due to structural growth. Using the nature metaphor, unit growth is equivalent to an increase in, say, rabbit population. Structural evolutionary growth would

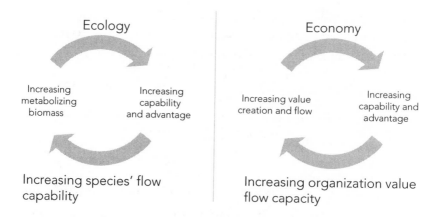

Ecology

Increasing
metabolizing
biomass

Increasing
capability
and advantage

Increasing species' flow
capability

Economy

Increasing value
creation and flow

Increasing
capability and
advantage

Increasing organization value
flow capacity

FIGURE 9.2 Compounding Positive Feedback Grows Flow Rates

occur if each of those rabbits grew five feet tall, increasing the rabbits per unit biomass (life) represented in the ecosystem. Either form of growth could increase the measured success of the species as measured by biomass in an ecosystem. Lollapalooza organizations adapt structurally, becoming more efficient while simultaneously expanding the volume of value delivered.

A retail franchise firm that is growing the number of stores it has while also increasing the profitability of each store per square foot is an example of combining unit and structural growth associated with a Lollapalooza. Figure 9.3 shows how a retail store Lollapalooza combines each store's earnings growth with a growing number of stores. Ino capabilities inside the cluster combine, making every store more profitable as measured by the same store sales (SSS) earning metric. This is structural evolutionary growth. At the same time, the addressable cluster (inter-cluster) growth, as measured by number of stores, increases as well. This is unit growth. The example in figure 9.3 combines a 7.5 percent SSS growth metric and 7.5 percent annual increase in the number of stores producing an annual 15 percent earnings growth rate. The combined effect yields roughly $8 for each $1 put in versus only $3 for a single store effect.

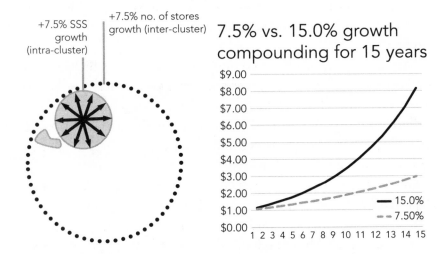

FIGURE 9.3 Long-Term Combined Inter- and Intra-Cluster Growth Is More Powerful

The Home Depot was a Lollapalooza in the retail sector, with increasing SSS earnings and a growing number of stores. The Home Depot had advantages of scale and volume, which meant that older, smaller hardware stores couldn't compete. Similar to Walmart, as more merchandise value flowed through their distribution system of stores, The Home Depot got better at positioning the merchandise, stronger at negotiating with suppliers, and better at attracting customers. This combination of accreting advantageous knowledge capabilities produced greater cash flow, fueling more growth and allowing the organization's capabilities to spread further and faster while at the same time becoming more effective.

As The Home Depot processed and sold more merchandise, it became more efficient at many retailing capabilities such as purchasing, distribution, and marketing. This is the equivalent of a single organization capturing the bulk of the economic advantages of an experience curve. The Home Depot's retailing efficiency advantages generated more cash flow for to allocate for exponential growth. This growth created yet more value throughput, leading to greater efficiencies, until the carrying capacity limit within the U.S. economic network for mega hardware stores was reached.[15]

The Home Depot had a competitor in Lowe's, which used a similar capability set and operational business model. The Home Depot correctly chose to grow in different parts of the country and not compete directly until the market matured and physically filled. In the early days a consumer's choice set rarely included both a Lowe's and The Home Depot.

The Lollapalooza value creation outcomes for The Home Depot shareholders are shown in figure 9.4.[16] The Home Depot had three stores in 1979 and was listed on the New York Stock Exchange in 1984. It had remarkable growth from 1984 to 2000 as it filled its economic "pond," the geographic United States, to carrying capacity with over 1,900 stores.

Lollapalooza firms create or dominate the clusters they compete in, using their mix of capabilities to encourage customer recognition as the easiest consumer choice. For retail category killers such as The Home Depot, Walmart, Toys "R" Us, and Bed Bath & Beyond, that

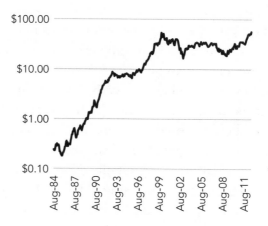

FIGURE 9.4 The Home Depot Share Price
Semi-logarithmic chart adjusted for dividends and stock splits.
Source: Yahoo! data.

meant identifying market locations where the firm's unique advantages could reap large returns on capital. Investing in Lollapaloozas early, prior to full geographic cluster saturation and the achievement of mature operational efficiencies, is key to maximizing returns.

Summary

The stability of margins is created by minimizing capability competitive threats. Profit and operating margin stability is the most important trait of the cluster to understand. It bears repeating—selecting a stable long-lived cluster at the correct development life cycle stage is as important as selecting the correct firm within a cluster. Clusters do not have equilibrium regions, fixed points, or "solutions" as traditional economics crudely implies. Rather, they are bombarded by constant storms of innovation and competition. Like ecological niches, clusters are born, grow, and disappear continuously in evolution's ever-adapting economic network.

The allocator should seek organizations that compete in or dominate and define a customer choice set for the long term. Avoid lottery clusters with high odds that lead to low adjusted risk payouts, and skip the Red Queen clusters, which pass value to customers. Seek firms in cash cow clusters and, if possible, the elusive Lollapaloozas at good prices relative to free cash flow yields.

Once the allocator has spotted a promising cluster, the next challenge is to identify firms with unique capabilities that deliver pricing power and margin advantage over many consumption cycles. The key to picking out a single firm within a stable cluster is to spot and measure the forces contributing to high returns on equity. As mentioned, these high, sustained, and defensible returns are called moats. The next chapters will dive into moat details. When selecting an investment within a stable cluster, the firm with the largest moat and highest long-term potential ROC is logically preferred.

PART IV
Moats

CHAPTER TEN

The Value of Moats

Live long and prosper.

VULCAN SALUTE FROM *STAR TREK*

FOR AN ALLOCATOR, success means investing in firms with sustained positive returns on capital in excess of inflation. Sustained 20 to 30 percent ROE in a low-risk, long-term stable environment are highly desirable. A moat occurs when some or all of a firm's capabilities combine, creating sustainable high margins. The confluences of capability and behaviors that lead to moats are exceptionally rare.

All moated firms share three traits:

1. A unique mix of capabilities not shared by any competitor
2. The ability to capture high margins, using pricing power relative to competitors
3. Durability to survive over multiple competitive product or capability and economic cycles

These traits create shareholder value via sustained high ROC. If any one of the three is missing, there isn't a moat. By keeping competitors at bay, a moat delivers high margins and thus high returns on capital. Moats are powerful—a study by McKinsey of the S&P 500 companies indicates that a 1 percent increase in pricing power (selling efficiency) or 1 percent decline in costs (margin efficiency) would equate to an 8 percent increase in profits.[1]

Most businesses don't have a moat to protect their profit margins. They mostly compete at negligible or negative returns on capital for brief periods. Value can be wasted or destroyed as management chases ongoing losses or unsuccessfully explores adjacent economic possibility spaces. The historical competitive record of a firm's capabilities can be seen in the retained earnings, dividends, and ROEs spread across years of annual SEC 10-K filings. These SEC filings are the corporate fossil records of earlier battles won and lost; the allocator should start studying these when trying to identify a moat.

The ecological equivalent to moats is the stable physical or behavioral traits a species uses to survive and grow as a population. Nature's moats are made of defensive and offensive capabilities. The 450 million-year-old horseshoe crab body shape is a great ecological dominant design creating a persistent moat.

Identifying the business equivalent to the horseshoe crab is a lucrative pursuit. Like animals' physical capabilities, economic moats take many forms with differing life expectancies. Firms adapt complex competitive forms in the cutthroat adaptive dance over many product and customer cycles. The allocator's goal is to identify a few moats, offering high margins and returns on capital while protecting and growing the value of assets and invested capital. Walmart's long-term share price from 1972–2002 reflects the value captured for shareholders by a rare excellent performing moat (fig. 10.1).

Moats Create Deep Margins for Long Durations

Value flows and grows through the company as it delivers products and services to customers. Relative competitive forces

FIGURE 10.1 Walmart's Share Price
Semi-logarithmic chart adjusted for dividends and stock splits.
Source: Yahoo! data.

determine, the company's ability to retain extra value in the form of profits.

Firm value creation begins at the ino, which is then expressed as the firm's capabilities. The mix of capabilities and behaviors may weave together to form a moat. For instance, a unique capability or strategy may evolve to give a firm minimal competition and high pricing power, allowing the firm to retain or hold back value for itself as higher profit margins. Low-competition situations means the clusters that selectively squeeze all the ino's created value downstream to customers.

Seemingly small but well-managed advantages can compound, offering profound rewards and acting like a profit and market dominance ratchet. To win at blackjack over the long run, you need to win more than 50 percent of the time. If you manage your chips smartly, even a 1 percent edge for a 51 percent win rate can make all the difference. Businesses compete in the same way; a 2 percent

(200 bps) operating advantage over the competition can become a significant edge if it's sustained over ten years. Given enough repeat winners (customer sales) and a stable process for winning (pricing power leading to high margins), significant value in the form of capital or further competitive advantage can pile up over time. These slight advantages in capital efficiency and value capture erode a competitor's effectiveness. Advantageous capabilities aren't typically based on single heroic victories or the revolutionary capabilities that make newspaper headlines. Instead, moats come about when a novel capability cranks out wider profit margins methodically with more sunny days than rainy days over years—or decades.

That such small extra-profit margins are initially involved explains why stability of the cluster is so important; having a 51 percent advantage in the game of blackjack isn't much help if in the middle of the game you suddenly find your chips riding on the spin at a roulette wheel or resting on a poker table instead. The stable cluster is equivalent to playing the same game with fixed rules over and over again, allowing a cumulative compounding advantage to work its magic.

However, it's not enough just to find a high margin "winning" firm in a stable cluster. Effective capital allocation means understanding the true nature and source of sustainable margin advantage. This can be a challenge, as the capabilities may be obscure or even hidden trade secrets. The efficiencies of great supplier relationships, strong, honest culture, or customer biases toward a favorite brand may not be directly measurable for the investor. These efficiency outcomes show up indirectly as excess margins relative to competitors or repeated earnings retained or paid as dividends on the balance sheet.

Take, for instance, a firm selling industrial detergents in bulk to institutions like universities, operating with low margins. Along comes another firm that reforms this bulk commodity with a few chemical and packaging changes and starts marketing it to consumers—as Tide did in 1946. Even though they are also selling chemical detergents, Tide is in another competitive and economic margin position altogether. Understanding the source of value that leads to the marginal difference between bulk detergent and Tide is one key to understanding the nature of its value. The excess value, repeatedly captured as higher profit margin, is the outcome of Tide's moat.

Competitive innovation can erode a firm's moat advantage, forcing the firm to either reduce the unit flow of value (fewer sales) or give up value to customers by lowering prices and margins (value capture per unit). However, the presence of a moat means the firm can weather competitive pressures more successfully, temporarily giving up excess margin without compromising core value-creating capabilities and ROC.

Moat Depth

Moat depth is measured by the extra profit margin per sale (act of selection) that a firm has relative to competitors. Deeper moats capture higher profit margins. High margins determine the long-term ROE of the firm and shareholders' returns, assuming management responsibly allocates capital back into high ROC activities or gives it back to the investor. If competitors earn 8 percent ROC on average over many years and a moated firm earns 20 percent, that means the moat is 12 percent deep.

Moat depth, in terms of relative ROE, is the outcome of years of excess company margins. A moated firm's record—if accurately presented on the cash flow and income statement—is lumpy, with a strong trend of solid margins showing up over many years. If there aren't high historical margins, don't expect them to suddenly show up tomorrow unless some dramatic catalyst has altered the cluster or firm.

Understanding the moat's depth relative to competitors and looking at historical performance helps an investor set long-term performance expectations. Strong relative moat depth indicates underlying advantages that may be sustainable or even expanding on a go-forward basis. It's important to track moat depth after investing, by monitoring the firm's capability to capture high margins and thus maintain high ROE.

Moat Duration

The second investor metric used to describe a moat is its expected duration. Moat duration is often linked with cluster stability. How long is the relative advantage that created the moat going to last? Making a one-off 30 percent return on capital is one thing; making a 30 percent annualized return on capital for ten years is something else altogether. Studying key product and capability cycle lengths helps one estimate moat duration. Reading business history and innovation case studies also helps. The most durable moats are multifaceted, using unique capabilities from Doblin's ten types of innovation capabilities, offering long-term relative advantages.

One key to measuring a moat's likely duration is its defensibility as measured by estimating the cost a competitor would incur trying to replicate a moat's capability mix. Businesses with high margins—over 25 percent ROC—may look appealing to someone with resources to throw at the problem. Even if it is irrational to do so, a high ROC may inspire a business manager with the resources of a giant multinational to give it a go for years. Thus the analyst must ask: what would it cost the smartest competitor to build and replace this firm's moat? How long would it take and what would the expected returns on capital be? This thought process helps assess the potential of a competing firm showing up wallet in hand to wreck the moat.

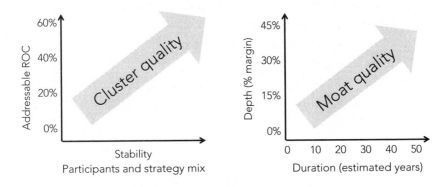

FIGURE 10.2 Measuring Cluster and Moat Quality

Moat Depth × Duration = Moat Value

A moat's value is estimated by its depth, in terms of excess margin capture, and its expected duration. Thinking through the capabilities driving the moat and cluster helps the investor select long-term allocations that are likely to provide higher ROEs. Competitive moats are as valuable as their combined depth and duration. Figure 10.2 shows a useful way of thinking about moat and cluster value.

The checklist can help you to assess the expected depth and duration of a moat.

The following are moat valuation questions:

1. How long has the moat been in place? Assess the moat's resilience to threats and past moat responses.
2. How long will it take a competitor to replicate the moat?
3. How quickly can the moat disappear due to bad management, bad luck, or innovation?
4. What is the dollar amount or ROE incentive for a competitor to replace the moat?
5. What is the firm's average ROE over the last ten years?

6. How does the ROE compare to cluster competitors?
7. How stable is the ROE over the last ten years?
8. How deep is the moat in terms of margin BPS (basis points) relative to peers?
9. What SPICE factors (Social, Political, Innovation, Cultural & Environmental), or other factors could change to shrink the moat?

Moats Working over Time

To capture meaningful value, moats must endure over many product cycles. Excess captured value builds reservoirs of capital, which can be paid out by management as dividends or retained as earnings to invest for expanding capabilities to capture more value, assuming acceptable ROC are available. Buying moats by investing in companies at good prices in stable or growing clusters builds wealth.

Reading corporate and industry literature alongside a checklist of the ten innovation categories can help to separate meaningful capabilities from fads. Over time, stable operating and capital performance ratios should emerge from a cluster. The efficiency advantages should be apparent in higher ROC and ROE outcomes. Figure 10.3 shows the difference between a fad business and a cash cow type of moated business.

As moats age, some of them experience wear and tear, whereas others become increasingly valuable relative to initial cost. Moats built on successful and efficient branding, for instance, may improve over time. Think about it: How long have you been using the same brand of toothpaste or laundry detergent? The apathy of consumers in switching from one product to another can give firms with a brand-based moat greater pricing power and higher profits, because customers won't notice the price increase of

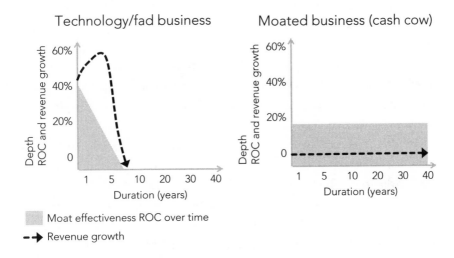

FIGURE 10.3 Fad Business vs. Stable Moat

toothpaste unless it's seriously out of line relative to other brands on the shelf. This type of moat involves spending early capital up front to create a long-term belief and behavior that may be maintained cheaply for years. Brand-based moats are best modeled by thinking about the lifetime value of a customer relationship rather than each single transaction.

Determining what causes a moat to wear out—or increase in value—requires some common sense. Moats may have fixed and/or variable costs associated with them relative to macroeconomic and cultural factors. Moat usage, volume, age, competitive threat, or innovation may lead to moat erosion. Although a brand or distribution network may improve with use and time, a moat based on physical infrastructure or machinery may need periodic infusions of capital after years of physical wear and tear. This doesn't mean that moats of the latter type cannot succeed; railroads and utilities can be lucrative ongoing capital suckers, but smart managers may manage the timing of long-term (ten- to twenty-year) capital asset investments by allocating when funding is cheaper than long-term future inflation expectations. The timing for allocation to these capex-heavy moats is discussed later, in chapter 14. Bringing capital spending forward when capital is cheap may mean fat margins in higher inflation periods, when prices can be raised in line with inflation.

Inflation is an important factor to consider when assessing how a moat will act over time. The relationship between moats and inflation is based on what I'll call the iron law of economic survival: The cost of goods must be less than the price for which they are sold, and the selling price must be less than the customer's perceived value of those goods. This sounds obvious but is often forgotten in manic periods. Figure 10.4 shows this relationship.

The capabilities that contribute to a moat must be maintained below the rate of inflation. Some moats thrive during inflationary periods. Brand-based moats, for instance, respond well in low to moderate inflationary environments. Production and distribution margins are the same, but the cost of maintaining the behavioral moat usually shrinks over time with each purchase.

Table 10.1 shows how an inflation-resistant moat allows for expanding margins during inflation. The table shows a single company selling a $100 product. Over time, inflation increases costs and value perceptions 50 percent, but the sunk cost of establishing the moat doesn't increase, yielding a significant increase in profits. (Note that this is a grossly simplified example.)

FIGURE 10.4 Iron Law of Economic Survival

Table 10.1
Inflation Resilient Moat

	Today	+10 yrs
Customer perceived value	**$110.00**	**$165.00**
Price	**$100.00**	**$150.00**
Excess value to customer	$10.00	$15.00
Cost of production	$45.00	$67.50
Moat cost	$45.00	$45.00
Total cost of production	**$90.00**	**$112.50**
Income	$10.00	$37.50
Corporate value @ 10 × profit	**$100.00**	**$375.00**

Table 10.1 includes customers' perceived value, which ultimately determines economic viability and separates the moat from other cost-of-production factors. Figure 10.5 uses data from table 10.1, highlighting the cost, price, and perceived value relationships. The marginal returns on the moat increase significantly, with profit increasing by 375 percent versus inflation growing 50 percent

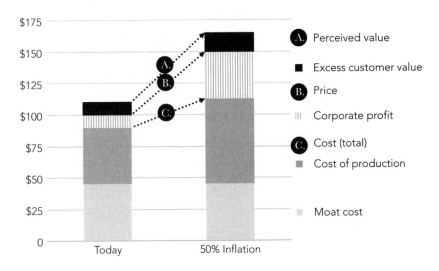

FIGURE 10.5 Moat Capability Metrics
Examples of moat capability effectiveness metrics.

over ten years. That is the power of a good moat. A moat may retain its relative value-to-cost advantage regardless of inflation as measured in relative value and not nominal terms.

The ultimate test of a moat is time. For this reason, looking backward can be helpful when trying to think forward. Historical ROC and capital efficiency of the moat may tell the allocator about a business' expected capital expenditures and cash flow yield potential. To understand the capital feeding needs of a moat, study as many years of operating history and financial statements as possible. Use these statements to assess the capital expenditures relative to unit revenues and wear and tear factors over time.

Finding moats in financial statements is easier said than done. Walmart's geographic positioning strategy never showed up as a line item on the balance sheet. Instead, good site locations and distribution positioning showed up as cheaper dollars/sq foot sales and operating margins. Seeing that Walmart had higher historical margins than competitors would be a signal that Walmart warranted deeper digging. This could lead to understanding the sources and capabilities creating the margins. High ROE, quick turnover, good dividend payouts, or large relative operating margins are the footprints of the moat, stomping across the balance sheet, income statement, and cash flow statements. Walmart's multi-capability moat showed up in excellent long-term ROE figures.

In the following section we will take a look at some ways of spotting these financial trails that moats leave behind. Like tracking an animal through the wild, certain signs provide clues to the nature and location of the rare organizational beast with a high margin and long expected moat life expectancy.

Financial Clues for Spotting and Tracking Moated Firms

Hunting for moats is like tracking big game across an endless information savanna. By looking at performance ratios and other metrics, you can identify the telltale signs and footprints through the accounting thickets and determine if you're tracking a real moated firm or a short-lived business.

The first step in the hunt for moats is spotting high stable operating margins. The next step is identifying the "why, how, and what" of the firm's excess value capture. Questions such as, "Why doesn't competition take away this high margin?" or "How long can this moat go on earning such high returns?" need to be asked and answered. Allocators should only invest in clearly understood moat stories. The key value-creating processes may not be obvious, but they should make sense once pointed out and explained. Simple moats are easier to monitor for margin erosion.

Studying at least ten years of balance sheets and income statements is a great start. It's not as painful or difficult as it sounds. Remember Henry Ford's saying that many people missed opportunity, because it showed up dressed in overalls and looked like work. Relative operational fitness shows up over time as excess margins. If the balance sheet looks interesting in terms of retained earnings and/or dividends paid, move on to the cash flow statement—it may help you determine if management captured value in the past. The questions you're trying to answer are: Does the firm have capital resources to weather competitive threats and foreseeable changes in SPICE (Social, Political, Innovation, Cultural and Environmental) factors? Has it been strong in the past?

Next, look at the operating income statement and series of cash flows. Retained earnings, high free cash flow, and dividends paid with high ROE signal sustained historical competitive fiscal strength and, maybe, responsible capital allocation by management. In your analysis, focus on cash flows and margin stability more than revenue growth or earnings. Here the questions are: How does value course through the veins of the company? Is value spent on capital expenditures and investment to continuously replenish the moat? Calculate an average ROE for each of the last ten years. Is it stable or erratic? The more stable and higher, the better.

Finally, look at the income statement again, not so much to understand excess income, but to understand it relative to other operating metrics. Does the firm run faster, leaner, and stronger than competitors? Be careful to make sure that operating margins are long-term sustained, not just one-year wonders. The value race isn't a quarterly sprint. It can be a decades-long run.

Coke, for instance, has an extremely durable moat that limits competitive threats. Competitively replacing Coke's global brand equity and distribution power would be extremely expensive, with a high uncertainty of success, which means Coke is unlikely to face direct competition from a new entrant among all its core products. Coke will likely battle Pepsi in the United States and other major soft drink distributors and vendors globally using its traditional strategies and innovations to enhance its unique capabilities.[2]

Long-term, high and steady dividend payouts may signal a moat, as can large retained earnings accreting to the balance sheet that are allocated effectively to grow over time. Dividends and retained earnings must make sense relative to free cash flow. High retained earnings should be associated with high-growing free cash flow—this means the firm is plowing earnings back into growth—or cash should be returned to investors. In stable industries with low or no real growth potential, a high dividend payout should be associated with a high cash flow yield. This means management is responsibly returning shareholder capital rather than gambling or wasting it.

After the numbers work is done, the allocator can ask the interesting question: Why does this company win the larger margins, beating others? Each winning firm has some measurable capabilities driving its moat's success. Measuring these capabilities' effectiveness relative to others becomes the measure of the moat's depth.

Each moat and cluster has unique key capabilities, which are the inputs to the moat. Measuring tail fins in the 1950s wouldn't have told one much about a car manufacturer's survival, as these were fads, not key capabilities. On the other hand, measuring a

Table 10.2
Inflation Resilient Moat Working for Ten Years

Value delivered to customer	Per unit of cost
Brand loyalty measured as pricing power and repeat purchases	Advertising spend
Tons of freight miles delivered	Dollar
Tons of polyethylene produced	Dollar
Meters of carpet produced	Dollar
Yearly revenue/customer	Square foot of retail space
Units of perceived value delivered	Dollar
Profitable insurance policies renewed	Marketing spend

railroad's debt load, the strength of its financial muscle, or the dollars per freight ton mile hauled can tell one about a railroad's financial and operational leanness. The output of factors like these combine to indicate a moat's health. Moat health metrics are expressed as competitive efficiency ratios involving a customer value delivered versus a cost (table 10.2).

Examples of Moat Capability Effectiveness Metrics

Spotting a historical moat is no guarantee of there being a future moat. Apple may have a moat in terms of 2013 margins, but its long-term ROE future is uncertain due to the short product cycles it competes in. Apple appears compelling, but it is beyond the skills of this author to understand its future possibilities, as it poses a valuation challenge more than four or six years out due to cluster uncertainty. If you can identify and explain Apple's moats in terms of the two key moat dimensions—the depth (margin) and duration (time of existence)—then maybe Apple is an investment for you at the right price. Another way to broach this question is: How would you have defined the moat and key clusters for Apple looking back to 1985, 1990, 1995, 2000, or 2005? How fast did they change and—more importantly—why?

As of 2013, Apple's fortunes may grow beyond its $400 billion market capitalization.[3] The questions to ask are: When does it end? How does it end? Are the ROEs sustainable? Will they produce a reasonable return on capital for shareholders? Apple may be a great twenty-year investment going forward; just make sure you can explain the moat and the nature of its excess value creation process. The six-year-old iPhone and four-year-old iPad contributed to the bulk of earnings in 2013. Can one really predict the success of the next i-"X" product five years out?

Valuing a Moat Differs from Normal Valuation Methods

Moats drive the valuation of a firm. In traditional valuation, the first consideration is book value, and so it is with the conservative nature of value approach. Book value is simply the estimated value of the company if all assets were sold to pay off all liabilities on the balance sheet. The remaining cash or equity owned by the shareholders is the book value. Assuming book value reflects the realizable wind-up value of the firm, it lets an investor put a loose theoretical value floor or margin of safety on the investment to minimize risk. The book value is the first and crudest way to assess investor risk.

Figure 10.6 shows a lemonade stand that produces $40/year in free cash flow (FCF). Free cash flow is made up of the operating cash flow less the capital expenditures. If a person buys the lemonade business for $90, they could shut it down, sell everything, pay off the liabilities, and pocket $10 in cash for a quick 11.1 percent return on their investment in the equity. Do that ten times a year and it promises to be lucrative.

However, valuing a firm on book value alone is a flawed method, as book value has many accounting assumptions about asset values and liabilities. For instance, book value doesn't consider the ability of the firm to grow and create value through moated operational cash flow, cluster dynamics, or the discount prices related to a fire sale.

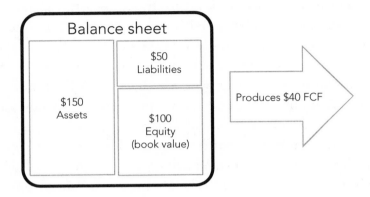

FIGURE 10.6 Lemonade Stand

In normal times, most firms sell for a premium to book value because the firm's capabilities are expected to create excess free cash flow on a go-forward basis. In the example above, the $100 in book value of assets creates $40 in free cash flow each year. Without knowing anything about the business, the anxious buyer paying $100 might anticipate a 40 percent return on his investment in the first year—$100 of book value plus $40 of next year's free cash flow. Other investors might see this opportunity for a 40 percent return and be willing to pay more than the $100 book value for the firm. The excess or premium paid above book value is known in accounting as goodwill. Paying $200 for the firm still yields a healthy $40/$200, or 20 percent current FCF yield. However, without understanding the nature of a firm's future possible value creation, paying more than book value doesn't sound like a sensible thing to do. Looking at goodwill on a balance sheet or paying a premium to book value is less important than thinking about how capabilities creating goodwill change going forward.

Understanding a firm's intrinsic value is the essence of value investing. Intrinsic value is a subjective number, reflecting all of the expected future-generated assets of the firm (discounted for inflation). Many economists consider intrinsic value equivalent to price at any moment in time; this is incorrect. As discussed in chapter 1 through the goose and balloon diagram, price reflects the intersection of two opposing guesses of value at a given time.

The investor's job is to make a judgment about intrinsic value based on faith in the underlying asset's capabilities to maintain a value-generating moat into the future. The stronger the moat in terms of duration, depth, and scalability, the more money the business will make for shareholders over its life. This requires estimating the future of an adaptive system in a cluster, so a wide margin of safety is required. The allocator's margin of safety is created by purchasing an asset at a large discount to its intrinsic value. Only buy the price balloon when it is way behind and to the left of your estimate of the goose's value location.

Basic investment analysis involves estimating the current free cash flow of the business, dividing it by the enterprise value of the firm (equity + debt – cash), and coming up with an expected yield on the business as an asset. Valuing a business on free cash flow is a useful starting point, but free cash flow isn't static. Investors rarely make the leap to consider difficult-to-quantify nature of value creation factors—like the moat's response to inos, cluster dynamics, and macroeconomic shifts. When estimating future cash flow in a moat context, one must separate the normal capital expenditures from moat capital requirements. Many moats and innovations don't get capitalized correctly, or may be invisible to simple balance sheet analysis. As mentioned previously, Walmart's early days of locating stores in small towns cost little and provided huge returns on capital for years due to structural advantages. This moat wouldn't have been apparent on the balance sheet and would require analysis of customers to understand.

Indeed, keeping the moat in mind when valuing a firm can help you avoid some of the common blind spots in valuation. For instance, many analysts and capital allocators only look at the firm in isolation, disregarding natural competitive dynamics. A financial model may show a firm growing revenues at 10 percent a year, expecting the free cash flow to grow at 10 percent as well. This analysis ignores capital requirements, evolving cluster dynamics and possible moat erosion. Thinking carefully about a firm's moat should help you determine if that 10 percent growth is sustainable or just a one- or two-year phenomenon.

Other simple linear valuation methods such as a 10 × PE (price to earnings ratio)[4] or other ratio-based multiples are also prone to naïve abuse when they're assumed to be perpetual. PE and PB (price to book value)[5] are meaningless numbers without estimates of how the firm and the moat will adapt in the face of SPICE (Spice, Political, Innovation, Cultural and Environmental), and macroeconomic changes. A cheap ticket on a sinking ship is never cheap enough to make the ride worthwhile. It is better for the allocator to analyze historical numbers first and then come up with a value, rather than starting with price as indicated by today's market.

Obviously the stronger the moat in terms of duration, depth, and scalability, the more money the business will make for shareholders over its life. The investor's job is to make a judgment about intrinsic value based on faith in the underlying capabilities to maintain the moat relative to the cluster and economy on a go-forward basis.

Summary

Moats are created as a firm's capabilities combine to form long-term, defensible positions allowing firms to create and capture excess value. Moats are found in stable clusters. Fast-moving product cycles don't lend themselves to moats, as few firms successfully make the transition from dominating one product cycle to the next. Moats aren't always visible and come in many unique forms that show up as higher operating margins, high retained earnings driven by high ROCs. We'll take a closer look at the different varieties of moats in the next chapter.

CHAPTER ELEVEN

How Moats Affect Cost, Competition, and Customer Forces

MOATS REDUCE THE SELECTIVE competitive pressures associated with three things: cost, competition, and customers. Some moats reduce pressures in just one area, whereas others can impact all three. Moats are formed when a combination of capabilities from the ten types of innovation lead to unique high-margin businesses with relative pricing power. Figure 11.1 highlights how capabilities and margins expand the economic boundaries of organizations and clusters.

To survive, a firm's cost, price, and the value delivered to the customer have to obey the Cost < Price < Value delivered relationship.[1] Figure 11.2 combines the earlier capability and cluster diagram to show how unique capabilities "push back" against the pressures of cost, competitive, and consumer choice, allowing for expanded margins.

We will begin by looking at how efficiency moats reduce cost relative to competitors. Efficiency advantages expand the margins and addressable market share in a cluster (fig. 11.3).

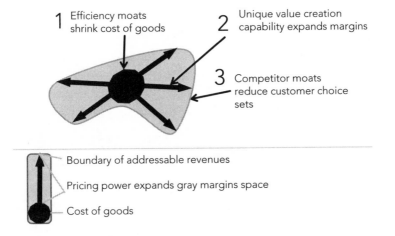

1 Efficiency moats shrink cost of goods

2 Unique value creation capability expands margins

3 Competitor moats reduce customer choice sets

Boundary of addressable revenues

Pricing power expands gray margins space

Cost of goods

FIGURE 11.1 Moats Shrink Margin Pressures
Moats can shrink the force of margin pressure from upstream costs, competitors, and customers.

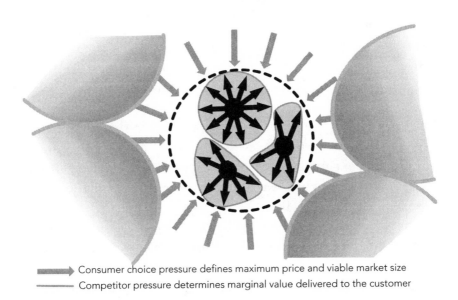

Consumer choice pressure defines maximum price and viable market size

Competitor pressure determines marginal value delivered to the customer

FIGURE 11.2 Moats Allow Margins to Expand
Moats reduce cost. Competitor and customer pressures allow margins to expand in the economic opportunity space.

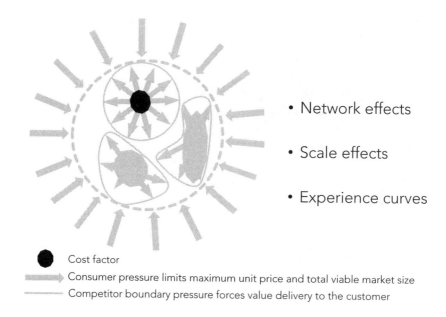

• Network effects

• Scale effects

• Experience curves

● Cost factor
▬▬▶ Consumer pressure limits maximum unit price and total viable market size
——— Competitor boundary pressure forces value delivery to the customer

FIGURE 11.3 Efficiency Moats Deliver Value More Cheaply
Efficiency moats shrink a firm's costs to expand margins and addressable cluster size.

Efficiency-Based Moats

Efficiency-based moats can be built around scale or on network effects. Scale-based efficiencies are the result of greater throughput driving experience curve cost reductions. Network-based efficiencies occur when increasing customers or links leads to exponential value growth.

Aircraft manufacturer Boeing is a good example of a firm with a deep and durable efficiency-based moat that is driven by scale of value flows. Boeing can make large aircraft relatively cheaply because they do it at volume; as scale increases, costs decline due to experience curve effects in the processing and production of their largest airplanes. From 1960 to 1990, Boeing's supply chain throughput meant in-house innovation and knowledge was being applied faster than among competitors. This created the dominant position held by Boeing for decades before the arrival of Airbus. The addressable market size and huge capital requirements meant there was limited room in the cluster for competing large aircraft manufacturers.

Network efficiency effects occur when the number of network connections drives qualitative or quantitative improvements in customer value. A network is defined as a set of nodes and connections that are informational or physical in nature. Network effects occur as the number of node connections increases the utility of each node, whereby the value of the network grows exponentially. Informational network examples include transaction markets in which buyers and sellers find each other, like eBay, or money transfer distribution networks like Western Union.

Networks can lead to significant cost reductions, as the network feedback effects lower the cost of providing content in the form of value flows across the network. eBay offered more value to buyers as more sellers signed up to its network resources. Conversely, eBay's sellers found more buyers in a positive value-creating feedback loop. Network clusters often become dominated by a single firm due to their winner-take-all nature. Payment and transaction distribution businesses such Visa, MasterCard, and Western Union are monetary networks of merchants and customers forming a locked-in behavior, like the buyers seeking sellers on eBay.

Social networks are also efficiency, winner-take-all networks. Like Gause's law for exclusive species competition, dominant networks push out other networks. MySpace was one of the first social networks to achieve critical mass in the social network cluster. By focusing on music fans instead of everyone, MySpace appealed to a subset of all potential network participants. Eventually most MySpace members moved to Facebook, as it offered greater value via more social connections and friend-curated-created content. Facebook's network provided more links for social ambient awareness than MySpace or Friendster.

Scale and network effects allow companies to operate more efficiently, giving them lower costs per unit of value delivered. Investors should seek out the broadest dominant network possible.

Competitor-Altering Moats Limit or Alter Competitive Pressures

Competitor-altering moats include physical geographic moats, patent moats, and government restricted or limited concession moats (fig. 11.4).

Geographic physical boundaries, like being the owner of a toll bridge or highway, form geographic moats. Local newspapers are another example of firms that operate in geographic moats. Local news is perceived as scarce and prized by locals; before the Internet, the newspapers and gossipy neighbors had the monopoly on local social information. Midsize or smaller

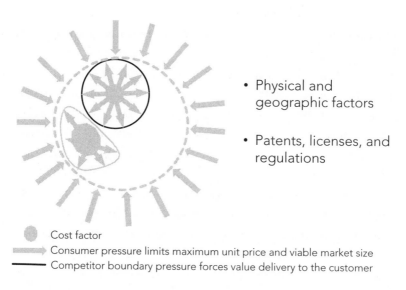

• Physical and geographic factors

• Patents, licenses, and regulations

🔵 Cost factor
⟹ Consumer pressure limits maximum unit price and viable market size
— Competitor boundary pressure forces value delivery to the customer

FIGURE 11.4 Moats May Reduce Customer Choice
Moats reduce customers' choice and competitive pressures on pricing.

cities supported one or sometimes two newspapers. Newspaper economies of scope and scale create monopolistic dynamics. Local advertisers want a focused audience. These two geographic needs create positive feedback effects leading to local monopolies on printed news in smaller cities. Newspaper geographic moats still exist, but the cluster of printed local news and advertising is shrinking due to digital alternatives and changing media consumption behavior.

Competitor-limiting moats can also be informational or legal in nature. Patents act as capability barriers, limiting cluster entrants. Issued U.S. patents lasting for twenty years are the foundation under many technology and pharmaceutical company moats. Competitors aren't precluded from inventing around patents, but patents temporarily minimize direct competition. However, patents alone rarely create moats; they often require substantial complementary capabilities for the firm to be considered moat protected. The uncertainty of judicial patent outcomes highlights patents' limited effectiveness as a sole line of protection for a business moat.

A competitor-altering moat can also be created by a restricted license or a concession from a government or regulatory body. Organizations with license- and concession-based moats can include ratings agencies, local trash haulers, government backed mortgage providers such as Fannie Mae, airport concessions, and other limited licenses or rights holders at local, state, or national levels. License and concession moats are no guarantee of value creation because they may not be limited enough or may be operated by reckless management, such as in the case of some licensed insurance providers. Sloppy management directed by wrong incentives may cause them to fail, as was the case with Fannie Mae and other government-backed mortgage providers.

Some moats are created through a combination of efficiency and competitor-limiting factors. For instance, if network efficiency moats are based on physical value flows, they often reduce customer choice. Take, for instance, mass transaction networks. These physical macroprocessing networks based on infrastructure such as natural gas pipelines, electricity transmission networks, cable networks, and railroads can have high pricing power. A physical network's high replacement costs or mutual exclusivity strongly limits direct competition. A physical network moat's pricing power is so strong, it is often regulated as a monopoly.

Consumer-Altering Moats Change Perceptions, Beliefs, and Behaviors

Consumer moats fall into three categories: physiological moats, sunk cost or switching cost moats, and belief or perception moats (fig. 11.5). Consumer moats may be based on rational behavior, but may have more complicated cultural or psychological bases. Psychology and culture may sound like soft things to base a business

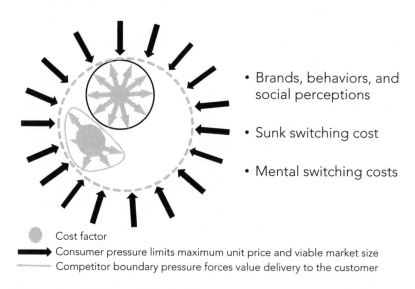

• Brands, behaviors, and social perceptions

• Sunk switching cost

• Mental switching costs

● Cost factor
➡ Consumer pressure limits maximum unit price and viable market size
━━ Competitor boundary pressure forces value delivery to the customer

FIGURE 11.5 Consumer Behavior Moats
Consumer behavior moats change or limit consumer behavior, creating pricing power.

on, but over the last forty to fifty years, it's become clear that attention to these factors can lead to profound business success.

PHYSIOLOGICAL MOATS

A physiological consumer moat offers either an addictive substance or a uniquely perceived consumer experience. Cigarettes, for instance, are physiologically addictive, and even certain unique or tasty foods can be mildly addictive, inducing cravings. Many firms seek "perfect" recipes, which will be perceived as unique enough to extract a premium price. Some perceived physiological moats are actually more psychological, based on branding and aspirational lifestyle stories.

Some physiological moats are experience related and are combined with geography, like a major amusement park at the edge of a midsized city. Delivering a roller coaster's thrill tends to be unique and capital intensive. It is unlikely a competitor would build another roller coaster next door unless there is untapped thrill seeker demand.

CONSUMER SUNK COST AND SWITCHING MOATS

The next type of consumer moat is based on sunk cost or the perceived cost to switch products. Sunk cost moats involve an upfront purchase or capital investment, creating high margin, locked-in repeat consumption behavior. A lucrative sunk cost moat is the Gillette razor blade type of business model. A large component of the system is subsidized up front—the razor body— and then repeat-purchase high-margin supplies provide an ongoing revenue stream going forward, as consumers purchase razor heads again and again. This limits the users' perceived product choice, encouraging them to stick with the current relationship and behavior. Hewlett Packard (HP) uses a sunk cost moat in the ink-jet printer business. As measured by margins and value created, it becomes apparent that HP's imaging division isn't in the printer business; rather, it's in the premium ink–selling business. The printer is merely a delivery mechanism.

An example of a consumer-switching cost moat is Apple's iTunes, which forms part of Apple's hardware and software ecosystem business model. Converting a few hundred dollars of media and exporting it from your iTunes library and your apps isn't worth the headache for the average iTunes user.

Sunk cost and behavioral switching moats are powerful but volatile in high-tech environments, as the depth of the moat may erode quickly, with competitors showing up from outside the cluster. Netflix wiped out Blockbuster this way, with mail delivery and then online streaming. Evolution's accelerating cycles mean today's "science fiction" becomes tomorrow's yawner consumer product faster, upending existing clusters and company's moat strategies.

CONSUMER BELIEF AND PERCEPTION MOATS

Consumer belief and perception moats can be immensely valuable. Belief and perception moats link the soft social sciences with economic value creation. Behavior, belief, and psychological motivations can be important sources of corporate value.

One way to think of these types of moats is as mental sunk cost moats, similar to economic switching cost and capital sunk cost moats described previously. Mental sunk cost moats rely on a consumer's resistance to switching products once a choice has been made. In these instances, the cluster boundaries are determined by the perceived ease—or complication—of switching to a competing product or service. A person may be able save $0.50 on a $10.00 book purchase at a site other than Amazon.com, but registering a new account and filling out the credit card details at Bob's Book-o-rama isn't worth the uncertainty and hassle for most people. That repeated extra $0.50 profit per transaction becomes extra potential margin for Amazon. Excellent strategy and experience design contributes to successful learned behavior moats. Amazon sells over 50 percent of all U.S. books using its logistics advantages, behavioral moats, and other unique capabilities.

Microsoft Office and Windows OS software are other examples of mental sunk cost moats. People spend hundreds of hours learning how to get the most from a software product; Microsoft Office may cost $150, but spending hundreds of hours learning a new application is also a real cost. The $150 represents the depth of the Microsoft Office moat.

However, this example also shows how mental sunk cost moats can erode. The Microsoft Windows operating system learned behavior moat is melting fast as more computing moves to tablets and phones. As computing and communication become less PC-based, the Microsoft operating system moat shrinks. Arguably the peak of Microsoft's cluster dominance came in 1997, when Microsoft invested $150 million into Apple computer in order to keep Apple alive as a straw man for antitrust purposes. Things have changed significantly since then. With the exception of a few product offerings such as the XBOX 360 and Kinect game interface, the sun appears to be slowly setting on the Microsoft empire. Microsoft Office and Windows likely have many value-creating years ahead of them due to their learned behavior and switching cost moats, but these moats are eroding quickly. Microsoft needs to develop inos and capabilities with longer duration cycles to meaningfully survive.

Trusted experience and familiar behavior drive learned behavior moats. Western Union's money transfer business has a strong position due to the trust developed after repeated use of its network. The Internet is an exponentially growing ino whirlwind, melting moats as the amount of value flowing through it adapts and grows. For instance, new challengers are emerging in the payment cluster as trust in mobile devices grows and smart phone functionality improves. In the face of this, Western Union's moat—strengthened by network effects and learned behavior—will likely be threatened.

Perceived geography moats are built on a firm's unique understanding of people's relationships to place. Perceived geographic moats are more subtle than true geographic moats, but still allow for cluster domination.

Let's go back to Walmart. They initially targeted small towns with populations of 9,000–15,000, with stores located on the outskirts of town. In the 1970s–1980s, other price discounters such as Kmart headed for bigger cities where the "action" was. Walmart correctly guessed that the inconvenience of driving to the edge of town versus the center was more than compensated for by its low prices and large selection. The added benefit for Walmart was that shoppers preferred a one-drive solution, doing most of their shopping at Walmart rather than making multiple stops at stores in the center of town. Opening up shop in small, isolated towns meant that Walmart's first competition was small, inefficient Main Street shopkeepers who typically competed with each other. This competition had increased Main Street rents. There was no real geographic barrier preventing other retailers from copying Walmart's strategy, but none immediately did, likely because they didn't understand the consumer psychology and behaviors driving Walmart's high-margin throughput.

Once their success became clear, Walmart's moat also altered their competitor's behaviors. If Walmart had a dominant share of the retail business in a small town, other price discount stores found it irrational to compete for the remaining cluster potential. If you were an early 1980s Kmart site location manager and Walmart was doing 25 to 35 percent of the addressable retail business in a small town, you would logically look down the road elsewhere. Walmart squeezed the margins out of small town retailers, eventually representing a dominant part of the small town's retail cluster.

Many perceived geographic moats are found in special services or niche goods that may be unique to micro clusters in towns. Dairy Queen is an example of a perceived geographic moat that relies on ritualized customer behavior. Dairy Queen ice cream is sold in highly visible, branded outlets, in small towns and off primary roads. Dairy Queen outlets become a ritualized treat destination and visible social gathering spot for locals. A person can buy cheaper ice cream in a store, but stopping at "your" local Dairy Queen to eat outside with friends and family is about a shared public social ritual or event more than a retail purchasing transaction.

Behavioral moats are built on a firm's understanding of people's psychology and underlying beliefs. Firms with these types of moats have figured out how to use advertising and branding to short-circuit rational economic thinking and leverage quick, automatic decision making. These brand-belief moats are constructed by weaving marketing into the consumption culture. A brand isn't what a company signals with ads; a brand is an asset held in the customer's head.

Brands create belief systems that are designed to cause repeat behavior and "default mental choice lock-in" for customers. Beliefs about a product's relative value are managed with stories shown in advertising using engineered social cues. Social signaling by wearing labels on your clothing means you work for the brand as much as it works for you. Perceptions change rapidly unless product experience is kept aligned with customers' brand beliefs.

Table 11.1 shows the value that twenty top brands add to their companies as measured by Interbrand,[2] a brand consultancy. Interbrand examines the three key aspects that contribute to a brand's value:

- The financial performance of the branded products or service
- The role the brand plays in influencing consumer choice
- The pricing power of the brand and its ability to command a premium price

Table 11.1
Brand Value Table

Value ($b)	Brand	Sector
$77.8	Coca-Cola	Beverages
$76.6	Apple	Technology
$75.5	IBM	Business services
$69.7	Google	Technology
$57.8	Microsoft	Technology
$43.7	GE	Diversified
$40.0	McDonald's	Restaurants
$39.4	Intel	Technology
$32.9	Samsung	Technology
$30.3	Toyota	Automotive
$30.1	Mercedes-Benz	Automotive
$29.0	BMW	Automotive
$27.4	Disney	Media
$27.2	Cisco	Business services
$26.1	HP	Technology
$24.9	Gillette	FMCG
$23.6	Louis Vuitton	Luxury
$22.1	Oracle	Business services
$21.0	Nokia	Electronics
$18.6	Amazon	Internet services

A brand is a type of ino adapted to hijack people's perceptions and behaviors. These could be value perceptions of trust, love, power, safety, social acceptance, sex appeal, style, fun—really, anything on Maslow's hierarchy of needs, and the higher on the hierarchy the better.[3] When successful, branding causes the consumer to assign these values to a product. Price sensitivity and pure functional "rational" choice criteria are distorted by brand value assignments.

Humans are unique among animals at assigning personality and psychological traits to inanimate objects. This unique trait is called anthropomorphization. Cigarettes, deodorants, shampoos, razor blades, etc., don't really have human traits like friendliness, courage or gender—we just believe and behave like they do. Images and slogans train us to assign emotional and social traits to products based on packaging and advertising cues. A significant amount of marketing is based on culture "hacks" to create social norms, ascribing extra values to products and services.

Brands are so good at training us to assign human traits to things that we rarely question them. For instance, in the heyday of cigarette advertising, things didn't get more masculine and tough than Marlboro cigarettes. The Marlboro man was perceived to be out on his horse rustling up cattle and generally being the manliest man around. When he wasn't growing body hair, chopping wood, or repairing fences, the Marlboro man was likely eating a big rare steak followed by an after dinner smoke, laughing with other Marlboro men buddies on horseback. The narrative and imagery cast a halo of masculinity over some rolled up, dried out leaves. You may be surprised to hear, then, that the manly Marlboro cigarette was actually created for women in 1924, targeting feminine sensibilities with the tagline "Mild as May." Beliefs and cultures can be hacked or changed with enough messaging: In the 1950s, the Leo Burnett ad agency made Marlboro manly with their cowboy campaign.

Consumers participate in the product characteristics and myths they want to experience by purchasing and consuming the stories they want in their lives. For many smoking men in the 1920s, being "Mild as May" likely went against how they wished to identify themselves or be perceived by others. The Marlboro cigarette physically didn't change in the 1950s; only the manufactured story did. We believe we are the stories fabricated with the goods and services we consume.

Spurred on by successful branding and marketing, people build their own coherent and congruent narrative archetypes by choosing products on the shelf. We all build these heuristic economic shortcuts; it's how we are wired. Ever wonder why shopping in a foreign country grocery store feels so weird? You don't have the narrative map to know which stories and attributes are associated with the products. The magic is gone and everything is a mystery or commodity with only strange colored labels and price to guide your defining choices.

When managed well, the emotional and behavioral forces created by branded goods and services show up in sustained higher operating margins. Branded products with sustainably high margins are often great moats, taking a long time to erode. Repetition and consistent experience delivery are hallmarks of successful brands. McDonald's reduces the uncertainty of dining cost and quality by offering consistency. The flavor of your Coke, burger, and fries probably won't perceptibly change much over your lifetime, and you won't want it to. McDonald's establishes trust via their brand—with a bit of novelty like the McRib to keep you coming back. Brand is one of the most powerful of the ten forms of innovation capabilities due to its potential for high return on investment, scalability, and durability.

One interesting subset of the brand belief moat is the luxury moat. As great apes, we are social animals wired to crave a higher social rank or position relative to our perceived peers. Our emotional "needs" and biases for positional rank can be hijacked by inos for value capture. Publicly consumed relative value goods such as luxury watches, handbags, clothing, and cars are used to signal relative positional social status and identity. Many people will buy and consume as many status items as they can afford in order to publicly signal or self-affirm their relative positional rank and success at the highest level affordable.

Rolex is an example of a firm with a strong luxury moat. If you could buy a genuine Rolex without the publicly visible logo and name on the face at half the cost, would you buy it? Not likely. There is a lot of valuable social knowledge embedded in that iconic tiny crown. The Rolex watch's value is held mostly in the consumer's belief of what belief about Rolex is held in other people's heads. The owner of a Rolex gets fulfillment in purchasing a known luxury, and this luxury value gets transferred as social status to the owner, leaving fat margins for the Rolex company. The Rolex company amplifies its inos with more public ads, endorsements, and expensive tennis sponsorships to signal how expensive and exclusive the product is. In a classic price-to-value paradox, the higher the socially perceived price, the more social value[5] ascribed to the item and its proud owner. Peacocks have feathers; we have luxury watches, high-end cars, and designer clothes. The cost reflects the extra energy and effort required to signal higher status via advertising.

Luxury brand moats may be suitable investments, but require careful brand stewardship skills. Luxury brands can suffer with economic changes or shifts of fashion associated with the brand. Heretics may point out that the emperor has no clothes, or a competitor may steal the valued premium position. A loss of faith in beliefs about quality, brand integrity, or prestige is disastrous for luxury brand–based companies.

In some instances a brand so defines a category as to be relatively unassailable in that category. American manufactured motorcycles are dominated by Harley Davidson, a global luxury motorcycle brand. The brand sells virility and authenticity— with a hint of rebellion—to a mostly middle class, nonrebellious male audience. As unique as we like to think we are, most of our culture's self-identified radical iconoclasts are easily sliced and diced into commodified archetypes for marketing departments to homogenize, repackage, and sell back to us.

Rolex has 36 percent of the luxury watch market and appears to have a moat in the midrange $3–15k luxury watch space. Groupe Arnault and LVMH are excellent luxury brand portfolio managers and stewards. Brands are often coupled with distribution network capabilities that give cost advantages or maintain a competitive geographic advantage for the product or system, like a Motorcycle or car dealership and repair network.

Brands, like companies, adapt and eventually die. If the product experience delivered is less than the brand promises, things won't go well. Schlitz beer was a long-lived American brand[2] that once rivaled Budweiser in awareness and popularity. In the 1970s, to reduce manufacturing costs, Schlitz changed its production methods and the quality of its beer suffered as a result. This, in concert with brand-deaf, egocentric management, killed the brand in a few years, as the shoddy product failed to match the brand myth. Management believed the brand power to be stronger than the real product experience. This was a fatal brand mistake. Brands, like politicians, can only stretch the truth so far before getting caught out.

The final belief moat is the default choice moat. Many consumer belief moats are based on an offering perceived as the "safe" or socially acceptable choice. For instance, Coke has a higher perceived social status than Walmart cola. Coke is ubiquitous, safe, and not the cheapest cola. Serving Coke at a party means a host will not be judged negatively for the choice. Serving Walmart cola may be perceived as cheap even if the taste experience delivered is identical to Coke.

International travel allows one to see brands in different contexts. In the United States, the Dutch beer Heineken is perceived to be a higher end imported beer. In Bahrain, on the other hand, Heineken is considered a low-end beer because it is consumed primarily by poorer laborers with lower social status. The beer hasn't changed, merely the relative value perception and story of who drinks it. As the value perception drops, the margins and pricing power associated with the drink and business shift. Most advertising mentally positions goods using images and stories of people with a slightly higher social demographic than the targeted consumer. And we as consumers buy and pursue our social aspirations by the branded bottle, watch, or clothing label.

As a former economic anthropology student, I always find it a little disappointing to see how easily meaning and social recognition get manufactured and consumed. We hand over value to associate ourselves with brand myths attempting to create meaningful self-narratives.

Summary

Moats are the key forces that allow organizations to capture excess value sustainably. Great moats reduce cost and competition and alter customer behaviors sustainably in multiple ways. The best moats combine multiple traits and unique capabilities, working to provide pricing power, long-term high margins, and high ROEs. If you don't understand the cost, competition, and consumer choices behind the moat, don't invest.

CHAPTER TWELVE

Managing Moats, for Value Creation Today and Wealth Tomorrow

GIVEN TIME, all businesses get the share price they deserve. Many investors wrongly believe that management's job is to increase the share price. But management shouldn't be focused on promoting opinion-based metrics like share price; they should be focused on processes and capabilities that grow value. Swaying opinions to drive short-term share price spikes doesn't grow intrinsic company value. Stock prices may increase temporarily with earnings spikes and accounting games, but these acts are short-term cheap magicians' tricks of misdirection.[1]

Managing capabilities, execution, and returns on capital sustainably requires a focus on long-term payoffs. Innovation-driven moat change typically unfolds at a gradual, Usherian[2] pace, interspersed with Schumpeterian periods of "creative destruction"—rare revolutions spurred on by radical innovation—much like the punctuated equilibrium changes seen in ecology. The gradualist management style required for moats won't appeal to glamour seekers; it is more suited to quiet craftsmen striving for process excellence. In some years the economic weather is good and some years less so, but the economic field in stable clusters remains stable and the incented manager works within the field's limits, patiently harvesting excess margins to yield excess free cash flow.

Unfortunately, many forces work against exercising a responsible and steady management process. For instance, although management teams incentivized by long-term ROE metrics are encouraged to acknowledge that they are out of ideas or places to effectively allocate capital, boards often prefer to use short-term metrics like recent share price or a focus on yearly or even quarterly earnings as a way to reward management success. When bonuses are determined by share price using short-term options, managers are perversely incentivized to take excessive or costly short-term bets and actions or retain excess capital. Shareholders or boards using wrong incentives should not be surprised with the results they get from their CEOs, because most CEOs and managers are as Pavlovian as the rest of us and behave in accordance with the rewards dangled before them.

As a result, CEOs who don't act or think short term are at a constant risk of replacement. A sobering indication of this trend is that many industry boom-bust cycles are longer than the current average CEO's three-and-a-half-year tenure. Announcing deals and launching trendy initiatives can briefly raise share prices with tales of anticipated earnings, even when these actions don't enhance the moats or long-term ROE driving intrinsic value. Lots of action, deals, and initiatives are mostly good press today and bad business tomorrow. Reams of academic and industry research show that mergers and acquisitions typically destroy value for everyone but lawyers and investment bankers. Despite this, short-term adventurist thinking continues to be structurally created by the incentive plans given by boards and institutional shareholders who don't recognize the nature of value creation and the sources of long-term ROE. The public's and the analyst's desire for near-term earnings growth can destroy shareholder returns, as moats gets pulled apart or surrounded by junk business divisions to entertain the crowd. Current business culture's desire for magazine front cover–worthy action, celebrity-style growth stories comes at the expense of really listening to a cluster's carrying capacity and the factors determining its long-term possible ROC.

Allocating to Moated Firms

Although "allocator" refers to the capital allocation decisions of investors and board members representing shareholder interests, "manager" or "management" refers to the CEO or business line managers running the day-to-day business. Managers and allocators should align to the same goal, namely, maximizing long-term share-holder ROE by enhancing the firm's ability to create future value.

A manager acting as allocator should be able to articulate his or her thinking about three choices:

1. Whether to allocate or reduce capital expenditure relative to the cluster and cost of capital
2. When to spend to sustainably capture margin and/or market share
3. When to do nothing, and return capital to shareholders

Allocating to moated firms at the investor or board level requires finding a quality business in a stable cluster. If you allocate too early, while cluster strategies are volatile, you have a high chance of being wrong on assessing the moat. The right time for allocation is when the following cluster conditions are met (assuming they ever are):

1. The cluster is mature or consolidating to a few dominant players and strategies.
2. The strategies and moat economics are stable, and the chances of new entrants, technologies, or disruptive capabilities appear minimal.
3. The business you believe to be cluster-dominant may provide margins and moat stability for many years or customer cycles.
4. The historical and expected ROE is right, offering a great moat at a good price.

This attitude toward allocation requires patience because the cluster consolidation process can take years depending on capability and product cycle duration. But the advantage of jumping in at a later stage allows one to skip the early "hot opportunity" or lottery stage. Alignment of the allocator and manager is essential to success in this game. When the board and shareholders start to itch to get in on peer activity, they may fire responsible CEOs in search of a transformative, visionary CEO, frothing at the mouth with growth aggression. This leads to a culture of firing CEOs for not chasing false growth while at the same time overpaying those lucky enough to be sitting at the right spot at the right time, even though they took bad bets. The fact is that most CEOs don't need to be visionary. Having visions all the time can distort reality. Visionary CEOs who crave business magazine covers and higher bonuses often leave behind train wrecks for others to pick up. Significant wealth could be preserved and strife avoided if boards and shareholders paid CEOs reasonable salaries and incentivized them to manage the business long-term ROE, instead of paying them like hit-seeking rock stars.

Managing Moated Firms

No matter how deep or durable a moat is, thoughtful and ethical management is required to maintain the moat and harvest value for shareholders. Unfortunately it is all too easy to mismanage a moat, squandering away the future wealth represented by a sustainable competitive advantage that may have been years or decades in the making.

The management team needs to:

1. Be truthful.
2. Know the moat.
3. Have the right incentive structure in place.
4. Allocate capital responsibly and patiently.

The CEO or manager sits in a position of trust, responsible for shareholder wealth. The CEO's primary roles are protecting the firm's assets and growing ongoing value-creating capability (wealth). This means defending the moat and allocating resources efficiently. Good managers are stewards of moats and shareholder value, intent on handing the moat over to the next manager in a better state than when they found it. A deep, durable moat can outlast many managers if treated well.

Unfortunately, many managers happily throw shareholder money into market share battles for "market leading" positions while lowering ROE. Forcing the cluster to grow with excess capital or radical strategies may destroy value or even kill the moat. After cluster carrying capacity is reached, allocating more capital for growth in a full cluster is like competing at a slot machine with more pulls.

Responsible moat management is mostly playing defense and overseeing organizational plumbing. It doesn't look exciting to outsiders; it requires a craftsman-like focus on process excellence, and an understanding of cluster constraints and capacities. Moat managing is more like a stewardship farming relationship than a pioneering adventure, as it involves repeatedly harvesting familiar customer territory. Good managers recognize that playing the quarterly earnings game with smoothed numbers to reduce earnings volatility does not enhance long-term intrinsic value. Accounting tricks used to smooth earning obfuscate the true volatility of the underlying business, masking the true risks. Take care of the moat, ROC, and customers, and the share price takes care of itself.

CEOs need to know that radical innovation is like radical mutation in ecology—very rarely successful. Scale your allocations appropriately. Few firms innovate successfully outside of their immediate operational sphere. If the cluster becomes untenable for a player or doesn't return a satisfactory ROC, the only option is to stop throwing money at it and exit the cluster or firm.

Reviewing a few years of CEO letters and asking around can reveal how boards and management understand the nature of their moat and cluster. This research will also give an indication of the likelihood for CEO capital abuse. Some managers are unaware of their own business' moat. This ignorance shows up as the manager tries to replicate a success elsewhere, only to find that pushing capital and applying a set of current successful capabilities to a new cluster destroys value and wealth. The fastest rabbit across the field isn't necessarily the fastest swimmer in the pond next door. Good managers cut losses rapidly, honoring and acknowledging their mistakes while learning their way forward. With proven moats, the way forward is often to harvest cash using variations on proven approaches.

A good allocator or manager can describe the return on capital capacities and constraints within his or her cluster. Warren Buffett is famously hands-off about management, with the one exception being capital allocation. Buffett scales capital allocations into and out of his collection of moats at Berkshire Hathaway, letting the managers run them at an appropriate scale relative to their cluster opportunity.

A good CEO conference call should be a report about "our" money, where it went and why, what it's doing out there, and how it's going to come home soon with extra value in its teeth, which it will kindly drop at our feet. Rather than self-promoting, good managers listen and respond to team concerns. When the team is always in full agreement, with no dissenting voice ever heard, there is likely something deeply wrong with the CEO's management style. Dissenting opinions, friction, and questioning feedback are signs of healthy listening and critical team thinking; all qualities that are needed in adaptive organizations. If the team facade is perfectly smooth, controlled, and polished, there may be deep structural thinking flaws being covered up.

When assessing managers, search for those needing to satisfy an internal intrinsic motivation for long-term ROE excellence. Seek out managers who define goals in terms of moats and absolute returns on equity, and beware of managers who define goals by a relative competitor's position or personal accomplishments.

Good investments don't need hype. The ROE numbers will quietly assert themselves over time. A dangerous "tell" to look for in management teams is aggressively selling or promoting the company's shares to investors. Beware of firms with active investor relations teams. The CEO's primary role is to serve customers and employees, not to solicit share purchases or kiss analysts' rings.

Action orientation or a strong peer competitive desire is not always the best trait in a CEO. Intrinsic motivation against an ROE goal is desirable. If you hand a CEO a bag of silver dollars, sit them down next to a slot machine, and carefully explain the odds and the house advantage, and then give them a day to "maximize value" with a "performance bonus" tied to their results, few will do the correct thing: hand back the bag of silver dollars untouched, which maximizes ROE given the nature of the game. In the early periods of such a challenge, many may see other "managers" sitting next to them who appear to be "winning" by putting money into the slot machine. Watching others "win" in the short term makes shareholders and the manager eager to do something to win. Winning such a game by doing nothing is simple to understand but not easy to do. As the brilliant seventeenth century French mathematician and philosopher Blaise Pascal put it, "All of humanity's problems stem from man's inability to sit quietly in a room alone."[3]

The best sign of someone who can manage trouble is someone who accepts responsibility, no matter what. The best managers and firms operate with internal scorecards and seek to improve on performances for the firm's well-being, not to gain recognition from others.[4]

Be wary of managers who never accept blame for mistakes or who say things they think people want to hear, such as:

- We are going to grow revenue (without moat explanations or margin impacts).
- Our margins will recover as we realize economies of scope, scale, synergy, without clearly articulating how.
- We are buying growth with this acquisition.

Reviewing many years of management letters will help in assessing management's understanding of their business. Past management letters should honestly acknowledge when past estimates were wrong.

Ethics of Capital

Capital ethics mean saying no to today's easy money that might undermine tomorrow's moat. The late Steve Jobs, CEO of Apple, stated he was as proud of what Apple had not done as for what it had done. The discipline of "not doing everything" reflects a desire for excellence in doing a few meaningful things. If Apple made microwave ovens or socks, Apple fans would pay a premium for them in the short term. But it doesn't mean that Apple would benefit in the long term from moving into these other sectors. Managing the moat for long-term ROE means leaving short-term money on the table today for the sake of greater value-creating wealth tomorrow. Apple's discipline from 2000–2012 reflected a deep understanding of excellence and what delivers value to customers and the firm longer term. The managerial discipline not to say yes to every saleable new product or quick-hit profit is worthy of respect.

If a firm can't produce a high long-term return on its capital, it should return the capital to its shareholders, not dilute returns on equity. This ROE versus earnings debate is sorely missing in many boardrooms as management focuses on increasing its salary—which itself is likely based on short term earnings and share price growth,[5] Earnings growth alone ignores the investors capital cost and higher ROEs investors may have gotten elsewhere.

Every good or service has an addressable cluster carrying capacity given a required ROC. In addition to being honest, disciplined managers must have margin ethics. Clusters, like ecological niches, have carrying capacity limits in terms of unit value flow, the number of competitors and participants they can accommodate. These limits define the relationships between a given ROC, a near-term maximum volume of revenue, and long-term harvestable margins. Margin ethics is the discipline to step away from a low-margin ROC project and correctly return capital to shareholders. The good allocator or board recognizes growth capacity limits in a given market and identifies other opportunities or returns excess cash to shareholders as dividends. Managing clusters with finite carrying capacity requires discipline in deploying or returning that capital.

In their quest for moving highly visible metrics like customers or revenue growth, many firms turn over every rock in uneconomic or low ROC places. There is nothing sadder than a manager taking a great small business with high returns on equity to beat it through shear will into a mediocre larger barely alive business with low returns on equity. A 15 percent return on $100m in equity ($15m) is better than a 10 percent return on $200m in equity ($20m). Think about that for a moment. Many firms' CEOs see the $15m in earnings as worth less than the $20m due to bad incentives focused on absolute earnings growth rather than ROE. Many firms focus on increasing earnings in absolute terms rather than cost of capital terms.

Low-return-on-capital businesses or less marginally competitive businesses are weak, but may not show it during good times. During bad times, these weaker firms can perish quickly. Over time, economic shocks and the cluster convergence process weed out low-return-on-capital firms[6] in the same way that a famine, drought, virus, or other environmental pressure thins a herd, reinforcing and defining the capabilities, traits, and behaviors needed for survival.

When the addressable market with high quality margins can't grow, pushing on it with a pile of money won't help. Beware of fights for market share, unless tied to sustainable competitive advantage with acceptable ROC. If market share truly deepens or extends the moat's depth or duration and supports the capabilities to achieve ROC goals, then go ahead and invest for growth. If not, stay away.

Management can go soft behind a moat. In some businesses, the competitive moat is so strong and stable that costs and operational efficiencies in other parts of the business get soft. This shows up as declining ROEs and cushy head offices with layers of bureaucracy that become more dogmatic and ritualized than responsive. Make sure managers can explain any project's impact on current value creation processes and moats in the cluster. If the manager can't or won't explain the moat impact, move on. The risk of wealth loss often outweighs any short-term benefits.

Creating a culture of ethics and truth seeking is a powerful organizational capability. Ethical behavior and an awareness of opportunistic limits builds better value and ROE. Shortcuts or unethical behavior compromise long-term wealth. Good sustainable business isn't about extracting value by cheating someone else. It is about thoughtful relationships that grow the pie by delivering sustainable value creation into the economy. A manager must make sure the means used to increase value creation and wealth are sustainable and never harm employees, customers, or society. Thoughtful capital managers behave ethically— even when this causes short-term setbacks. If given the chance, ask a manager to share a personal anecdote about the short-term cost of ethics. If they don't have an example at hand, beware. Forgoing immediate profit for the sake of doing the right thing reflects thoughtful long-term thinking, and is a good sign in a manager.

Investor allocation means trusting in ethical managers, by assessing their ethics, incentives, and capital discipline, as discussed. Cultural ethics are deeper than having a corporate social responsibility web page or yearly contribution to the CEO's favorite charity. Ethics should be ingrained and lived throughout the corporate culture. As CEO Bruce Black taught me, "A corporation's ethics and corporate culture are what happens when no one is looking and no one will find out what happened." Never allocate to a team with questionable ethics.

Summary

Ethics are integral to managing moats and attaining success. These ethics include truthfulness about the required return on capital and truthfulness with workers, investors, and customers. Long-term thinking and constantly seeking economic truths are critical advantages for firm survival. Firms with managers who are comfortable operating in opaque or gray areas are not worth the allocator's time or capital.

PART V

The Economy

CHAPTER THIRTEEN

The Economy as a
Macroprocessing Network

Nature is wont to hide herself.
Everything flows and nothing stays.

HERACLITUS OF EPHESUS (535–475 B.C.)

NOW THAT WE'VE COVERED all the principal components of the economic panarchy, it's time to take a look at how everything fits together forming the organized economy as a whole, defining the Nature of Value approach to understanding the economy. But before looking at the economy as a whole, it might be helpful to quickly review each level of the economic panarchy, shown in the following list (fig. 13.1).

1. *Inos* are units of information that get expressed as organizational capabilities and behaviors. They are analogous to biological genes. Surviving replicated inos reflect accrued knowledge that has been competitively selected, reproduced, and amplified by evolution's process.
2. *Organizations* ingest energy, resources, and capital while using their inos expressed as capabilities across the ten innovation categories to convert these inputs into goods and services. They are analogous to organisms as a form of adaptive marketing structure.

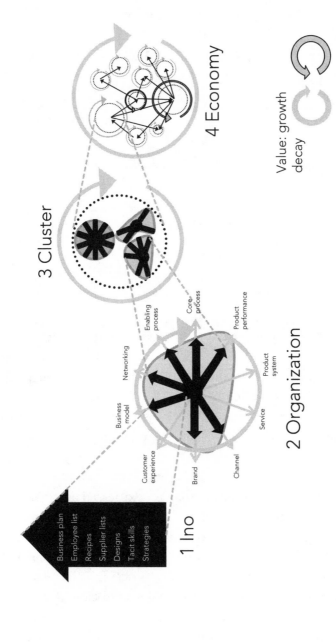

1 Ino
- Business plan
- Employee list
- Recipes
- Supplier lists
- Designs
- Tacit skills
- Strategies

2 Organization
- Customer experience
- Business model
- Networking
- Enabling process
- Core process
- Product performance
- Product system
- Service
- Channel
- Brand

3 Cluster

4 Economy

Value: growth
decay

FIGURE 13.1 Evolution's Economic Process Across Levels

Value flows through the network, adapting as it moves from one level of the panarchy to the next.

3. *Clusters* are the competitive network spaces that firms operate within. They are shaped by competitive and consumer pressure. They are analogous to ecology's niches. Selection occurring within clusters is the macroprocessing mechanism that determines what information will be selected for value delivery and turn into surviving knowledge.

4. The *economy* is the adaptive network of organizations and clusters that seek survival and growth. We will cover the economy as a whole in this chapter.

One advantage of considering evolution's economic process in aggregate as an analog to biological evolution is that it allows us to pose interesting questions about the trajectory of the economy based on concepts learned from evolution's ecological trajectory. Put more simply, it allows us to consider the predictability—or not—of the economic system.

As has been said, predicting the exact future state of any complex adaptive system is impossible. However, trends that show up across evolution's biological domain may point to events with a greater propensity to happen—and so it is with evolution's economic domain. Understanding these propensities may give one an ever-so-slight gambler's edge at seeing the future—and even a small edge can lead to great advantage amplified over time. As discussed in chapter 3 (now's the time to return to it, if you decided to skip it earlier!), all evolutionary systems evolve to consume and dissipate energy more effectively through the use of selected, replicating informational structures and patterns. Through the acquisition and retention of survival knowledge, these systems grow, by "adaptive learning," to harvest all accessible resources. As new information is expressed as capabilities in a system, it's either replicated or destroyed via competitive and selective mechanisms, as shown in figure 13.2.

Economies are just another form of evolutionary expression writ large and fast, driven by available resources and applied knowledge. As with other evolutionary systems, although it's

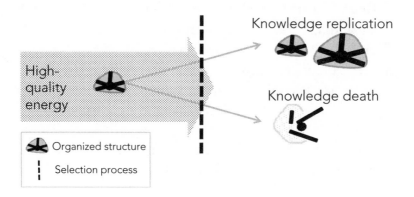

FIGURE 13.2 Evolution's Ascending Cycle
Evolution's cycle: energy flows through organized forms selected to replicate or die.

impossible to predict the specific innovations and knowledge that will deliver long-term GDP growth, overall general patterns can be discerned with some certainty.

Economy Unpredictability

Before getting into some of these generalized patterns, however, I'd like to focus for a moment on why the economy is so unpredictable. Understanding the factors driving unpredictability can help one better understand both the economy and the nature of value approach. The economic network's lack of a fixed balance or equilibrium point, seemingly random external shocks, continuous adaptive change in network links and flows, and death or removal of participants are all factors that contribute to the unpredictability of an economy.

Nonequilibrium

Traditional economics obsesses over predicting outcomes by applying neat linear equilibrium- and fixed-state models for prediction.

However, in reality, equilibrium and stasis can't exist in any of evolution's domains for a meaningful period. Economies can have occasional points of seemingly arrested development, for instance, when a company with a very strong and durable moat seems to hit a point of unchangeable stability for a few decades. However, even these periods of perceived stasis only exist for short periods in small localized areas of a flowing economic network. Keynes's "bliss" has not and will not come to pass. As an open system an ecosystem has no equilibrium outside of absolute death, and neither does the open system of an economy.

External Shocks

A basic rule of networked systems is that their elements and links don't always respond in a simple linear or expected way to big shocks. Economic shocks can take many forms—technological, like the disruptive arrival of the dotcom era; monetary, as with the entrance of the euro into the global financial system; political, in the form of coups or other major shifts of power; physical, in terms of natural disasters or climate change; biological, in terms of epidemics and other public health events; or even social, when consumer behavior changes abruptly. These kinds of shocks to an economic network will not see every linked component niche or cluster respond immediately or proportionally. Some sectors may be hugely affected, whereas others hardly show any change; some industries may experience immediate upheaval, whereas in others, the shock impact takes years to materialize. Even within organizations, knowledge, capabilities, resources, and flows respond differently. Although some shocks themselves might be somewhat predictable, the full impact a shock will have on the economic system isn't predictable. How shocks resonate through the economy is an extremely interesting question and one that deserves an allocator's special attention. This question is considered later in this chapter.

Adaptive Network Change

Evolution's networked domains, such as the economy, constantly adapt, by re-routing, shutting down, and creating new structures. These topological changes are contingent on an almost limitless number of factors—and even these factors themselves change over time. This makes specific cuasal prediction such as x always causes y almost impossible. It is possible to reduce all adaptive systems to simple physical and causal microinteractions, but this reductionist approach can't scale to predict macrobehaviors. Evolutionary systems (macroprocessing) have too much feedback and complex new structures being created. There are simply too many contingent pathways to be able to correctly anticipate value's next change in flow or expressed bifurcation.[1]

Looking at the complex paths evolution discovers to create and spread economic value and amplify knowledge across the economic network can be bewildering. Even a simple raw input such as a pig being macroprocessed by the economic network is complicated. The flows into an incredibly complex mix of value-increasing products flowing through multiple clusters, as seen in figure 13.3.

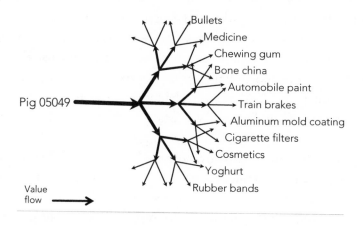

FIGURE 13.3 Pig 05049 Macroprocessed by Economy
Pig 05049's value diffused and maximized across 185 network clusters.

In her book *Pig 05049*, Dutch designer Christien Meindertsma followed a single pig as it was transformed from raw inputs into 185 end products, including chewing gum, bone china, automobile paint, train brakes, coating for aluminum molds, cigarette filters, cosmetics, medicine, yogurt, rubber bands, bullets, and many other surprising things.

The complex bifurcations and information represented by a single economic input and subsequent macroprocessing illustrates the difficulty of predicting the exact flows of an economic network's current or future pathways for value flow.

Economic Death

Another factor that makes prediction difficult is the fact that the mix of participants and capabilities in evolution's networks constantly change. New economic forms explore and emerge to fill adjacent possibility spaces, whereas death and extinction empty other spaces, leaving voids and dead pathways.

Ecology and the fossil record allow us to study how the elements in biological networks come and go. One of the most dramatic examples of this in ecology occurs during large-scale extinctions, in which 20 to 50 percent of species can disappear completely. Figure 13.4 shows the earth's major eco-network extinction events.

The timing of these specific large extinction events is unpredictable. However, like many network systems, the extinction events do follow what's called a "power law," which directly relates the frequency of an event with its magnitude. Avalanches and earthquakes follow power laws as well. Most simply put, the longer it's been since an earthquake-prone region has experienced an event, the bigger the next event is likely to be.[2]

In his informative book *Why Most Things Fail*, economic author and thinker Paul Ormerod shows how corporate and economic extinctions follow power laws as well, in which the size and

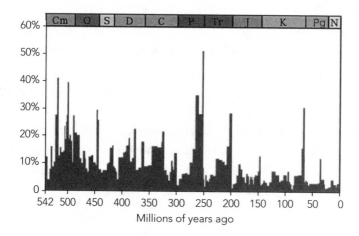

FIGURE 13.4 Four Hundred Fifty Million Years of Network Extinction Cascades
Four hundred fifty million years of extinction among marine species provides a
record of death required for the network of life to ascend.
Source: http://en.wikipedia.org/wiki/Permian_extinction

frequency of extinctions are related by a simple exponential relationship. He coined the term "the iron law of failure" to describe
this. Just as with earthquakes and avalanches, Ormerod states that
it's impossible to predict exactly when these economic events will
occur, but it is possible to discern patterns in their occurrence.

There are other discernable patterns in the death of participants
in the economy. For instance, in the short term, the new firms entering the U.S. economy experience a steady attrition rate as participants exit the economy due to bankruptcy or organizational death.
For instance, figure 13.5 shows the attrition rate for a cohort of all
new firms that entered the U.S. economy in 1994. The economic
attrition rate will not always decay so smoothly, but figure 13.5 is
indicative of aggregate attrition across an entire economy.

Just as in nature, selective death constantly thins the herd. These
organizational deaths have a productive function; they recycle
the economy's resources, energy consumers, and knowledge,

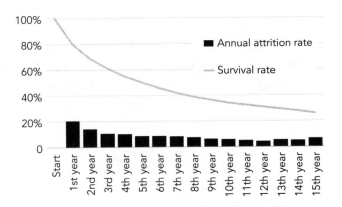

FIGURE 13.5 Attrition Rate of American Firms Born in 1994

reallocating them to maintain the most efficient, growing value-creating organizational forms. Individual and broad sector economic death allow evolution's knowledge creation macroprocess to adapt and progress. Although exact economic network changing events are mostly unpredictable, there are discernable patterns in the frequency, magnitude, and rate of events—just as there are across all of evolution's domains.

Summary on Economic Unpredictability

The constant flux and change of evolution's adaptive structures means much of evolution's next steps are a mystery. Adaptive changes in structure and knowledge combined with external shocks, death, and extinction make evolutionary processes look wildly unpredictable. Even growth and renewal occur in unpredictable ways. Fortunately for the allocator, evolution shows clear broad patterns over many domains. These patterns won't allow one to predict the precise future state or events unfolding in an ecological or economic network, but the patterns can be indicative of general trends and can help the allocator understand where things are headed. Like the blackjack player with a card counting edge, we don't know what will happen in evolution's next deal, but if we can be right 51 percent of the time, that may just be enough to make all the long-term difference. The next section looks at some patterns and trends across evolution's domains.

Economic Predictability

> How should scientists operate when they must try to explain the result of history, those inordinately complex events that can occur but once in detailed glory? Many large domains of nature—cosmology, geology, and evolution among them—must be studied with the tools of history. The appropriate methods focus on narrative, not experiment as usually conceived.[3]
>
> Evolutionary Biologist Stephen Jay Gould

To understand the evolutionary network's behavior, all we have to go on is a chaotic history spread across domains and time scales. However, these systems do express a few patterns that may aid in predicting their future behavior.

- Evolutions networks adapt to operate in a certain range of energies and operating conditions, and in doing so increase Φ_m throughput capacities.
- Evolution replicates and amplifies structured information by macroprocessing it successfully as knowledge.
- Evolution bifurcates knowledge into an ever more complex structure of mellifluous forms and flows.

Although these rules may look vague and theoretical, there are practical lessons the allocator can learn from them. First we look at each of these predictive patterns in greater detail, and later show how these rules can inform the allocator's understanding of the economy as a whole system.

Predictable Environment and Growth Behavior

In ecology, the complex chemistry structures able to organize themselves into functional proteins and cells occur within a limited range of temperature, nutrients, and electrochemical gradients that must be just right. Systems with having too little energy running through them are too "cold" and lack the ability to capture and retain structured knowledge via a selective process. These frozen systems are nonadaptive and effectively dead, unable to macroprocess biological knowledge. At the other extreme, too much energy throughput prevents a system from forming large, biological information- and knowledge-accumulating structures, destroying biochemical feedback links and creating randomness (statistical entropy). These "too-hot" systems are equally unsuited to biological adaptation. Biological adaptation needs a "goldilocks" sweet spot, with enough energy flow to keep things moving, but not so much that large interesting bits fly apart (fig. 13.6).

Similarly, economic adaptation operates best within or near an optimal range of factors. Just as ecologies flourish best in a specific environmental contextual range, economies seem to flourish in a viable sweet spot defined by certain ranges of network contextual factors and governance. Things that interrupt the flow and creation of economic knowledge inhibit an economies value flow and growth. High levels of corruption and bad governance are two factors that can somewhat predictably limit economic growth.

The growth rates of economies that exist in the "sweet spot" have other predictable characteristics. As a general rule, as discussed in chapter 3, evolutionary systems consume more energy more efficiently as they grow following their own experience curve. Economically, this trend manifests as a tendency to create more

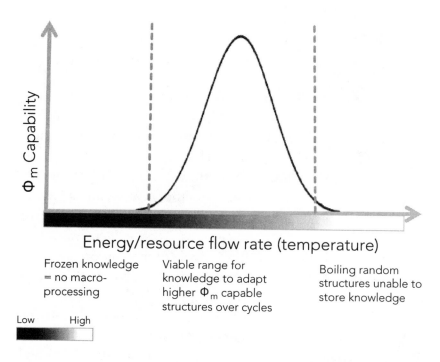

FIGURE 13.6 Environmental Conditions Required to Support Knowledge and Growth

value overall, by consuming more energy more effectively. There is a strong relationship between economic value flow rates (GDP) and the human condition as measured by the human development index (HDI).[4] Economic growth fueled by knowledge and energy distributed across an economy[5] is associated with a broadly improved human condition, providing that the value flow is sustainable.

There are other economic principles following this general trend toward increased value flow, and allocators can use these principles to guide their understanding of a growing economy. For instance, experience curve effects are some of the strongest predictive patterns available to understand an economy's trends. Specifically, Moore's law (a variation on the experience curve) states that the number of transistors on a computer chip doubles every

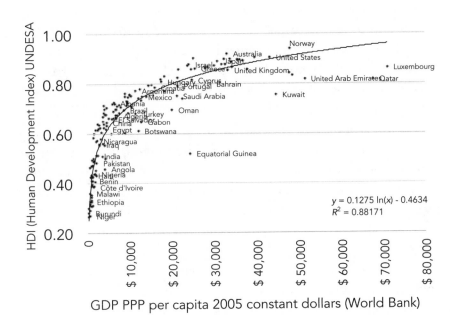

FIGURE 13.7 GDP [Purchasing Power Parity (PPP)] vs. HDI, 2011

two years; generally, this means that computing power increases exponentially over time.

Although Moore's Law is the most celebrated example, similar experience curve laws are present in many manufacturing and service delivery processes, not just computing. A research paper from the Santa Fe Institute that examined six proposed economic capability laws and curves found that all exhibited similar predictive traits with 95 percent confidence. In each case, the laws predicted efficiency gains driven by production flow or system throughput. Research wasn't focused exclusively on techy stuff like microprocessors, DRAM, and hard disk storage. The research included goods such as beer, polyvinylchloride, magnesium, refined cane sugar, and aluminum, among many others. The paper found that the laws they tested were accurate to within 2.5 percent a year—a pretty impressive predictive accuracy rating for exponential processes measured over decades.

Another specific example in which experience curves have proved accurate in their predictions is in the measure of the capability for maximum velocity of manufactured vehicles. In 1953, the U.S. Air Force's Office of Scientific Research plotted a line graph of these maximum vehicle velocities over prior centuries, and found (unsurprisingly, given the preceding discussion!) that the result was an exponential curve. This exponential trajectory shockingly projected that humanity would create a vehicle with enough speed to leave the earth's orbit in four years' time; in 1957, Russia launched Sputnik, right in line with the U.S. scientists' own evolutionary capability projection. The multi-century vehicle speed capability curve created in 1953 also approximately predicted the U.S. moon landing in 1969.

In their ability to accurately pinpoint the rate of growth in capabilities and the economy, these power and flow type laws almost seem to reflect evolution's increasing macroprocessing pace as value flows faster through the global economy. These findings highlight the fact that certain types of economic growth are generally predictable—a powerful insight for an allocator trying to understand where an industry is going next. Faster value flow accelerates knowledge creation, leading to faster capability development and even increasing value flow measured as economic growth.

Predictability in the Amplification and Replication of Knowledge

The experience curve effects and power laws described go hand in hand with the amplification of knowledge and adaptation within a macroprocessing network—another broad and predictable trait of evolution. Evolution expresses survival knowledge in a bewildering, ever-changing set of forms, relationships, and structures. The general trend is the association of increasing evolutionary progress with increased complexity found in the structures and capabilities created using the knowledge. Where new forms of knowledge creation and amplification are thwarted, evolutionary systems shrink or stagnate. Extremist political or cultural ideologies antithetical to change, education, and knowledge creation are rarely rich beyond their easily extracted resources.

In his groundbreaking book on evolution *The Selfish Gene*, Richard Dawkins talked about genes as having an intrinsic motivation for replication, and moved forward from there to show how these "selfish" genes drive evolutionary processes. This rhetorical device helped many to better understand genetics and evolutionary progress. In looking at the process of economy, a similar analogy is useful. One can consider economic progress as driven by selfish inos that have the simple goal of exploring every economic possibility space to replicate themselves by maximizing value delivered. To this end, an economy can be seen as evolution's extended, post-ecology step, with the economy growing to spread resource capturing and macroprocessing knowledge beyond that of the ecological systems capabilities. This is demonstrated with the increased Φ_m factors found in evolution's economic domain mentioned early in chapter 2.

As discussed, knowledge in this context has a very specific meaning. Knowledge is the special subset of information with a propensity (in the Popperian sense) to adaptively replicate and thus maintain itself against the constant forces of entropy represented as structural decay.[6] Figure 13.8 shows how evolution creates knowledge across ecological and economic domains.

Predictability of Evolutionary Systems with Growing Complexity

In order to more efficiently accommodate increasing energy flows, bifurcations occur in evolutionary systems that cause them to become informationally and structurally more complex over

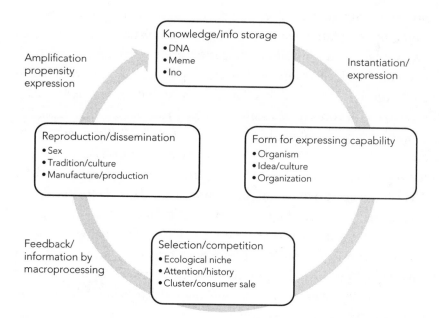

FIGURE 13.8 Evolution's Knowledge Cycle at Work in Ecological, Cultural, and Economic Domains
Knowledge is the information that is selected to replicate through the network.

replicating cycles. In the ecological domain, bifurcations are represented by the countless networks of organisms, each intent on metabolizing all available resources to spread life's network. In the economic domain, these bifurcations are expressed as countless goods and services that capture and efficiently dissipate energy, leading overall to greater value flow as the economy grows.

As the Duke from Giuseppe Di Lampedusa's book *The Leopard* said, "In order for things to stay the same everything must change." He was referring to feudal Italian civil society in the nineteenth century; as the estates' power faded, the very structure of the Italian sociopolitical network had to structurally change to accommodate the rise of an eventually richer unified modern democratic Italy in 1861. Structural change in politics allowed for accelerated socioeconomic development for the Italian people.

Summary on Economic Predictability

Evolution's next step is not exactly predictable, but may be generalizable. By looking far and wide, certain trajectories and patterns emerge. The factors related to energy flows, energy-dissipating capacities, knowledge amplification, maturation, and constant structural change may hint about what evolution has in store for economies. That being said, economies are shaped and defined in the near term with that most capricious of quasi-rational creatures, humankind. This leaves economies like ecologies—semipredictable domains to explore in the next section.

An Allocator's Look at Types of Economies

As discussed, economies are unpredictable but show general patterns and trends similar to evolution's other processes. The challenge is to understand how these unpredictable and more predictable changes interact. Evolution's predictable economic trend toward growth and change seems to be held back mostly by knowledge and value flow blockers such as greed, abuse of power, and corruption. Understanding these factors may help investors pick economies that are viable for investment. This section looks at how the more general evolutionary trends discussed in the preceding section can help the allocator identify economic systems that are promising for investment.

Inclusive and Exclusive Economies

Economic growth has a long-term predictable upward trajectory, but only if there are no social and cultural forces in place limiting growth. The allocator must be able to understand and recognize these forces in order to best predict the behavior of an economic system. Daron Acemoğlu of MIT and James Robinson of Harvard have categorized economies into two groups—"extractive" or "inclusive"[7]—and these two categories are a good place to start looking at how these forces come into play and impact economic progress.

To maintain optimal growth, economies must live in a sweet zone of social equality, rule of law, good regulation, limits on cartels, protections of customer safety and the environment, and stability in banking and insurance. Economies operating in or close to this sweet zone allow more people a chance to contribute by competing sustainably. These are called inclusive economies because everyone in the system is a potential participant. Successful capitalist economies limit cartels and monopolies for the sake of long-term socioeconomic development.[8] On the other hand, political corruption and damaging levels of concentrated financial, regulatory, or political power and wealth can damage an economy's growth prospects. Factors like this are present in exclusive economies, named as such because cartels of dominant firms or political actors extract value from society by controlling supply and price—effectively breaking the adaptive cycle and the cluster pressure that delivers the broadest social benefits.

I start by taking a closer look at inclusive economies.

Inclusive Economies

Inclusive economies exist in a sweet spot that allows for knowledge amplification and value creation. This sweet spot lies between the governance extremes of absolute libertarian, zero governance, chaotic, random failed states such as Somalia, where individual actors can forcibly extract value and destroy knowledge, and the dead, crystallized tyranny of North Korea that fully controls every aspect of the economy, thereby arresting the ability to effectively accumulate new knowledge. Figure 13.9 shows the economic sweet spot of inclusive economies, analogous to evolution's sweet spot for knowledge accumulation and growth.

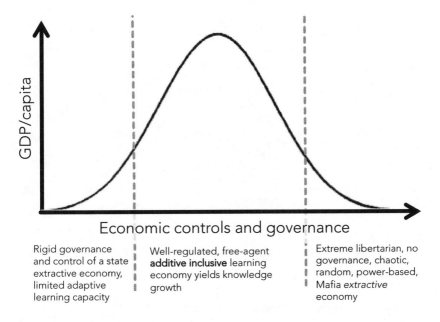

FIGURE 13.9 Government Control of Economic Actors vs. Long-Term GDP/ Capita

Within inclusive economies, new organizational capabilities compete freely to capture value, accumulate knowledge, and explore new clusters. This competition and exploration leads to adaptive bifurcations and growth in the economic structure, increasing value flows to consumers. All in all, inclusive economies accumulate knowledge and human wealth, creating potential in the form of organizations and capabilities that more efficiently deliver goods and services.

Inclusive economies are regulated and structured to encourage and protect open, competitive participation rights. This requires equitable laws that are justly enforced, private property protection, and non-monopolistic competition. The cluster models presented earlier in this book assume the presence of a functioning inclusive economy, in which managers and entrepreneurs apply

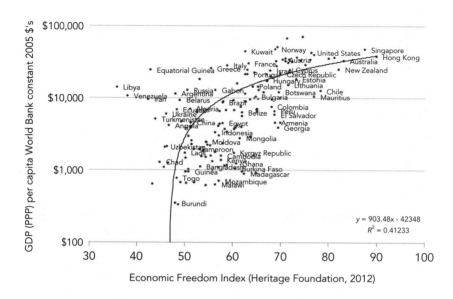

FIGURE 13.10 Inclusive (Economic Freedom) vs. GDP (PPP)

inos and knowledge while attempting to extract profit from a cluster by adding extra consumer value.

The relationship between healthy economic growth and inclusiveness is shown in figure 13.10, which uses the Economic Freedom index as a proxy for economic inclusiveness. As shown, there is a direct correlation between economic inclusiveness and GDP. It is important to note that economic freedom is extremely limited in extreme libertarian states having almost zero central governance.

Extractive Economies

Corruption, abuses of power, and other uses of force that interfere with knowledge flow, capability development, and free competition inhibit economic growth. Political or religious tyranny can also arrest growth by crushing the economy's knowledge-creating capacity. Broadly speaking, these factors are associated with extractive economies.

Extractive economies are filled with corruption and are characterized by political or absolute power structures that extract value from citizens and organizations using the power of legal or extralegal threats—or even physical violence. Extractive economies slow evolution's path by degrading its selective knowledge discovery macroprocessing; this, in turn, limits value flows. The cancer of concentrated power is itself maladapted ino, stopping normal adaptive change for the sake of its own self-preservation. Extractive economies are associated with minimal or even retarded economic growth, diminished human capability expression, and/or negative per capita growth flows.[9] Fortunately, evolution's creative destruction process means that all power structures eventually change or die, allowing for exclusive economies to potentially become inclusive in time as the restrictive political or cultural belief structures are replaced.

Corruption, one of the most prevalent features of extractive economies, limits economic development in infrastructure, costing lives[10] and lost human opportunity in developing countries. Extractive corruption correlates highly with lower life expectancy, lower literacy, and lower human development index scores. Sadly, many economic development and aid programs fail to address the predictable infeasibility of stimulating economic growth and nation building in such extractive economies. The untreated root causes of poverty—namely, extractive regimes—significantly diminish the potential impacts of development aid. This leaves much development aid active only during crisis response. Throwing money at problems like chronic poverty and human suffering is hugely important, but may only temporarily treat acute crises, and not address the root causes of economic underdevelopment.[11]

The second-order impacts of widespread corruption include limited competition, shoddy goods, black markets, reduced system throughput, and fewer taxes collected for nation building. Extractive feedback loops amplify corruption's impacts, depriving citizens of basic goods and infrastructure services such as electricity, sewers, running water, health care, and education. When basic services[12] are available, they are of significantly lower quality in relative cost terms than in less corrupt countries with inclusive economies. Figure 13.11 shows the relationship between corruption and reduced GDP per capita.

In a functioning inclusive economy, each cluster a product or service flows through on its path to the customer adds more value to the product. In extractive economies, on the other hand, value diminishes as a product moves through the economy. As figure 13.12 shows, if you start with a raw input value of $100, it could grow to a final value of $244 in an inclusive economy. In an exclusive economy, the value diminishes to $32 due to extractive forces such as corruption, poor resource utilization, or just plain extortion. Starting with the same potential, the simplified example in figure 13.12 shows 7.6 times less economic value available for consumers in the extractive economy's value chain. For the poorest among us, life literally is squeezed out of them by extractive political and cultural forces.

Those who live or have traveled in corrupt countries have likely seen the results of extractive value chains, materialized in things like enormously inflated prices on imported commercial technology; failing physical infrastructure; and inefficiency and incompetence in soft infrastructure like education and medical care. For those interested in this, see work by Nobel laureate development economist Amartya Sen on the true human costs of corruption in underdeveloped states.

Not only corrupt kleptocratic states have extractive economies. Centrally planned economies are extractive and limiting to knowledge creation by design, as they inhibit the entrepreneur's exploration of local adjacent possibility spaces. No centrally planned system works as effectively as it should at discovering

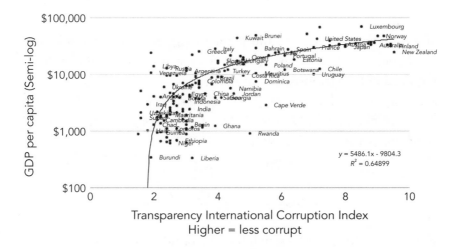

FIGURE 13.11 GDP (PPP) Per Capita vs. Corruption Index, 2011
Source: World Bank & Transparency International

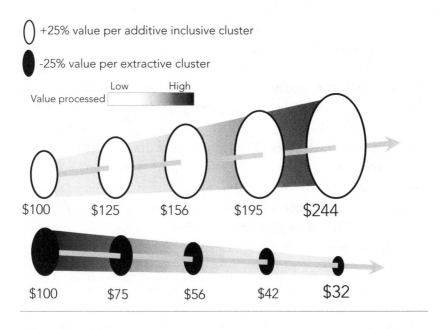

FIGURE 13.12 Value Chain Conversion Process: Additive vs. Extractive Cluster Processes
Inclusive chain delivers $244 in value, equivalent to 760% more economic value than $32 from the extractive value chain.

and applying knowledge and resources across the economic network, because of the exponentially increasing variety of responses required in a distributed economic operating environment and the centrally controlled system's inability to rapidly structurally adapt. centrally planned and controlled economic systems are extremely poor macroprocessors of value.

Implications for the Allocator

Extractive economies—much like unstable clusters—are not easily investable. The high uncertainty and brittleness associated with extractive regimes makes responsible long-term investment almost impossible. Although many developing economies have growth opportunities that might allow for short-term returns on capital, from a long-term nature of value perspective, extractive regimes are wholly inappropriate for consideration. On the other hand, it can be argued that from a humanitarian perspective, investing knowledge and capital can help accelerate political change via the rise of an enfranchised middle class that may then lead to the development and future stability of inclusive structures in these economies. Two hundred years ago, for instance, the United States was a small collection of territories, emerging from a guerrilla war with a population that had literacy rates below 10 percent, life expectancy of only 40 years, and high infant mortality. The nascent state had a poor infrastructure, a penniless federal government, and atrocious property rights. Over time, however, the state turned out fine.[13] The decision and rationalization to invest in unstable or emerging economies is ultimately up to the investor.

Generally, however, extractive economies are riskier for investors, because they are less stable and more brittle, with little capacity for adaptation or resilience. Investors should stick to or ideally advocate for inclusive economies and related policy changes.

Summary

Economies sit high at the top of evolution's panarchy of hierarchical systems. The evolution of the economy—as of any complex adaptive system—is not exactly predictable, but does have some general trends and trajectories. Economic networks consume and process energy at a growing pace and convert it into value and knowledge ever more efficiently. The key to economic growth seems to lie in allowing knowledge to amplify and spread by maintaining inclusive open economic network governance policies.

An economy's governance structure on the additive inclusive versus extractive economic continuum determines its ability for growing GDP flow and human development. Economic regulatory governance must not distort the knowledge and value flows within an economy. At the same time, enough good governance and regulation must be in place to protect and maintain an inclusive, open environment that will allow consumers and competitors to freely express and explore innovative capabilities. Finding the economic sweet spot of inclusiveness leads to positive social development and human well-being associated with sustained economic growth.

CHAPTER FOURTEEN

Monetary Shocks and Their Implications for the Allocator

WITH THESE GENERAL ECONOMIC trends and types of economy in mind, let's take a closer look at how the nature of value approach may help us understand economy-wide events, such as inflation, deflation, and other major economic shocks. Being able to identify and even potentially anticipate these events can help allocators find unexpected investing opportunities, and can also help the thoughtful allocator recognize when it's best to avoid getting involved.

However, before delving into this discussion, let us return to a topic touched on in chapter 1—the difference between price and value. This relationship is essential when it comes to thinking about economic events, with one more important variable to add to the equation: money. In chapter 1, I remarked that price is really just an opinion of value at a given time. The way we represent and communicate this value is through a type of social information known as money.

A Closer Look at Money as a Shared Mental Construct

Money, in its countless forms, is symbolic information used to measure current and expected value. Money can functionally represent value only when a group believes that it represents value; without this belief in place, the relationship between money and value breaks down. The fact that money is a form of belief means that anything can become money, as long as others have faith in it too.

The beauty of money is that it allows value to flow more efficiently through the economy by separating and abstracting physical things from their represented value. Most money has no intrinsic value of its own—it's just beliefs and social conventions assigned to computer bits, paper, or pieces of metal that refer to a value flow expected in the future. This future exchange could be anything from the transfer of an ice cream cone over a countertop to the expected delivery of currency against a bond coupon in twenty years' time. In order for something to function as money, its only essential requirements are that the group of people using it believe that it is:

1. A relatively stable representation of value[1]
2. A fairly stable informational unit of account
3. A medium of exchange believed to be shareable across an economic network of other money believers

All forms of money live only within the boundaries of the social network where and when the preceding beliefs are held. This chapter begins by looking at the most common forms of modern money used to represent value and belief in expected value. It then goes on to show how economic beliefs in expected value can cause price gyrations, inflation, value flow contractions, manias, panics, and crashes.

Currency, Debt, and Equity

Currency is what most people think of when they think of money. Currency is useful in day-to-day life, because it typically has instant social acceptance as a fairly stable representative unit of value. Stable currency units provide an efficient shortcut when compared with, say, a barter trading system. Knowing that a Warhol painting is worth 5 million cans of soup, and that those 5 million cans of soup are worth 110,000 barrels of oil, doesn't make it very easy to understand the painting's value. Currency serves as a mental lubricant for normalizing economic transactions by acting as a collectively shared, information unit that lets the art dealer thinking in Warhol units of value exchange with the oil baron thinking in oil barrel units of value. Currency units are a socially shared language of value acting as an infinite translator between different parts of the economic network. Think, for instance, about what happens when you travel abroad. You will most likely do continuous currency conversion processing in your head to understand the "value" of things in your familiar home currency, just as you might at first mentally translate a foreign sentence into your native language before you're able to answer it.

The ubiquity of currency means that most of us rarely think about just how artificial and belief-based a currency is—and how temporary. Indeed, all currency units have life cycles of their own.

Some currency is born after the painful death of another currency or political system. At other times, the birth of a currency is greeted with a political hurrah, as with the euro in 1999. Following a familiar currency—the dollar—through its origin story can help the allocator appreciate just how fickle the mental social magic of currency really is.

The dollar was originally a fifteenth century Spanish currency concept[2] that in turn was based on gold. The word "dollar" was derived from a Bohemian silver coin called the Thaler (pronounced "taller") that circulated successfully for four hundred years. The success of the Thaler provided the brand leverage needed for the dollar as a unit of value. The American colonies settled on the term "dollar" as a name for their currency after the Continental, the original American currency unit, failed because of over-issuance and counterfeiting in 1781.

In its early years, the United States set up a few central banks to issue its federal currency, but these initial banks failed because of corruption and lack of political support. After the third federal central bank—confusingly named the Second Bank of the United States—closed in 1836, the United States entered a thirty-year period of "free" banking in which each state loosely regulated its own banking and currency issuance and each local bank issued its own version of U.S. dollars convertible into a fixed amount of gold. During that time, it's estimated that there were more than thirty thousand variations of dollar banknotes circulating[3]—the ever-adapting dollar even saw a tea company in New York issue a pink $0.25 note. Customers and merchants had to use guide-books to calculate dollar exchange rates, and 30 percent of the dollars circulating were estimated to be counterfeit. Because of a lack of faith in most versions of dollars, many dollar banknotes traded at steep discounts to their gold redemption face value.

Congress killed the state banking system after the Civil War in the 1860s by taxing banknotes at a rate of between 2 and 10 percent. To reduce the frequent liquidity and gold redemption panics, such as the one in 1907, a Federal Reserve system of twelve regional banks began operating in 1913, with each member bank issuing its own dollars backed or representing a claim on gold. These dollars became the exclusive U.S. legal tender and other issued U.S. dollars were phased out. The Fed's 1913 version of the dollar unit lasted twenty years, until its gold redemption ratio was cut from $20.67 to $35 per ounce of gold. This 1933 version of the dollar lasted thirty-four years, until 1971, when the gold redemption feature was removed completely.

The 1971 version, which is still in use today, has no redeemable value other than its ability to settle tax obligations and to be recognized as legal tender. Most currencies no longer directly represent physical value; they represent pure faith in people's acceptance of the currency itself with no convertible link to a metal or other asset. This non-redeemable currency feature creates flexibility in a currency's circulating amount, providing a necessary debt-pain relief valve during debt money crises, as central banks almost always print their economies out of trouble, deflating recurring economically overwhelming debts. Large-scale currency issuance performed by central bank asset purchases is an economy-wide reset of the informational value of the currency. Like any form of economic pain relief, creating currency to diminish the relative value of fixed money debts can be abused and cause hyperinflation, as we shall see later in this chapter, or even lead to the to the informational utility and functional death of the currency.

People's economic need for the economic utility of a currency is so strong that even when the original issuer disappears and the notes are mere collectible artifacts, people still use the currency. This happened with the Somali Shilling after the 1991 collapse of the Somali central bank. The Somali people needed the utility of a paper currency so much that they collectively traded a heavily discounted Shilling years after the central bank disappeared. The central bank had died but the zombie currency lived on.

As the origin story of the dollar makes clear, the relationship a currency has to value changes over time. In order to keep functioning, the essential thing is that a currency retain its believability as a stable informational unit for representating value. This point is illustrated powerfully in the story of the island of Yap, told by Peter Bernstein in his book *The Power of Gold*. The inhabitants of the island, as Bernstein relates, used giant round stones as a form of money.[4] These stone coins, weighing from several pounds to many tons, were proudly displayed in front of houses. Their value was based on the ocean distances the stones had traveled and the history of their ownership. In one instance, a large disk weighing more than a ton was being transferred from a wealthy Yap family to another, but while on its journey at sea, the coin sank. Fortunately for the new owner, the belief in the story was so strong that the other Yap island-ers acknowledged the new owner as still "owning" the stone's value and the wealth it represented. You may think it sounds silly to recognize wealth based on faith in an unseen and nearly irretrievable asset sunk beneath the waves. If so, consider this. At the Federal Reserve Bank in New York, there is a vault fifty feet below sea level believed to be filled with an estimated 23 percent of the world's mined gold. The vault is sectioned off, with each zone associated with a different country. As these countries swap money, bars are physically moved from one section of the room to another. Physically, countries rarely access these functionally useless piles of gold metal—but everyone believes they are there, and that knowledge is good enough for the money informational effect to work.

People's persistent belief in a currency's symbolic value can be blindingly powerful. The anthropologist William Henry Furness tells how, when the island of Yap was purchased by the Germans in 1898, they tried offering the islanders paper or metal money to get them to build roads.[5] It was to no avail—the islanders were not motivated by and did not believe in German forms of currency. Their German currency, after all, was only flimsy bits of paper and metal—nothing compared with a huge stone coin trusted and owned for generations.

So the Germans introduced another form of money—debt. They put black marks on the islanders' giant coins, claiming them as their own. With the islanders having publicly "lost" their assets to the Germans, they felt compelled to work to earn back their stone coins. Once they'd worked enough, the Germans publicly removed the black debt marks.

As this Yap islanders story shows, debt is also a form of money. Debt represents faith in the expected delivery of future value in the form of currency. Anything representing a claim on value, or future value representation, can serve as money. Equity, for instance, is also money. Equity is the expectation of future value delivery, in either dividends or a claimable share of the company assets upon its sale. Shares in the Coca-Cola company are a form of money because they are expected to deliver future value to shareholders and represent a claimable share of the firm's assets or book value.

Debt and equity as far away future claims are more variable and uncertain than currency; securities are often pledged as collateral or loaned against obligations at large discounts, reflecting the uncertainty in their ability to represent value. In certain exchanges, however, shares and corporate debt are widely used as a purchase currency. Corporate takeovers, for instance, are often paid for using shares or are funded with the aid of debt. Just as with owning currency, owning debt and equity are forms of wealth because they reflect the belief in expected future delivery of value.

Debt and equity money serve a different purpose than currency and have different characteristics. Currency, for instance, is very well suited for day-to-day exchanges. Shares in GM or Amazon, on the other hand, would make for a terrible unit of account due to their high price variance. They could be used as units of account for extremely short intervals, but for the most part are too uncertain for long-term use. This difference between the two types of money can allow us to usefully classify them into two types of value representation: near money, like currency, and far money, like debt and equity.

Near and Far Money Represent Near and Far Expectations of Value Delivery

Currency is near money in that it is immediately near-term transferable into things like hamburgers and bicycles. Far money, like long-term debt and equity, represent expected value flows over time. Near and far money are deeply interrelated. One buys or sells far money bonds or equity using near money currency in the anticipation of eventually receiving currency of greater value. Plenty of forms of far money are highly liquid, that is, readily convertible into currency. Debt decays or is typically paid back with currency, and shares can be bought back and retired by companies or swapped for cash in acquisitions. Forms of near and far money are constantly created, destroyed, and transformed into each other.

Table 14.1 shows some forms of near and far money along with the informational belief boundaries they operate within. These forms of money behave differently over time, in terms of their relationship to value. The value of most near money decays over time, due to inflation related to central bank currency creation and issuance. The value represented by far money also varies, but less predictably. This variance is illustrated in the constantly changing prices of stocks, for instance. Far money can increase in value over time, but it can also decay to zero value when the issuer/creator goes bankrupt. Due to uncertainty and anticipated currency decay expectations, far money often trades at a value discount to near money based on inflation. This discount is reflected in the extra yield or amount of extra future currency delivery that far money buyers demand.

Figure 14.1 shows various forms of money and how much faith they represent as future representations of created value. As figure 14.1 illustrates, different forms of money have different beliefs associated with them, in terms of their belief function as a store (stable representational unit) of value. Different types of money have different expected currency yields; the differences in the expected yield (extra currency delivery) justify the price differentials across various forms of money. Thus, the price of far distant money represents the uncertainty of far money's ability to deliver future value relative to the currency into which it decay.

Table 14.1
Table of Money Forms

Form of money	Time distance (near /far)	Cultural/geographic boundaries	Issued/created by	Redeemed/destroyed by	Special feature
U.S. Federal Reserve paper currency	Near	Nearly global	Federal Reserve banks	Fed Asset sales	Mild value decay
U.S. Federal Reserve electronic currency	Near instant	SWIFT or Chips bank clearing system	Federal Reserve banks	Fed Asset sales	Not redeemable
Paper checks	1–30 days	Near trusted groups (merchants, friends)	Individual citizens	Bank clearing against account	Represent a form of personal and corporate near money
Personal IOU	Near	Trusted friends	Individual	Individual full repayment	Rarer form of informal money
Money market instruments	30–90 days	Typically country specific	Corporations	Redemption for currency at term	Recent panic of 2008 caused temporary money liquidity function failure
Short-term debt	90 days–5 years	Government debt accepted institutionally	Governments and corporations	Interest payments and currency redemption at term	Issued at auction, price subject to ratings agency opinions
Long-term govt. bonds	Far; 5–30 years	Government debt accepted institutionally	Assumed stable governments	Interest payments and currency redemption at term	More volatile form of money due to long duration

Long-term corporate debt	Far; 5–20 years	Exchange traded	Larger corporations	Interest payments and currency redemption at term	Less liquid. May be linked to specific collateral or be a general claim.
Mortgage-backed securities	Far; 10–30 years	Bundles of mortgages require other specialists to assess. Limited boundary of circulation.	Major institutional banks	Interest payments and currency redemption at term	Over valued form of money in 2008. Far money used to inflate housing price bubble.
Publicly traded corporate equity	Far	Exchange traded within countries	Organizations	Bankruptcy, dividend payment or buyout (currency redemption)	Highly liquid, rare redeemed feature only used during takeovers and buybacks. May pay discretionary dividends.
Gold	Near	Cross-cultural	Miners	N/A	Limited functional value. Gold's money:value ratio subject to disbelief.
Casino chips	Near	Limited to inside a casino	Casino	Currency redemption	Redeemable into currency. Often novelty colors.
Christmas fruitcakes	N/A	Universally recognized and heavily discounted	Unpopular relatives and factories	N/A	Traded globally as unwanted gifts, with negligible trade or nutritional value

(*continued*)

Table 14.1 (continued)

Form of money	Time distance (near /far)	Cultural/ geographic boundaries	Issued/created by	Redeemed/ destroyed by	Special feature
Somali shillings	Near money	Parts of Somalia	Former Somali central bank	n/a	Original issuing central bank no longer exists. Still used due to need for currency.
CDO (collateralized debt obligation)	Far; 5–20 years	Limited to math and finance specialists banks	Major banks and institutions	Bankruptcy, dividend payment or buyout (currency redemption)	A form of money so complicated that its creators and some consumers severely miscalculated its money:value ratio accelerating the multi-trillion dollar real estate crisis
Bitcoin and digital currency	Near money	Global	Algorithmic hard-coded issuance/circulation	Loss and breakage are permanent	Limited supply/known issuance rate/digital, physical and metallic expression/pseudonymity

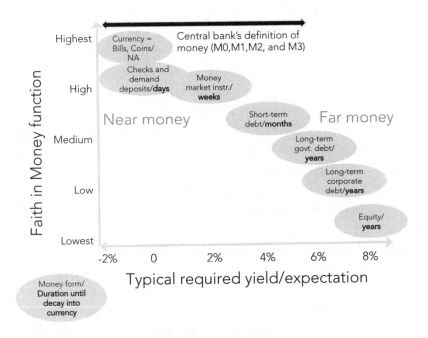

FIGURE 14.1 Money Risk and Inflation Premiums
The "faith in money function" is the faith in money's representational belief as a unit of account, store of value, and means of exchange.

Once one thinks about money as expected value delivery beyond currency, it becomes obvious that different types of money, as representations of value, have lives all their own.

Money × Value = Price

This brings us to a key equation representing the relationship between these three variables: Money × Value = Price. Or to put it in words: Price is a ratio of expected money to expected value. The MV = P equation is a canonical representation of how money, value, and price work together. Money is a representation of value, and value is perceived, which means that price—as discussed earlier in this book—is mostly a matter of group opinions and beliefs. Each one of the variables is stretchy and elastic due to people's changing expectations and behaviors. The big-picture implication of this is that economics is a behavioral and social science, not a mechanical or physical one like physics or chemistry. Many economists believe in a perfectly rational market that will always keep the MV = P relationship stable. This belief is itself highly irrational and shows much of economics to have a reckless misunderstanding of human behavior and history across thousands of cultures spanning thousands of years.

A stable representational information system of near and far money can accelerate the growth of real value and wealth (expected value) for as long as its participants agree to believe in it. The money system works because of the societal agreement that near and far money are claims on near and far value that will be fairly upheld and acknowledged, and that the currency won't be overproduced, diminishing the value of future credit obligations too greatly. Without sensible limits to currency creation, Currencies can die rapidly, leading to economic network shocks to value flows, wealth destruction and human misery. Money death and the loss of faith in currency can make flows of value through the economic network seize up. Effective management of a monetary system is a key component of a healthy, growing economy and stable government.

Central Banks

Central banks are at the heart of most modern economies' near and far money management systems. Central banks typically operate with a single mandate[6]: Maximize long-term value flow (GDP) growth by keeping the near money to value relationship—that is, the price of things—stable. The overall goal is to grow the V (current and expected value flow or wealth) in the MV = P relationship. Changes in the balance between near and far money and near and far value show up as price changes for current value (goods and services) and far value debt and equity wealth.

Most importantly, a public/private central bank doesn't have a monopoly on money creation and issuance. Far money equity is mostly issued and retired by the private sector, and debt is also issued and retired by the public and government sectors. Central banks manage the MV = P relationship by applying pressures to public and private money-creating capability and flow via short-term interest rate changes, open market purchases of private near and far money,[7] bank reserve requirements, and the sale and purchase of government debt with currency. In order to achieve price stability and maximize value flow growth, central banks attempt to anticipate what the future real and perceived growth in wealth and money flow may be. The central bank's challenge is to use a simple set of public tools to loosely guide private money creation rates, which itself is driven by beliefs and future value flow expectations, while at the same time coordinating its own behavior with the government's own fiscal tax and debt issuance policy.

The importance of a stable and well-managed MV = P relationship is best demonstrated by looking at what happens when the money or price factors get out of line with value, causing money bubbles and crashes. Here's a recent example: For years under Allen Greenspan, the U.S. Federal Reserve acted as if housing bubbles fueled by private money in the form of easily created equity or debt were not a concern for central banks, the rationale being that the "free market" feedback mechanisms always priced value correctly and would most effectively manage the creation and destruction of money relative to the real value expected and outstanding. This "rational markets" assumption proved a grotesque misreading of common human foibles and how an economy really works. Homeowner tax and financing subsidies and technocratic debt institutions, like Fannie Mae, further distorted housing's role in the U.S. economic network. These distortions occur easily in a positional goods market as more money competes for relative positional value rather than intrinsic value or wealth. The result was a large multi-trillion dollar debt-fueled asset bubble from 2002 to 2007. This massive creation of money and associated resource allocation led to an acceleration of price that got way ahead of intrinsic value. The end result was significant money and value destruction, price declines, and temporary value flow (GDP) decline—in other words, a recession. U.S. home prices were ahead of housing's value by a $6.6 trillion factor representing over a third of the annual economic GDP flow,[8] with trillions in mortgage debt issued that ultimately proved to be worth far less than the value it was supposed to represent. The extreme price dislocation fuelled by cheap money distorted the economic network's resource allocation function by encouraging others to overallocate resources to housing-related activity. As the network destroyed the cheap far money creation debt machine in 2008 and resolved structure closer to a "normal state," millions suffered and lost jobs. As of 2013, the amount of cheap debt was still not deleveraged to normative levels relative to real economic value flow. This presents a risk of further dislocation shocks or poor network flows until the money and debt service to value relationship resolves itself. This confusion of relative value in a positional good is also occurring in U.S. higher education as subsidized student debt fuels an arms race for what is increasing a positional credential rather than an absolute knowledge good.

Focusing on maintaining a stable MV = P relationship is thus one of the major keys to avoiding economic meltdowns. It's no easy task, as the mix of near and far money—the components of this equation—are in constant flux. Too much money relative to expected value or purchasable value creates inflation; too little money or demand creates dangerous deflation. Deflation, which increases fixed debt burdens relative to incomes (individual value flows), can shrink aggregate value flows (GDP) in a value flow contraction feedback loop just as badly as too much inflation. Figure 14.2 shows how buckets of money and value are typically balanced, while being filled

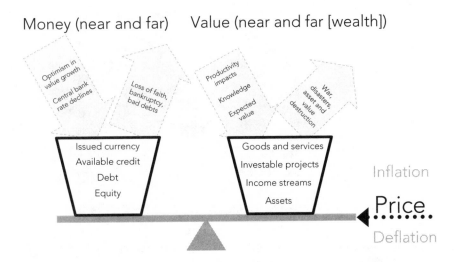

FIGURE 14.2 Money and Value's Creative/Destructive Flows Tip the Price Balance

and emptied continuously by economic activity. Value delivered and expectations of future value are destroyed and created just as money is continuously created and destroyed. Inflation occurs when the value and wealth bucket weighs less than the money bucket. Shocks that create inflation can come in the form of excess money creation relative to the outstanding value of assets. Wars and other destructives forces that suddenly destroy value create inflation by shrinking expected far value (wealth) relative to available supplies of near and far public money (created to fund wars).

The shifting relationship between money and value determines the direction of the economy, as shown in figure 14.3. Most central banks strive for policies that move the economic network into the "stable growth zone," aiming to minimize the variance between far money and wealth (expected value creation). Economic and political stability are tightly linked, so understanding how to keep value flowing and maintain the correct amount and types of money in an economy is important for all citizens' well-being.

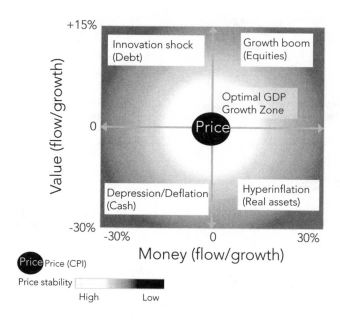

FIGURE 14.3 Environmental Stability Fosters Economic Growth

Stable environments are required for sustained ecological metabolic[9] network growth, too.

Ecosystems that are stable over many life cycles become populated with organisms that express extreme structural diversity and many unique capabilities. Because organisms in stable environments do not need to adapt the physical capacities needed to deal with extreme environmental variation, they can instead adapt new exotic forms of energy capture and throughput rather than expending resources on resilience. Desert and arctic regions with wide environmental variability see less variation in species and less biomass in weight per unit of land, as fewer species are able to develop the capabilities needed to survive such inhospitable environments. The networks are sparser and less dense measured in connections, biomass density, species and organism variation, metabolic throughput, and Φ_m. Likewise, economies that move into the volatile far corners of the chart in figure 14.3 support limited organizational diversity and value-creating capability per unit of resource, as fewer firms can adapt to survive extreme and unfamiliar economic pressures in volatile resource network.

Economic expectations of stable inflation rates get baked into business models, supply chains, operations, consumption behaviors, and contracts. Stability in resource, information, and value flows allows for greater risk-taking and the exploration of new value-creating economic possibility spaces that create sophisticated, diverse organizational forms and economic networks. As collective faith in inflation expectations stabilizes, more far money is created for allocation toward longer-term and larger value–creating projects. These projects often grow the value flow capacity of the entire economy. Stimulus advocates recommend public money debt creation to replace private money debt during crisis of confidence to induce monetary flow stability and consistency relative to the economic network's value.

Many economists and central bankers consider low-level stable price inflation of 1 to 2 percent annually to be optimal for long-term GDP and economic network growth.[10] Of course, no economy perpetually remains in a stable growth zone. At some point, an economic "shock" to the MV = P equation upsets the relative balance and moves through the economic network of value flows, altering the network's relationships and capacities for the clusters and firms living in it. Understanding how these shocks operate and how they impact economic systems is important for the allocator hunting for value.

Inflation and Deflation Shocks

Most shocks don't affect all things at once; rather, they occur at various entry points in the economic network and are absorbed by firms, which either pass on the shock or die during the transition to the new post-shock economic network structure. Large shocks distort resource flows, causing value macroprocessing inefficiencies across the firm, cluster, and economy. Large shocks often punish far money debt and equity issuers and holders making large infrastructure and other new capital-intensive projects more expensive as far money credit creators demand large or unfeasible yield premiums due to expected inflation and increased economic uncertainty.

During inflation shocks, equity holders often see real inflation-adjusted share prices decline, as the risk premiums over pricier bonds require higher equity yields to justify the expected risk in the Money to Value relationship. For some firms, inflation can be advantageous. For instance, for inflation-invariant moated firms, such as utilities or FMCG brands that derive their pricing power from consumers' relative competitive choice relationships, slow stable persistent inflation may provide significant long-term competitive and ROE advantages. In the rest of this chapter, I take a closer look at inflation and deflation, and examine how the allocator can best understand and react to—and possibly even on rare occasions anticipate—these events.

Inflation

Stable monetary inflation, measured in absolute terms, isn't terribly dangerous. Money is really just a unit of account—a score-keeping mechanism that helps balance the $MV = P$ equation and that lets V grow as the knowledge effects of inos work their magic. Inflation, that is, doesn't change the intrinsic value of a thing. If tomorrow every single cost, price, contract term, coin, account, and currency note in the world had an extra zero added to it, it wouldn't make any difference. The 5¢ bottle of Coke in 1959 is just as refreshing as today's thirty times pricier $1.50 bottle.

The inflation problem comes from how the money and/or price shock distorts, stretches, and twists the economic network, straining the flows and links between real stores of value, expectations, clusters, and supply relationships. Inflation affects each of these pieces in different ways and at different velocities; as a result these links and flows are distorted and uncoupled. For instance, contract terms debt, and interest rates are often fixed based on "normal" inflation expectations. When large price shifts occur, these financial flows and links operate differently. The overall result is that value creation slows or even stops. Of course, there's always a silver lining—near-term shocks to equity prices can create a value purchasing opportunity for the investor able to act during a crisis and separate the underpriced wheat from the inflated chaff.

The most dangerous type of inflation shock is hyperinflation. It is the killer of entire economic networks, currencies, and far monies value representation. Hyperinflation is often defined as broad consumer price inflation greater than 50 percent per month. It occurs when currency fails in its three basic belief functions: belief as a store of value, belief as a stable unit of account, and belief as a medium of exchange. A currency fails or falters as the illusion and reality of its value-storage capability disappears. This is most devastating to holders of debt (far money) that is redeemable in the rapidly devalued near money (currency). Volatile, weak currencies limit the creation of private sector debt and equity, which is needed for economic growth. Extreme near money currency creation often cascades into a far money shortage after the price shock has passed, as risk-averse far money creators are slow to believe in the stability both of the currency to value relationship and the future economic network's value flows.

Hyperinflation's ecological equivalent is an extreme factor shift, such as a radical rise or fall in temperatures. Extreme cooling or heat wipes out populations and entire ecosystem networks. The Permian extinction,[11] known as the Great Dying, saw 95 percent of species in the ecological network become extinct. Hyperinflation caused by excessive debt or conflict-driven economic and political crises can have a similar extinction impact on organizations across whole economies.

The United States hasn't experienced hyperinflation since the destruction of the earliest U.S. Continental currency in 1791 and the Confederate dollar in the 1860s. The Continental went from being worth $1 gold to 1¢ to eventually nothing. (This is how the phrase "not worth a Continental" was born.) The Continental's decay was an accelerated version of the normal erosion of value purchasing power that takes place with most central bank issued currencies; since 1930, for instance, the U.S. dollar has lost 96 percent of its purchasing power. And yet, evolution's economic value ascendency has still seen annual GDP per capita value, in real terms, increase from $21,249 in 1971 to $42,671 in 2011[12]—a successful increase in real value flow per capita. Even with a steady slowly decaying unit of information—that is, money—economic macroprocessing resiliently adapts and selects the knowledge needed for increasing value creation and flow.

Hyperinflation, on the other hand, shrinks an economy's value flow capacity in real terms. Deep recessions in economic activity, measured as real GDP contractions in which either money flow or demand shrinks, cause even greater loss of efficiency and flow. This can create a lethal feedback spiral for firms. A company creating lemonade at a real cost of $1.50 per glass and selling it for $1 per glass won't survive long. Large inflation shocks often increase far money related capital costs, while shrinking planning horizons and addressable working capital capacities. The paradox in such situations is that price inflation, driven by an overabundance of near money rather than a resource availability crunch, can occasionally induce far money scarcity due to uncertainty of future economic network volatility. Long-term projects become impossible to finance because their real expected returns measured in near term local currency units or "known" value are wildly uncertain and thus must offer extremely high yields relative to the newly scarce and expensive far money.

Assuming demand holds up, hyperinflation in brief periods is less damaging to asset-intensive firms that have debt priced in fixed terms and assets that allow for delayed capital spending. Railroads, utilities, and debt heavy infrastructure are all examples of this; they may suffer declines in use and mild deterioration due to low capital investment during hyperinflationary periods, but their moats retain their value-creating ability. This may allow them to eke by until relative price links in the network stabilize and a normal interest rate environment returns. The cash flows of infrastructure and heavy capex-related industries can then roar back once inflation subsides and operational efficiencies and demand return. In general, the real moatable value of a business—assuming it survives the strains of hyperinflation and associated political upheaval—may recover rapidly as inflation and expected currency decay rates normalize.

As mentioned, the MV = P equation plays out differently across network value flows and different forms of near and far money. Many are surprised to learn that stock markets in hyperinflationary Weimar Germany and more recently Zimbabwe[13] went up significantly in nominal terms. During the Weimar period (1919–1924), for instance, there was a rush of stock speculation as climbing prices for equities (far money) convinced many to incorrectly assume that shares were gaining in value and might offer an economic escape hatch as the currency (near money) and debt instruments (far money) collapsed. The problem was that growing equity prices did not increase fast enough relative to the currency's declining purchasing power. Thinking in value terms explains this clearly. The wealth (expected future value creation) measured in real purchasing power terms declined faster than general inflation due to economic network dislocations associated with the hyperinflationary economic shock. Shares lost real absolute value as firms suffered real economic damages due to increased working capital and capex financing costs along with diminished unit demand. This is another example of the dangers of confusing price and value when currency creation gets crazy and the currency fails to perform its informational function for the network to macroprocess.

An even more flagrant example of the fundamental confusion between price and value is illustrated by the behavior of the German central bank in the 1920s. In the midst of the Weimar economic crisis, the head of the German central bank urged the Reichstag not to panic, saying he had secured enough paper and ink to supply what he saw as the demand for money—clearly mistaking MV = P attractor model with the M = P equillibrium model. From August 1922 to December 1923, prices doubled every 3.70 days.[14] Using a faulty interpretation of the mechanistic Walrasian equilibrium economic model, which didn't take value into account, the Weimar central bank had come to the conclusion that printing more currency would eventually lead to price stability and an equilibrium between the currency and value.

The reality was that people didn't believe in the currency. They were desperate to get their hands on their salary in near money (currency) quickly so they could spend and convert it rapidly into anything that might act as a store of value. The rush to spend currency (near money) fast in order to make the most of the eroding MV = P relationship is a trademark behavior during hyperinflation. At times like this, items that may retain value become traded as near money proxies—easily recognized luxury goods and expensive liquor brands—become particularly sought after stable money. These luxury buying behaviors occurred in Weimar Germany's hyperinflationary period[15]; unfortunately, the British ambassador in Berlin mistook the frenzied purchasing and spending on "luxuries" as an indication that the economy was active and thus strong. He suggested that Britain continue its demands for World War I reparations payable in gold-backed currency. This debt pressure increased the value extractive burdens on a collapsing economic network. Weimar Germany, with an economy that was actually shrinking in terms of value throughput, found that the push for reparations in hard currency increased the debt to GDP ratio (estimated by some at 9:1[16]) beyond a sustainable point. (To put this into a modern context, as of 2013, Japan has one of the highest government debt:GDP ratios in the world at 2:1.) As the excess currency flows required for debt service became an increasingly large percentage of overall economic network value flows, money for new investment and working capital for real value flow was choked. This led to the economic network suffering a value flow contraction feedback loop or death spiral ending in, network collapse, social chaos, and a political vacuum.

Eventually the Reichsbank Mark was replaced by the Rentenmark, which saw twelve zeroes cut off the prior notes in the conversion process. Adam Fergusson's book *When Money Dies* provides excellent insight into the chaos using insider accounts of Weimar Germany's hyperinflation.

More recently, in 1990, Brazil experienced hyperinflation, running at 80 percent a month with prices doubling every thirty-five days. Faith in the future currency value representation and far money collapsed, as price increases became daily events. As in Weimar Germany, people began panic buying, purchasing value in stores as rapidly as they could to get rid of cash. Store clerks would rush through stores with price marking sticker guns constantly updating prices. Many consumers made a point of running ahead of these store clerks in order to get better prices.

Firms suffer severe stresses managing resource flows during periods like this. A Brazilian beer maker that went out of business because it couldn't raise prices fast enough to keep up with production costs provides a useful case study. The one- to two-week brewing and production time was too slow relative to the price increases the brewer could pass on to consumers. The internal working capital strains distorted costs and margins, and although this only lasted briefly, it was enough to bankrupt the brewer and many others who hadn't adapted the resilience capabilities and behaviors needed to survive the hyperinflation shock period. In order to survive, the brewers would have needed to make tough choices for survival: perhaps shrinking the amounts of beer produced to reduce working capital needs, securing very expensive financing, or forcing commercial customers to prepay for their beer. These are all difficult choices in a shrinking money environment.

In order to escape hyperinflation, the Brazilian central bank turned to economists for help. Brazilian economist Edmar Bacha and his colleagues approached the problem by thinking like sociologists, understanding that near money currency is just a collective belief in a unit of information and that the belief in Brazilian Cruzeiros was failing. With this in mind, they took a twofold approach. First, they stopped overissuing Cruzeiros. Second, they created and marketed a new theoretical money unit called a unit of real value (URV). The URV was a kind of monetary unicorn. Since no one had really seen it, even scant evidence served to shape people's perception of it.

Every day for six months, the local newspapers showed a slowing rate of Cruzeiros price inflation next to a stable URV price for consumer staples. The URV price numbers didn't move, of course, because the URV didn't exist. The URV was just a made-up column of numbers created by economists and printed next to the Crusero prices in the daily newspaper. The URV and its $MV = P$ relationship existed only in people's minds as a shared psychological anchoring mechanism. No URV ever existed or was spent; it was an economist's perfect currency, a form of beautifully pure belief expressed on paper that never failed to represent value or lost purchasing power because it never had to exist in the real economy.

In Weimar Germany a more tangible device was used as a unit of information to represent value; people related the daily price of money to the price of an egg. The egg became a trusted unit of value helping people understand the Reischmark $MV = P$ chaos. The Brazilian URV idea, like the egg, was a psychological anchor showing people that a locally created currency unit could hold a stable value relationship—which, being nothing more than a column of numbers, wasn't so difficult. Currency is a collective belief system, a shared social experience enabling efficient macroprocessing of resources and information into value and nothing more.

From 1986 to 1995 Brazil created six currencies[17] before stabilizing on the Real, which remains in active circulation today.[18]

The Brazil example shows that it's not the absolute value of goods that shifts during inflation; rather, it's the relative amount of near and far money available to buy goods and assets. Milton Friedman stated that inflation is always and everywhere a monetary phenomenon; this is correct only in that inflation changes the relationship between a supply of near and far money, and value or expected value. To put it more simply—increasing prices doesn't directly change a thing's intrinsic value. As mentioned earlier, if every single contract, input cost, unit of money, and price suddenly had an extra zero added to it, nothing would change. The $MV = P$ relationship would hold roughly true subject to people's psychological anchoring on past price. Of course, this isn't what happens. Instead, price increases propagate at varying rates as they cross different linked sectors of the economy network, and it's these relative price and cost differences stretching and distorting economic links that can ruin organizations and entire economies. We'll take a closer look at how shocks move through the economy later in the chapter—but first, let's look at deflation.

Deflation

Deflation comes in good and bad forms. Generally "good" deflation is associated with applied knowledge that improves value-creation efficiency of goods and services. In this case, prices drop relative to value delivered. "Bad" deflation is caused by factors that limit available money, which retards demand-driven value flow as measured by GDP in real terms.

Bad deflation is associated with contractions in the near and far money supply, leading to a decrease in real demand-driven value flows. In the worst cases, deflation causes a devastating feedback loop, as the lack of near and far money leads to a lack of money creation for demand-driven consumption and organizational capability building. Shrinking money available to drive demand accelerates price declines and also shrinks the value of far money like debt or equities that is based on expected profits and debt service currency flows. These declines in far money assets combined with increasing near money demand for operations and near-term debt service cause the cost of existing debt service to grow relative to shrinking cash flows and incomes. Shrinking incomes make consumer purchasing power weaker. Currency and existing near money measured in real terms becomes scarce as people struggle to pay down their now relatively larger debts. Servicing far money debt becomes more difficult while their wealth commands lower prices due to a market flooded by expectations of reduced future value flows. Everyone is selling and there is little money for buying, leading the economic network's money and value flow to shrink devastatingly, leading to widespread capability underutilization and significant unemployment.

The ultimate result is drastically reduced value flow rates, as was seen in the Great Depression in the United States in the 1930s. A severe deflationary feedback loop occurred as land, shares, and asset prices crashed, and credit (private far money) nearly disappeared, while interest payments on existing debt grew relative to available personal and corporate cash flows. Output and prices declined by a full 25 percent in the 1928–1933 period.[19] Prior to 1933, the United States is believed to have suffered nine bouts of deflation, with the worst period occurring in 1875–1879,[20] after the U.S. railway mania mired in political land corruption burst in 1873.

When debt-fueled asset bubbles collapse, the price of the asset and the money fueling it are often both destroyed. Bad deflation often follows, depending on the central bank policies and scale of the bubble. In the early 2000s, Greece (like many developed countries) had an inflationary real estate bubble fueled by a far money creation frenzy in the form of securitized mortgage securities. Bankers and homeowners confused rising home prices fueled by money creation with rising intrinsic value. In 2009, when real estate values reverted to normal income-to-property value ratios, the mortgage debt that had been created still needed to be serviced. Near and far money became scarce as individual discretionary incomes and new debt and rollover financing for bubble assets collapsed. Historically, the Greek central bank would have printed Drachmas, using them to buy the banks' bad money real estate loans while stimulating demand by creating temporary make-work jobs, keeping the economic value flows in nominal but not real terms. The printing of Drachmas, of course, cheapens the currency (near money to value relationship) at the expense of far money debt holders. Using the Euro, however, meant that the traditional inflationary economic option (printing currency to buy bank debt, effectively targeting nominal GDP flow) was not available. The combination of a growing debt service-to-income ratio and contracting value flows was devastating to the Greek economy and its people. Similar scenarios occurred in Portugal, Ireland, and Spain.

But as mentioned—not all deflation is bad. Deflation can also be caused by an *innovation shock* entering and cascading through an economy. These types of shocks impact the economy positively in the long term by increasing economic value flow capacity and expected flow wealth with a "good" knowledge-driven deflationary force. Although innovation-driven knowledge shocks have a net positive effect, some firms with suddenly outdated capabilities suffer or fail as evolution kills them, processing them out of the network as no longer adapted as fit for purpose. For instance, the production of cars in North America jumped from roughly 8,000 in 1900 to 9.2 million per year by 1920,[21] leading to increased throughput and greater efficiency while simultaneously dislocating or eliminating many existing transportation clusters, such as horses, carriage makers, and manure haulers. The Internet, a relatively new "network of networks" was highly deflationary for many clusters, replacing them entirely as it grew new capabilities and explored possibility spaces for increasing value flow.

Emerging economies in Africa, Latin America, the Middle East, and Asia are experiencing a mobile phone innovation shock, with market penetration going from negligible to more than 70 percent in under a decade. It can be hoped that cheap smart phones will enable information and knowledge explosion shocks that could help convert developing countries from extractive poverty traps into more inclusive, sustainable growth economies.[22]

Good broad based deflation caused by "revolutionary" innovation shocks may be preceded by strong equity price rises and manias[23] driven by the innovation's anticipated wealth creation. As is typical of lottery clusters, these manias cool as the competitive macro process pushes and diffuses innovations into other firms, contracting margins and increasing the value flow to consumers. As the innovation shock diffuses, aggregate productivity and GDP may increase just as equity prices and margins decline at the realization that not every firm will survive to share in the bonanza. Today's breathtaking revolutionary technology is tomorrow's dominant design yawner. The original iPhone captured the world's imagination; five years later, the iPhone 5 captured a jaded shoulder shrug.

Absorbing and Diffusing Shocks Across a Network

Inflation and deflation shocks distort the linkages among the economic network's elements, stressing fixed versus variable cost relationships and working capital needs. The absolute level of inflation or deflation over time is usually less important than the shock's magnitude and duration. In general, a broad price inflation macro shock diffusing through an entire economy increases the nominal and real[24] price of many downstream products, while impacting far money prices, like stocks and bonds, negatively. During inflationary periods, organizations, clusters, and economies may run suboptimally, with less throughput as they adapt to suddenly expensive far money and currency $MV = P$ informational uncertainty. This throughput decline compounds the temporary damages of value flow dislocations, making it more difficult to bounce back after the shock has passed.

For the most part, however, the ratio of relative value to nominal price[25] will not change much after the inflation shock diffuses through the system. An economy's network of value-creating capabilities is resilient, typically snapping back by reforming the adaptive links and flow structures to those seen before the inflation shock dislocation. When an economy hasn't evolved to be elastic and resilient to inflation impacts, economic value flows contract severely as measured by real GDP. Companies operating too efficiently or too leveraged increase the risk of profound impacts from inflationary and deflationary shocks. As Warren Buffett says, you can only tell who is swimming naked when the tide goes out. We'll look at how shocks impact organizations in more detail in the next section.

The concept of clusters shows how inflation shocks impact economies. Clusters are linked together in value chains; when a money shock hits, the cluster will attempt to pass the price/value shock down the chain. A significant price increase in raw materials moving through the economy looks a bit like a snake eating an egg, if one imagines the snake's diameter to be the cost of goods as a percentage of revenues and the egg's diameter to be the cluster's value flow capacity, measured as working capital needs. By passing this money or price shock through the value chain, both margins and relative $MV = P$ value can return to normal after a few turnover cycles. The cost increase is passed downstream in the form of higher prices or lower quality into the economy. This assumes, of course, that the inflation shock hasn't crushed operating efficiencies or temporarily killed the cluster, like a forest fire momentarily wiping out the network of competing trees and related flora (fig. 14.4).

A large inflation shock shrinks the amount of value that can flow through a company, as working capital becomes scarce and expensive relative to unit value production costs. Coupled with

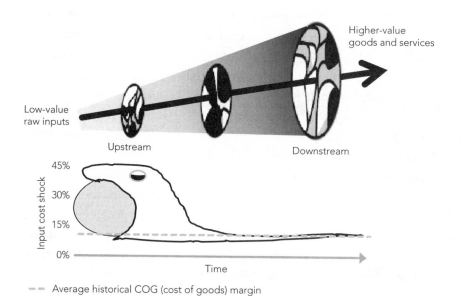

FIGURE 14.4 Inflation Shock Passing Through Links in a Value Chain
Inflation shocks compress margins as they move through linked value chains.

this, at the macro network level, is a potential decline in consumer demand. As the inflationary shock works its way through
the value chain, from cluster to cluster, it stretches and strains
money and value flows through fixed and variable price inputs
and outputs. The stresses in organizational flows show up as compressed or even negative profit margins. This can degrade system
flow performance, measurable as reduced value flows (contracting real GDP) and recessions. To keep value flowing, either the
working capital cycle must shrink via faster payment conditions
(difficult during scarce money periods) or the firm must reduce its
delivery capacity, serving fewer customers and passing less absolute economic value down the chain. A risky but not uncommon
way to temporarily maintain value flow is to take on increasingly
expensive debt at a time of diminished income in order to fund the
higher working capital requirements (fig. 14.5).

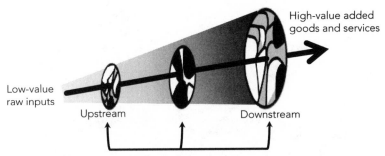

High-value added
goods and services

Low-value
raw inputs

Upstream   Downstream

Working capital cycles and requirements

•Inflation increases working capital costs across the chain

•Inflation shrinks capacity, viable chain lengths & flow paths

FIGURE 14.5 Inflation Increases Working Capital Costs
Inflation increases working capital costs, shrinking the capability to deliver real value.

Money shocks, such as rate hikes, bank collapses and increased debt service to income ratios, can rapidly change money creation, value flows, and the entire economic network's capacity to flow and accumulate knowledge. In extreme cases, inflation shocks and the resulting economic distortions bankrupt firms, clusters, and entire economies.

Figure 14.6 puts some major historical shocks into their respective contexts. Some shocks impact a single organization or cluster; others impact the entire economy. The oil shock of the 1970s falls into the latter category, as it rapidly diffused through the entire U.S. economy and affected all prices. Figure 14.6 is more illustrative than exact in its representation of the scope of various shocks' monetary/value impacts.

Sometimes, the inflation shock egg is too big, killing firms, clusters, and entire branches of value chains in the network. Entire economic sectors can seize up. Although this usually doesn't lead to failure of the economic network as a whole, far money debt and equity holders suffer significant losses in value purchasing ability

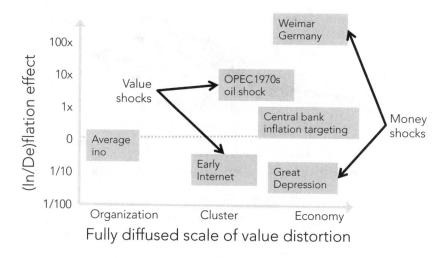

FIGURE 14.6 (In/de)flation MV = P Shocks vs. Scale of Flow Distortion

and price. Like an earthquake, the more extreme the magnitude and duration of a shock, the greater the danger to the economy.

Shocking Organizational Impacts

Broad-based and long-term stable price inflation (say, 5 percent or less) is not necessarily economically destabilizing.[26] It acts more like a tax on cash holders and savers, making far money available but priced at relative premium yields,[27] reflecting expected near money decay and slightly elevated default risk. Most firms retain a memory of the last ten to twenty years of inflation and have adapted resilience to it, making them able to survive and even prosper in stable periods of inflation. Loss of resilience occurs as part of the normal process of collective cultural and organizational "forgetting." Of course, to some extent, this type of forgetting is organizationally required in the struggle for efficient survival today—companies living too thoroughly in the past can't take advantage of new opportunities. But forgetting the past ultimately leads to its inevitable repetition. And so cycles of debt and crisis bubbles endlessly percolate through economic networks on waves of discovery and forgetting, as evolution's capability and capacity ascend through the economy.

However, as the rate and magnitude of an inflation or deflation shock increases, so too does the danger to firms. In order to weather these types of shocks, a firm must be resilient enough—and prepared, managerially and monetarily—to survive temporarily in an extreme environment. The challenge is that these precautions cost like insurance eat into the day-to-day effectiveness of the firm, making it more difficult to remain short-term competitive. Organizations provide value for society more efficiently when they can focus on competing to add value rather than insuring themselves for macro uncertainties, such as hyperinflation or severe political shocks. Of course, short-term overoptimized firms that are run too efficiently and capital lean without resilience insurance are most susceptible to economic shocks. Thus, firms must find a way to operate efficiently while still leaving capacity "in reserve" in case of economic turmoil (fig. 14.7).

Long-lived organizations manage for uncertainty by correctly operating suboptimally in the short term, storing contingent capacities and resources as insurance against dramatic economic environment changes. They balance resilience measures against the efficiencies required to compete effectively in their cluster(s) in the long term. As with other long-lived adapted complex systems, firms in the economic network accumulate recent cycle survival knowledge, adapting toward a "normal" viable growth range; this makes them most resilient to the recently experienced range of shocks. Thus, firms' co-adapt operating behaviors and resilience capacities that are heavily weighted toward their recently accumulated knowledge. This means that if a shock is severe and of a type not recently experienced by the cluster, even the strongest firms can crumble.

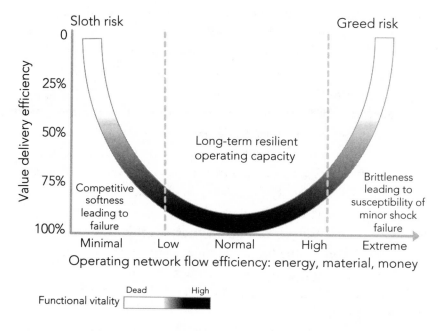

FIGURE 14.7 Extreme Environment Pendulum Shifts Lead to Tension or System Failure

Another danger during shocks is that firms will react as if the shock is the "new normal," making expensive permanent adjustments in response to a temporary economic circumstance. This type of behavior is especially prevalent in the face of innovation shocks. In this situation, a Red Queen cluster effect occurs as the group's belief in high future value flow forces the majority of competitors to throw capital spending at innovations—effectively overinvesting for efficiencies or resilience in a dying cluster.

On the other hand, competitive pressure to adapt new innovations quickly can also force whole clusters to lose resilience, leaving them vulnerable to economic shock. This is a tragedy of the risk-taking commons. Take the example of farmers who transition to mono-crop agriculture in the face of competitive pressures. Each farmer's drive for efficiency leads to capability (crop) homogeneity across the group. This near-term co-adapted efficient homogeneity comes at the expense of resilience to pestilence associated with natural ecological diversity.[28]

"Tragedy of the commons" cycles like this lead to cyclical economic booms and busts within clusters, as competition swings the resiliency pendulum back to using riskier efficiency capabilities, such as using higher operating leverage. Likewise, in times of stable inflation, businesses with raw commodity inputs may adopt hedging mechanisms or other strategies to dampen upstream cost shocks or limited duration spikes. These peer-driven, short-term strategies require tradeoffs of growth and efficiency for near term survival that may come at the expense of resilience.

Managing for Resilience and Efficiency

The best way for organizations and clusters to maintain resilience is to correctly calibrate their internal and external linkages and flow needs. The manager's goal of long-term shareholder ROE is met by keeping the web of flows stable, trading off between the opposing goals of operating efficiency on the one hand and safety measures that facilitate adaptive and responsive resiliency on the other. Managers don't want resource stockpiles too high and capital flows too loose, which is inefficient in terms of ROC. Managers also don't want the links too tight, which would make the organization vulnerable to total failure under shock, affecting returns or even survival. Achieving this balance is challenging, but the payoff is the ability to survive the tough times that may upend competitors.

Organizations' internal metabolic resource flows form a small network of parts linked together like springs. Managers can find it difficult to keep these links and flows competitively efficient even in noninflationary economies; for instance, inventory may get ahead of sales, which increases warehousing costs, or a factory may work at overcapacity before new operations are brought on line. Typically, economists find that a network of manufacturers processing at an average 80 percent of capacity is associated with overall optimal economic value flow and growth. More than 80 percent leads to inflation, whereas below 80 percent is suboptimal and reflects unused capacity. Economic networks operating at 80 percent of capacity sit on the critical edge of self-organized optimal and resilient growth. When inflation is high, these links become more volatile and vulnerable. Compress a spring—say, reduce available working capital— and cost margins or turnover cycle times will have to shrink in order to maintain organizational throughput capacity or efficiency.

Many longer-term contracts, accounting assumptions, and corporate obligations are designed for viable operation in expected low or steady-state inflation environments. Fixed operating constraints can make firms' internal flow networks brittle and vulnerable to shocks due to declines in demand or increases in working capital needs. Depending on an industry's price elasticity, high inflation may shrink volume demand (with the exception of the mania stages of asset bubbles).[29]

Inflation also affects a firm's external linkages, which are more difficult for the manager to control. Inflation exerts pressure on both sides of a firm's economic relationships, significantly altering input costs and output value. Firms typically first experience an inflation shock as increased input costs, followed by working capital stresses. If interest rates increase and money gets scarce, capex may increase. Consumer demand may simultaneously decrease, shrinking throughput efficiencies. Together, these can shrink payback horizons, increasing doubt as to future funding and stability.

The unbalanced relationship between input costs and the value of outputs may lead to negative profit margins, as short-run pricing power and volume can't keep up with input cost increases. In the face of a diminishing viable working capital payback period, the need for working capital can increase dramatically per unit of output. Together, these factors can be lethal for firms—take the

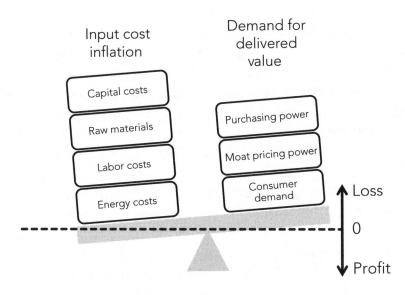

FIGURE 14.8 Inflation Strains Profits as Costs Exceed Consumer Value Demand

Brazilian brewer mentioned earlier, for instance. Margin compression often self-corrects, but in the meantime businesses with long production cycles or high working capital needs can fail (fig. 14.8).

Indeed, working capital–intensive firms with long cash flow cycles often become unviable during hyperinflationary periods, going extinct just as the wooly mammoths did in the relative heat wave at the end of an ice age. Inflation does less harm to asset-heavy firms, assuming they have minimal working capital requirements during the shock period and have fixed rate debt service obligations.

Shocks can be beneficial in the long term for prepared firms because they weed out reckless, margin-eroding competitors. As inflation pressures clusters, smaller firms that are being squeezed to the survival point may engage in aggressive price-cutting. Shocks can drive all cluster firms to the extreme of temporary negative margin pricing tactics as a temporary way to maintain metabolic flow—similar to burning fat stores to maintain critical body functions. These situations lead to cluster consolidation as weaker, less resilient firms with poorer balance sheets get forced out. When the shock subsides, the survivors capture the freshly relinquished market share, realizing higher ROEs because of throughput efficiencies and greater negotiating and pricing power.

Whether inflation is a problem or an opportunity for a firm depends on how the inflation percolates and scales through an economic network and cluster. In fixed asset–intensive firms using fixed rate debt, profit margins may slightly increase as debt service shrinks relative to operating cash-flow margins—assuming prices can be raised proportionally (in line with the MV = P equation) with minimal volume falloff. The manager lucky enough to run a moated firm will likely see pricing power and increased relative profit on the other side of the macroeconomic shock.

Organizations with enough resilience[30] survive the inflation shock's diffusion. As available money and demand rebound to earlier volumes after consumers' "sticker shock" wears off, like a forest that starts to regenerate after being scarred by fire or pestilence, the economy reshapes and regrows into a new expression of its previous form. In some ways, the landscape will improve. In the wake of a low or moderate shock, stable higher nominal prices and more resilient firms will foster increased throughput and growth, supporting the previous real GDP flow rate and wealth-creating trajectory. However, not everything bounces back—owners of previously issued fixed-rate debt and money, which are absolute representations of expected value (wealth), will see their real purchasing capabilities permanently eroded by currency decay/default.

Inflation's Effects on the Allocator

Shocks can often be a good opportunity for a canny and prepared allocator. From the allocator's perspective, near money in the form of cash[31] provides an option to purchase value instantly during a crisis, when others may not have available cash. Crises often see share prices (perceptions of far value) decline rapidly as panicked demand for near money sharply increases, accompanied by declines in available far money (debt and short-term debt) and the sale of equity. The yields of shares and other far monies go up as prices come down.

Responsible central banks typically react to liquidity crises by initially offering abundant public near money and equivalent liquidity resources at punitive prices following Walter Bagehot's rule, which is often summarized as "lend without limit, to solvent firms, against good collateral, at 'high rates.'" After the liquidity crisis is resolved, the central bank may lower their near money interest rates, intending to extend the private sector's capacity for near and far money creation in order to maintain nominal money creation and value flow rates through the network. During these liquidity crises, the allocator with cash on hand may snap up bargains as prices drop. During liquidity crises, as sudden fear makes the price of a previously $1 chocolate bar fall to 25¢, it would be nice to have a spare $1 around to buy four chocolate bars and then own the $1 bars as the network of relative MV = P value relationships resolves itself by reverting back to normal ranges. This resolution can be challenged if overproduction of debt is the root cause of a major MV = P imbalance. These situations typically require central bank currency creation to reset the MV = P resilience boundaries. Producing currency shifts the information value of the currency used for debt service, and thus somewhat resolves the overly created far money debt.

For the allocator holding cash is opportunity insurance. This cash opportunity insurance allows the investor or allocator to act when others panic or lack the capacity to act. Keeping this call option on value has a cost equivalent to the current inflation rate and/or near money return rate.

Keeping an eye on expected inflation rates can help allocators identify periods of opportunity. For instance, in the United States in the 1980s, three economic trends converged to create an ideal environment for equity value investors. By using high interest rates to shrink the supply of near and far money, Fed Chairman Volker was able to break the 10 percent or more annual inflation price loop, creating a long magical period for stocks. The U.S. equity bull market initiated after the early 1980s saw short-term U.S. interest rates start a decades-long decline from their annualized 18 percent peak. The extraordinary flourishing price of equities and value growth over this period had a number of powerful forces driving it:

1. Increasing economic demand due to increased efficiencies and economic throughput, as near and far money rates returned to normal and the oil crisis price shock was absorbed
2. Declining real interest rates that allowed for cheaper capital expansion in real terms, encouraging the funding of longer-term projects and increased capital investment
3. Declining monetary inflation that reduced the cost of working capital, increasing the amount of free cash flow in the cash flow cycle process—overall, increasing real and nominal returns on capital
4. Declining U.S. corporate tax rates that increased returns on equity
5. Lower equity yields demanded relative to declining debt yields, which pushed up share prices

The allocator with an eye for these rare extremes in economy-wide money (credit cycle) changes can move when opportunities arise.

The allocator should always look for firms that will benefit from moderate inflation. If a firm's source of value, advantage, or moat is related to a historical sunk cost input or an inflation invariant capability, then price inflation can expand ROE margins significantly. Stable minimal inflation rates are highly beneficial to businesses that create value with inflation invariant moats, in which the

MV = P relationship holds value through a shock. Inflation-invariant value-creating advantages will quietly work their compounding ROE magic, allowing the firm to outperform and dominate a cluster. Over time these businesses may extract excess value from the cluster by delivering value to customers more effectively.

One type of firm that prospers during (and especially after) a time of moderate inflation is one that has a moat based on non–capital related advantages based on relative advantages—such as brand. If a customer values Coke today and will pay a 30 percent premium relative to selecting a no-name cola, his price sensitivity may increase temporarily during economic stress, but will likely return as the economy stabilizes. The "premium" relative value perception of Coke as a preferred drink is a fixed sunk cost; as such Coke's ROE for early investors will scale faster than inflation. Assuming demand and consumer relative value perception remains the same, inflation increases the rate of return on Coke's brand equity—the trust relationship between consumer experience and firm offering. Future margins and the moat's return on equity can be grown later. The costs and inefficiencies needed to maintain resilient capabilities such as customer trust are a form of moat insurance that pays investors huge long-term, post-shock rewards.[32]

Of course, during times of inflation the allocator must protect existing investments in addition to looking out for bargains. For the value-focused allocator, inflation is typically benign as long as value-creating capabilities survive. The goal of the investor is to maximize terminal wealth (expected value-creating ability), so if the allocator or investor owns a firm that is growing its capacity to produce real value, then its nominal share price in money at any given point is largely irrelevant. If one invested in a chocolate bar costing $1 and hyperinflation raises the cost of the chocolate bar to $5, the "taste value" of the chocolate bar doesn't change, only its value relative to other choices, which determines it potential for pricing power and excess margin. The same idea holds for the factory producing the chocolate bars.

The allocator has two goals during a shock.

1. Stay afloat.
2. Protect the moat.

The first rule for an allocator during an inflation or deflationary shock is to protect wealth (the capability to create future value). To protect wealth, the allocator needs a deep understanding of the firm's unique capabilities he or she's invested in; price shocks usually aren't a huge concern for the long-term investor, as resilient, moat-based firms can survive the shock by virtue of their excess value-creating ability and balance sheet margin of safety. As an equity holder, the company only needs to die once for all value to be wiped out. Thus, it's crucial that allocators understand enough about a firm's moat and cash flow needs to understand how the firm will react to various economic shocks. Looking at competitors' moats and ROC strategies may show which firm will suffer the most during periods of expensive capital and/or slowed demand. Margin compression shocks rarely impact competitors equally.

Moats and balance sheet links stretch and strain differently during money or value shocks, depending on the sources of economic margin, moat wear and tear, and leverage. Working capital needs may increase or they may shrink. In some cases it may be better to reduce activity; in other situations, to buy aggressively. Prior to periods of maximal economic stress, thinking through the impacts of inflation and eventual "normalizing" of relative value relationships among surviving competitors can allow for cheap asset purchases.

When anticipating a period of growing inflation or increasing interest rates, the allocator should consider the impacts on working capital, capex, and debt service. Typically, increasing interest rate environments punish equity investors due to higher working capital costs and the increased yields required for equity versus debt money. If a high inflation environment is anticipated, the best place for the allocator to hide is in moated assets requiring minimal working capital, which will retain relative pricing and earning power after the inflation shock subsides. Firms with long-term variable rate debt service-heavy moats—such as some utilities and infrastructure-related firms—can find it challenging to pass on inflationary cost increases if demand shrinks significantly. Successfully anticipating inflation shocks or financing capex-heavy firms with cheap far money during good times may allow them to bring capability spending forward using this cheaper fixed debt. This can allow for margin expansion later, as the debt service remains fixed while pricing power increases in line with inflation. The goal is to manage relative margins and relative pricing power capability over the long run for maximal long-term ROE over inflation cycles, to increase terminal wealth. The free cash flow and margin boost doesn't last forever, as capital-intensive assets eventually need re-investment at the now higher prices, but with hopefully cheaper money relative to generated free cash flow.

In order to best understand how a firm will fare during and after shocks, the allocator should carefully consider the firm's history of inputs, processes, and output.

Inputs

The first thing to look at is a firm's inputs. A candy maker might have inputs like sugar, labor, energy, and packaging. If a firm makes beer, then grain, fuel, and glass may be important inputs to study. During times of inflation, smaller players often get squeezed harder because they have less negotiating power with suppliers and receive worse credit terms. Scale can help bigger firms' moats, increasing survival chances during periods of economic stress, assuming the larger firm is competitively nimble and resilient.

Low level inflation often shows up in the form of sporadic input cost rises. Most cluster participants will experience temporary margin competition and will try to digest rising input costs with one-off profit margin compression. The manager's initial thinking may be to accept a temporary compression instead of losing customers, volume throughput efficiency, or market share. Although this is a good strategy in some situations to protect the customer price:value experience, accepting compressed margins can be dangerous as lower ROCs and expensive debt pile onto the balance sheet as margins are surrendered in the hopes of better future pricing days. Moated offerings with pricing power are the antidote to such problems.

Process

Inflation's effect on a firm's processes and capabilities involves understanding the cost drivers of the means of production, margins, and the operating capital required. A fixed asset business—like a railroad—may have long-term capex costs, which can be shifted forward or backward in terms of debt service depending on the firm's ability to manage price increases and variable costs. Firms needing significant amounts of working capital relative to competitive offerings suffer greatly as the true cost of working capital increases, stressing the balance sheet. Tilting toward processes requiring less working capital makes sense in inflationary environments, assuming this doesn't negatively impact the moat.

Output

Inflation affects the firm's output of end products and services. Quality investible firms have pricing power, allowing them to pass proportional input cost increases on to customers. Being the last competitor to raise prices may help a firm retain or even gain market share as consumers adjust to new price information across the economy. It is important, however, that firms not cut quality during shock periods, as this may impinge the relative value moat, resulting in a true loss of future value-creating ability (wealth).

During World War II, See's Candy was known for periodically closing stores rather than selling inferior products during wartime shortages. See's correctly recognized that customer belief in the product was integral to the moat, and that short-term economic pain helped the See's brand earn a long-term reputation for quality. Focusing on excellence in product quality or capability can lower short-term efficiencies while providing resilience and higher long-term returns. Good management knows that surrendering margins today to maintain quality may be the cost of insuring tomorrow's wealth-creating moat.

Inflation's Impact on the Moat

The moat's depth (extractible excess competitive margins) will temporarily change due to inflation shocks, but its duration shouldn't be altered. Many moats are assessed using a replacement value argument. How much would it cost a competitor to replace the value perceived by the customers? If a firm's moat depends on heavy capital investments, then expensive money during inflation makes incumbent participants relatively stronger, assuming they have secured previously cheaper fixed rate debt. When viewed in terms of ten- or twenty-year capex investments, the incumbent's lower earlier effective cost of sunk capital may increase the barrier for new entrants in long ino cycle clusters, increasing the expected moat's duration.

Small machinery or fast-eroding technical capability advantages purchased with expensive fixed rate debt during inflationary high periods may be disadvantaged in falling rate environments as competitors retool with newer equipment that is cheaper to finance.

At the peak of an inflation cycle, good assets with moats may be purchased cheaply (at low multiples) relative to the anticipated margin and volume expansion associated with declining inflation rates, lower volatility, and increased value flows. By definition, high ROC moats require less capital per unit of free cash flow than competitors'. Moats get more efficient at providing excess cash flow as the business grows and the cost of working capital in terms of inflation declines. Demand-driven throughput volumes will likely increase, creating a virtual cycle for the firm's intrinsic value growth during interest rate normalization periods similar to the 1980s in the United States mentioned earlier.

Allocating Capital When (M)oney × (V)alue Is Far Away from (P)rice

I started this chapter by looking at the MV = P relationship and the part it plays in our understanding of the economy. I'll end it by looking in greater detail at how the MV = P relationship can be used to inform the allocators about the impact of shocks on the economy and particular firms.

The MV = P relationship is the normal stable economic relationship, occurring as value and money flow through the economic network. Each of the variables is in constant flux due to changing beliefs. When the MV = P is close to balance, the economy hums along with a stable increase in MV and P. Most economists consider optimal growth in V (real GDP) flow to occur when P grows at a stable 2 percent per year. As value flows through the network, it gets more efficient due to adaptive knowledge learning curve effects enabling the more value flow (economic growth).

Figure 14.9 is similar to the earlier figure 14.3 showing the Money × Value relationship. Think of it like a curved sink basin with square edges at the top, with the darker edges higher than the light center. The "normal" relationships between money and value see Price attracted to the lower center of the basin. This point is an attractor in math terms and not a stable point. The farther Price

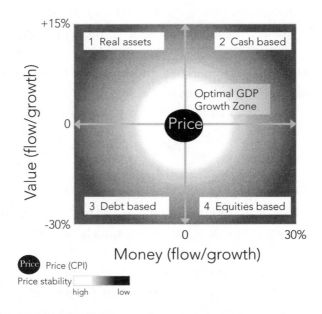

FIGURE 14.9 Moat to Own Based on MV = P Location Relative to Attractor Basin
Note that the value flow vertical axis is not linear, reflecting the bias in extremes to the negative rather than the positive. Acquiring the recommended asset at the extremes, yields high rates of return on the "snap" back booming or busting to normal conditions.

strays from the center, the more it is likely to snap back, booming or busting to a normal state and long term growth rates. The MV = P relationship overshoots before wobbling back to return temporarily to the MV = P attractor location in the center of the basin.

Prices, indicated by the CPI, move through the four zones, as shown in figure 14.9. Normally the MV = P balance in developed countries is stable and near the center, with a bias for growth that shows up as slight increases in value flow, money, and price inflation over time. Shifts in price to the extreme corners are the result of extreme economic forces and trends that are mostly impossible to predict. The only predictable truth is that extreme dislocations from the MV = P attractors point in the basin are unsustainable in the long term.

Extreme dislocations pushing MV = P out to the corners of the diagram have many causes depending on the factor and direction of the dislocation. These dislocations may be caused by changes in real economic value flows, expectations driving public and private money creation and spending, or interest rates. Let's look at a few of the most common displacements, and their causal factors.

Extreme money growth dislocations may be caused by the following:

- Asset class bubbles—such as the recent housing (mortgage) and technology bubbles—that fuel private money creation and are due to excess far money created incorrect future value by expectations
- Public money currency issuance, when central banks purchase assets and effectively "print near money." Hyperinflation is the worst and thankfully rarest version of this type of money growth. Public far money creation occurs in the form of government-issued debt. Recent 2012 monetary policy, for instance, saw the U.S. Federal Reserve buy bonds and effectively put hundreds of billions of dollars into the economy in an effort to replace private (mostly bank-created) money flow shortfalls and stimulate more private money creation via low public money yields. All of this was done to maintain nominal value flows through the economic network. This would hopefully keep value flowing and minimize impacts of a shift in the income to debt service burden associated with deflationary value flow contraction.

Extreme declines in money and money flows can occur due to factors that include:

- Rapid declines in private money and flows are associated often with asset price busts after a bubble has popped. Suddenly high debt service to income ratios may also cause rapid declines in private money creation and value flows.

- Public money creation shrinks during austerity measures as the government reduces services and issues less debt. This effectively shrinks value and money flows as most OECD governments represent 20 to 45 percent of GDP spending.
- Central bank controls—such as increasing interest rates and increased reserve requirements—may also shrink both public and private sector far money creation and related flows.

Extreme value flow growth (economic flow expansion) can be driven by factors such as:

- Knowledge, experience curves, and increased efficiency cause private sector value flow growth and wealth (expected future value delivery). Cheap or easy money associated with a money bubble distortion can cause the private sector to experience unsustainable growth spikes above trend due to misallocated capital flows.
- Government money creation, causing public sector value flow growth, can occur for many reasons. For instance, in the face of private sector money and value flow shrinkage, the government may spend stimulus money in an attempt to stabilize the economy by temporarily maintaining money flow rates. Wars and large government programs can also impact value flows. The public sector is generally considered less efficient at creating knowledge and increased value flow. The public sector does have an important role to provide services the private sector is unable or unwilling to provide effectively such as education, social safety nets, defense, and fundamental research.

Value flow declines (economic recessions) occur for fairly familiar reasons:

- Private sector value declines may be related to bubbles bursting, bankruptcies, declines in demand, increased debt service burdens relative to revenue flows, or other factors associated with declines in either available money or consumer demand.
- Public sector declines in value flow are driven by unwinding of stimulus spending, austerity measures, and other instances of shrinking the public sector, which decreases economic value flow.

When the economic network of real value and money flows deviates far from center, it eventually must return close to the MV = P relationship. This may take many years, as bubbles and manias can be surprisingly persistent social value delusions. Eventually, like a rubber band, things snap back to MV = P. The path from the dislocated corner isn't always straight to the center and may overshoot depending on the magnitude of policy and belief changes. Based on major actors like central banks and the fiscal spending policy responses to the causes of variance, the path back to stability may lurch from one dislocation away from center to the next before landing back in the center. This two-dimensional MV = P elastic behavior is similar to the one-dimensional price to value relationship shown in chapter 1. As mentioned earlier, currencies can die and governments can fall before normal MV = P normalizes. The mismanagement of MV = P by central banks or governments can have large impacts on political stability.

Depending on the degree and direction of dislocation, certain assets will perform better during the reversion-to-center period. The allocator should think about what asset to own based on which type of extreme dislocation is occurring. Ideally, the allocator should

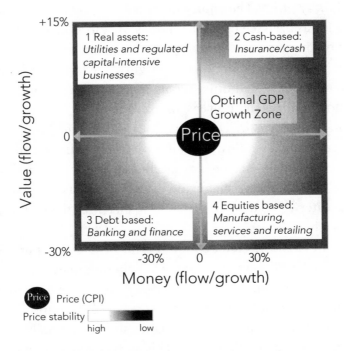

FIGURE 14.10 Berkshire Hathaway Business Categories and the Moat to Own during extreme MVP dislocations prior to a "boom" or "bust" back to normal MV = P attractor basin.

build a balanced portfolio of moat types corresponding to the four MV = P extreme dislocations. This way, the portfolio will hopefully be able to survive all four dislocation scenarios.

The allocator who has excess cash can pursue opportunistic purchases of moated firms that may be relatively cheap during extreme dislocations. Figure 14.10 indicates the opportunistic positioning the allocator should target for each of the presumed dislocations. The moat/asset types are explained in the following.

1. *Cash moat:* This isn't really a moat; it is holding cash. The high GDP and high money creation mix often involves unsustainably high prices. Ready cash can allow for fantastic bargain buying.

2. *Equity moat:* The equity moat is based on relative value, such as branded consumer goods. As the money and value flow increases, consumer price sensitivity declines, meaning expanded volume and margins. Well-positioned consumer and distribution moats that benefit from increased flow and pricing power can excel.

3. *Real asset moat:* During periods of extreme money and reduced value flow, tangible assets—such as railroads and utilities—are cheap. Declining interest rates should allow for cheap refinancing of debt-based assets, whereas greater value flow and cash flow increases the real return on those assets.

4. *Debt moat:* As credit conditions improve due to improved value flows and margins, the supply of money grows and rates come down. The increasing money growth means more revenues, whereas the increased flow improves the debt assets quality on the balance sheet potentially reducing reserve requirements. This is true for banking and finance-based spread businesses that create far money.

Figure 14.10 also shows the four business categories that Berkshire Hathaway self-identifies in its annual reports. These categories conveniently map onto the four corners of the MV = P model, providing a diversified set of growing assets able to respond as the MV = P relationship changes. This portfolio of moated businesses has proved to be robust over the past forty years.

Understanding the nature of MV = P as a stable state attractor for growth, and how economic network money and value flows deviate from this state, are powerful for the allocator. The careful allocator will not be able to call top or bottom extremes as MV = P dislocations stretch from center to the extreme edge, but the allocator may patiently position him- or herself for a reversion to the norm as dislocated prices and links in the economy are attracted back to their natural economic state of MV = P.

Summary

Currency is an act of ongoing faith across the social network, which aids in accelerating trade, investment, and ultimately value creation. Currency is near money; far money in the form of debt and equity represents future expected value and currency flows.

The MV = P relationship among near and far money, value, and price is complicated by the nature of uncertainty associated with an adaptive value-creating network. The price and amount of money created, in circulation, and destroyed continuously changes as individuals and institutions assess expected currency informational and representational value about the uncertainty of future value creation.

Understanding an organization's ability to generate relative value across various GDP flow and inflation scenarios is a critical allocator skill. Ultimately all far money converts into decaying currencies, organizations fade, and knowledge is usurped by new knowledge. To grow wealth, the allocator should own a portfolio of growing moats balanced across the four scenario quadrants that positive and negative changes in money inflation and value growth can deliver. The portfolio should create greater value for the allocator, as evolution pursues its unpredictable adaptive flowing dance.

PART VI

The Nature of Value

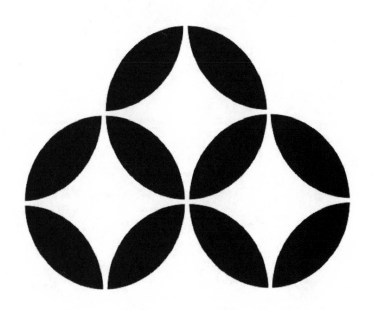

CHAPTER FIFTEEN

The Nature of Value Allocation

THE NATURE OF VALUE APPROACH to investing informs the allocator's understanding of economic value flows, from the smallest unit of information (the ino) to seeing the entire interconnected economic network acting as one of evolution's adaptive network panarchies creating ever-increasing Φ_m capacities. There are some practical ways a nature of value approach can improve your allocating success. Here are a few thoughts on the implications for allocators.

Missing the Hits

The economic and ecological domains are like hits-based businesses; over time, one either makes a killing or gets killed. There isn't a lot of sitting around, and things are constantly either growing or dying out. Instinctively it seems like chasing the fast growing hits would be a lucrative pursuit. The problem is that as one concentrates a portfolio to chase hits, the chances of underperforming the average increase as well. Let's take a closer look at why this is the case, and what this means for the allocator.

Index Funds

Buying and holding broad indexes—versus chasing the "hits"—is the safest means for the majority of people to benefit from the nature of value creation at the level of economy.

With 388 funds managing $1.1 trillion dollars, index funds are the undisputed allocator champion strategy.[1] Index funds that follow stock market indexes are naïve or purely random, uninformed strategies, and embedded in them is the assumption that one can't predict future winners and losers. Broad stock market indexes reflect a whole economies network of public growing and dying clusters, filled with firms struggling to create excess value and live. A naïve index represents the arithmetic mean performance of shares[2]; academics broadly call this result beta[3] or the market.

Professionals use indexes to benchmark their performance and to set investors' expectations. Figure 15.1 shows the 110-year inflation-adjusted index returns for various major economies. Most active managers will underperform these metrics (I'll explore why in a moment) while charging investors 0.70 to 2.00 percent annually for the favor.

The S&P 500 index, for instance, is a set of rules for buying and holding the five hundred largest firms in the U.S. economy, with a bit of rebalancing. This buy and hold approach may sound easy to outperform, but it's not. There are 178 million U.S. equity mutual fund holders who trust fund managers with $11 trillion dollars to beat the S&P 500 index, but despite that faith the long-term returns of the S&P 500 stock market index beat almost all professional managers and investors over time. So—why is a naïve "buy and hold" index strategy so difficult to beat?

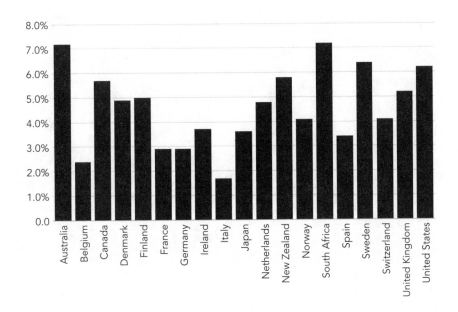

FIGURE 15.1 1900–2011, Real Equity Index Returns
Source: Elroy Dimson, Paul Marsh, and Mike Staunton, *Credit Suisse Global Investment Returns Yearbook, Credit Suisse Research Institute* 2012.

Take a look at figure 15.2, which shows the lifetime return of U.S. shares broken into performance buckets. Notice something weird? This distribution has a really long tail of big winners rather than a normal bell-shaped curve distribution. Only 5.25 percent of shares return more than 100 percent in a year, but a few rare lottery ticket–type companies produce returns far greater than 200 percent. The stock returns are shrunk on the right into a few bins for presentation on the page, but the basic meaning remains; the extreme positive performance outliers significantly increase the average (arithmetic mean) return. Out of three thousand yearly companies over twenty years, the median annual return is 4.9 percent less than the arithmetic mean annual return. This tells us the most likely annual occurring company return is 4.9 percent

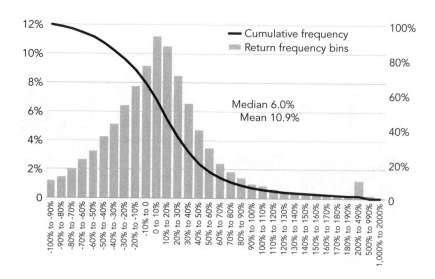

FIGURE 15.2 Cumulative Frequency and Histogram of Annual Returns of 3,000 Equities, 1991–2011
Source: Longboard Asset Management

lower than the market index "average" return. This factor, along with others, contributes to managers underperforming the index.

A concentrated "rifle shot" bet on a few shares during any given year is likely to underperform by 4.9 percent, with a few concentrated bets hitting their target and outperforming. Without understanding the nature of the moat inside a firm and the cluster dynamics, the allocator is left to predict others opinions of price if they want to beat the mean or index.

To clearly illustrate how this works, let's examine a grossly simplified model economy with a stock market of one hundred companies and a very fat tail. Every year each company starts out with a value of $1/share. The price of one of the companies then climbs to $9/share, returning 800 percent. The arithmetic mean of the index is 8 percent, but the most likely mean return for any company is basically 0 percent (fig. 15.3).

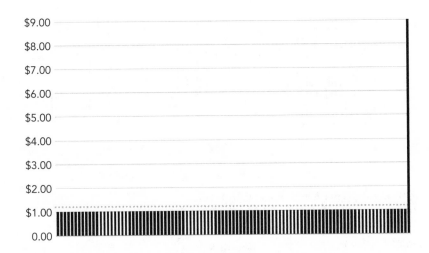

FIGURE 15.3 Profile of 1:100 "Hits" Index
A "hits" index returns 8 percent per year when 1 out of 100 firms is a hit returning 800 percent.

Clearly, chasing the 800 percent return target is a seductive strategy, and many will wish to pursue the 800 percent brass ring. Of course, if the manager allocates to only one firm in the hopes of achieving a full 800 percent return, he or she has a 99 percent chance of a 0 percent return. More moderately, if a manager uses a shotgun approach and randomly buys 50 shares, he or she has a 50 percent chance of a 16 percent return and 50 percent chance of a 0 percent return. This sounds like an interesting bet until one thinks like a mutual fund manager and considers personal career and fund risk. The manager or fund returning 0 percent in an 8 percent year could be shown the door rapidly. If the mutual fund manager wants a 90 percent likelihood of having a job next year, he or she would purchase 90 shares equally. This creates a 10 percent chance of returning nothing (getting fired) and a 90 percent chance of returning 8.8 percent or beating the index by 80 bps to keep his or her job.

Over time one might argue that our manager's performance would revert to the index average. In reality, this is highly unlikely.

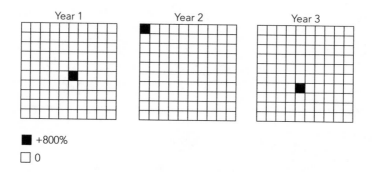

FIGURE 15.4 Hits Are Impossible to Predict
Predicting the location of next year's +800 percent hit company is nearly impossible. (The three Fama-French factors are an exception to the random distribution of returns.)

If a manager only understands price and not value, the movement of the 800 percent winner target appears quite random over time. Over the years, the 800 percent "winner" will show up in different sectors of the economy, as shown in figure 15.4. When the allocator chases the moving target sector, market, or area that had last year's winner, he or she can suffer from not choosing randomly enough. In selecting securities, this increases the chances of missing the target and underperforming.[4]

By aiming at last year's winning cluster or tilting portfolio exposure to the "hot" sector, the manager increases the likelihood of missing next year's randomly occurring winner or chasing last year's winner that may be reverting back to long-term median performance. Transaction costs will also impact returns. Misunderstanding the nature of value and chasing price increases is equivalent to picking random stocks—and as we saw in figure 5.4, in a random picking situation, the safest thing to do is to naïvely equally weight across all shares and hope to perform near the index by capturing the extreme positive outlier or outliers.

Clusters and Sector and Narrow Index Exchange Traded Funds

The middle ground between an index strategy and picking individual stocks are tools that allow investors to bet on a number of firms within a single sector. Sector- and narrow index-based Exchange Traded Funds (ETFs) are an example of this. Sector and narrow index ETFs trade like stocks, and often hold a portfolio of highly targeted, sector-specific stocks. Sector-based ETFs differ from clusters in that clusters are defined by customers, whereas sector-based ETFs often represent sectors or industries. However, they are similar enough that sector ETFs provide a good proxy for cluster and inter-cluster complexity.

When times are exciting in a product or sector, an investor might think, "I like this industry, so I will diversify and spread my bet around with an ETF." However, people forget that a sector ETF allocation is actually a bet on the distribution of value capture among competitors in a cluster. Anticipated revenue growth means increased value will flow through the cluster—but does not guarantee sustained profits for any single firm, much less the aggregate cluster of firms. Competition and cluster instability can limit the cluster's retained profits and the sector's ability to retain value or build wealth.

Many forget this and approach "growth" sectors with the belief that by betting on the whole sector using an ETF, everything will work out. But if an index is equally weighted and 95 percent of firms go bust, the 5 percent that emerge victorious must grow twentyfold for the index to break even. In hyped sectors, due to individual lottery pricing psychology effects, price is often far ahead of value for most participants. To illustrate this, let's examine how an ETF with all firms trading at a "discount" to individually touted expectations can still be a loser.

Take a sector ETF with ten firms, in which each of the firms is valued at $1 billion with future expected earnings of $100 million—but with all firms chasing a $1 billion revenue cluster opportunity. Each firm may claim it deserves a $1 billion valuation due to 10 percent future earnings margins and a 10 percent yield or 10:1 PE multiple. Firms will seem to be trading at a 90 percent discount relative to "their" $1 billion golden opportunity just around the corner. With a hundred firms each telling and selling the same story, the reality is potentially $10 billion worth of market capitalization chasing maybe a $1 billion opportunity. Remember that the final surviving firm or firms has to make the $100 million in earnings and trade at a 10:1 PE ratio; but even if this happens, it means a 90 percent loss for the "safe" index investor spreading bets across the ten firms.

The Internet phenomenon is a real-world example of a hyped sector like this. The Internet bubble 1.0 was built on expensive firms with impressive top-line initial revenue growth, many of which were quickly eviscerated by highly unstable clusters and hypercompetition analogous to a mini-Cambrian explosion. Many single-product or feature-based innovation markets can grow to billions in annual revenues but never pay a penny in aggregate net returns to investors when measured at the cluster or index level. The Internet bubble combined incredibly short product innovation cycles, uncertain clusters, and hyped prices to destroy allocated capital. The person who got "in on the Internet" by index investing using the Internet Holders Index (HHH) at its launch in 1999 was down 36 percent, not including inflation, taxes, and fees, as of late December 2011.[5] Due to Siegel's paradox, a 57 percent return from December 2011's prices is required for breakeven after holding the index for twelve years. Many narrowly targeted indices and ETFs in "hot" innovation or story sectors are like this; the clean tech/solar sector in the late 2000s did the same thing.

Consumers and society at large won the Internet 1.0 bubble due to the knowledge and capabilities for value creation that diffused into the economic network. A handful of companies are lottery winners, but Internet firms in total haven't done much for the lottery ticket investors. Narrative survivorship bias means people easily recall the storied giants like eBay and Amazon, but not the hundreds of tiny noBays that didn't survive. The investment bankers selling lottery tickets, IPOs, and M&A deals did well for themselves. Putting on a suit and tie to sell dreams is easier than competing to deliver them.

The Internet and solar sector ETFs are examples of lottery clusters that turned into a collection of mostly Red Queen clusters, offering limited value capture potential. Too few innovation diffusion effects and too little price discounting was factored in relative to final value capture.

Other Things Working Against Trader Returns

Many factors are at work that erode returns below the index or arithmetic average, besides just chasing the "hot" firm or sector. Other major drags for traders and portfolio managers include psychological biases, taxes, and transaction costs.

Psychological Biases

One return shrinking psychological trait exhibits itself when many people act as price traders with an asymmetrical reaction to pain and reward. As is evidenced in many studies, people have a psychological bias to let losing trades run long and take money off the table with winners too early. This lets them feel secure and avoid the pain of accepting a loss. This bias means that extreme positive outliers, like the Walmarts and Home Depots of the market, become under-represented by portfolio managers selling early. After a huge gain and in the absence of understanding the forces growing value are still at work, many people convince themselves to "take some money off the table and not be greedy."

This move to safety effectively truncates the right-hand long tail side of the distribution, pushing the realized portfolio returns to the left below the index returns. Cutting off the tail is psychologically comforting in the absence of any other information about value. What would you do in the earlier 1 in 100 portfolio after your single "lucky" share price initially jumped 500 percent? Would you hold on for the full year's 800 percent? If you wouldn't, over time you would underperform the index.

The act of selling or pruning large price "winners" from a portfolio is often justified as an act of portfolio rebalancing or de-risking by diversifying. Allocating based on an understanding of the nature of value rather than price can mitigate this risk as increased price should reflect growing value. The flawed idea behind pruning large, significant winners is that it de-risks overly concentrated portfolios. This focus on overconcentration is correct from a short-term naïve statistical perspective, but incorrect when one has an understanding of the nature of the source of value in the underlying portfolio firms. Deeply understanding a few sources of value creation beats knowing nothing about many sources of value creation. The paradox of doing well by humbly understanding nothing about everything (the index) still stands as the best strategy for most investors.

Tax and Trading Issues

Continuous transactions contribute to long-term underperformance due to tax and transaction impacts. Thinking long term can show how these seemingly small impacts contribute to long-term significant underperformance.

Taxes vary for each situation. A simple example of tax impacts: imagine our portfolio manager selling his 800 percent annual winner at the end of the year. A theoretical 20 percent tax would yield a $1.60 cost to the initial $100 portfolio of 100 shares each initially priced at $1. The 8 percent annual index yield of $8 would now become a post-tax 6.4 percent yield.

Active trading costs also impact returns. Even with high-frequency algorithmic trading and other high-tech financial techno-wizardry, there is still a real cost to trading. Most managers want to be seen "managing," which often means an annual portfolio turnover of more than 85 percent in many funds. Using a conservative estimate of 0.25 percent cost per transaction in our $100 portfolio, this works out to a 0.21 percent yearly cost, which is yet another drag on performance. On top of this, managers and management companies need to get paid. Another 1.30 to 0.80 percent is a likely cost factor weighing down the pursuit of beating the index.

Investors can have a negative impact on managers' actions as well. Mutual fund managers trying to beat the S&P 500 are often stuck with short-term management guidelines or incentive structures driven by flighty investors' assets under management who are intent on seeking out the latest hit. According to DALBAR research in 2012, over twenty years investors underperformed the index by a massive 5.7 percent annually just due to the investors' own buying high and selling low of the funds in which they invested. Investors who chase yesterday's seemingly random victory tend to catch tomorrow's mean-reverting defeat. Buy and hold if you know nothing else.

Nature of Value Portfolio

So if ETFs and hit-chasing stock picks won't help you beat the index—and with biases and transaction costs adding to the problem—what *will* help the allocator find portfolio success? My answer is understanding how and why value performs. Buying a moated firm at a discount and holding on for a long time is a solid approach. Looking for growing moats with high ROEs that respond well over time to inflation is likely they best way to allocate capital, although it is very hard work.

Berkshire Hathaway's strategy probably reflects one of the best nature of value type approaches to investing. By owning companies

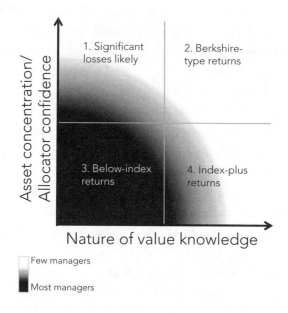

FIGURE 15.5 Investor Confidence and Knowledge Level Drive Portfolio Outcomes

and allocating capital internally between firms, many of the tax and transaction costs are avoided. Capital allocation is performed highly efficiently. Berkshire Hathaway's use of insurance company float as a form of ready capital and leverage is another unique strategic driver of its returns. Insurance company float is beyond the scope of this book, but a truly fascinating topic worthy of study for those deeply interested in capital allocation efficiency.

To understand the power of Berkshire's value knowledge applied compared with a typical mutual fund, take a look at figure 15.5. The y-axis shows portfolio concentration, as a proxy for allocator confidence. The x-axis shows a party's understanding of the value of his or her portfolio. This maps out four quadrants:

1. A highly concentrated portfolio combined with a low understanding of value. This increases the risk of under-performance, as discussed previously.

2. A highly concentrated portfolio combined with a high understanding of value. This is rare and difficult, but exemplifies nature of value investing when done right.

3. A diversified portfolio combined with a low understanding of value. This is how most mutual funds are structured and is usually sold as a safe bet, but the misunderstanding of value or structural short-term incentives and costs can lead to below index returns.

4. A diversified portfolio combined with a high understanding of value. This usually means outperforming the index. As figure 15.5 shows, misunderstanding the nature of value can be equivalent to picking random stocks. In a random picking situation, the safest thing to do is to equally weight across all shares hoping to perform near the index—which is tough after transaction and management fees. Figure 15.6 illustrates the risk of concentration and why understanding the nature of value is so

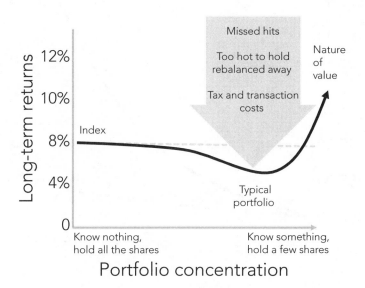

FIGURE 15.6 Humble Know-Nothing Index Returns Beat Concentrated Ignorance

important if one wishes to concentrate a portfolio. If you want to skip the broad-based index approach and are willing to do the work required, then nature of value investing might be for you. Most investors don't have the time, desire, or skills to study individual organizations in the required depth, but nature of value allocators have fun reading 10Ks and past annual and industry reports. The goal is to understand and allocate to a few firms with proven moats that can create good cash flow yields, and to hold them for many years. Charlie Munger and Warren Buffett claim the bulk of Berkshire's value came from twenty buy and hold decisions made over the course of forty years.

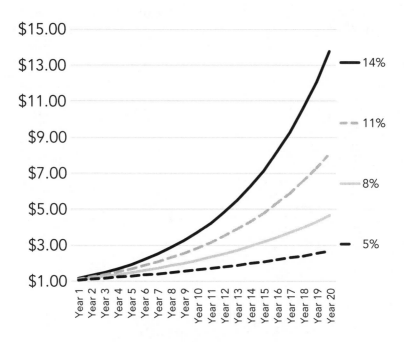

FIGURE 15.7 Impact of Twenty Years of Compounding Growth

The nature of value approach requires patience, research, and effort. These skills must be met with equally large doses of humility on the behalf of the manager and his or her capital resources thinking in five- to ten-year increments versus quarterly or annual performance metrics. The work required to apply the nature of value approach can be substantial, but the payoffs over time are great, as seen in figure 15.7 and table 15.1.

Table 15.1

Twenty Years of Growth Compounded

	5%	8%	11%	14%
Year 1	$1.05	$1.08	$1.11	$1.14
Year 2	$1.10	$1.17	$1.23	$1.30
Year 3	$1.16	$1.26	$1.37	$1.48
Year 4	$1.22	$1.36	$1.52	$1.69
Year 5	$1.28	$1.47	$1.69	$1.93
Year 6	$1.34	$1.59	$1.87	$2.19
Year 7	$1.41	$1.71	$2.08	$2.50
Year 8	$1.48	$1.85	$2.30	$2.85
Year 9	$1.55	$2.00	$2.56	$3.25
Year 10	$1.63	$2.16	$2.84	$3.71
Year 11	$1.71	$2.33	$3.15	$4.23
Year 12	$1.80	$2.52	$3.50	$4.82
Year 13	$1.89	$2.72	$3.88	$5.49
Year 14	$1.98	$2.94	$4.31	$6.26
Year 15	$2.08	$3.17	$4.78	$7.14
Year 16	$2.18	$3.43	$5.31	$8.14
Year 17	$2.29	$3.70	$5.90	$9.28
Year 18	$2.41	$4.00	$6.54	$10.58
Year 19	$2.53	$4.32	$7.26	$12.06
Year 20	$2.65	$4.66	$8.06	$13.74

Summary

The simple broad-based index system which captures most of an economy's returns is tough to beat. Indexing means placing faith in an entire complex economic network[6] of information and value flows while humbly acknowledging total ignorance about any single companies, and yet ignorant indexing is probably the best way for 99.9 percent of people to invest. Most managers and investors have many things working against them. Managers may not understand the sources of value or may be forced to chase price in a game that is weighted against them.

The nature of value approach involves long-term allocation to a few well-understood moated firms. The implications of long-term transaction reduction, tax reduction, and compounding effects associated with a nature of value capital allocation approach should not be underestimated.

CHAPTER SIXTEEN

Conclusion

NEW IDEAS AND INFORMATION are often rightfully ignored, as 99 percent of innovations fail or fade away quickly. Hopefully a few ideas presented here have provided you with a new view on the origins, flows, and creation of economic value. The ecology and economy are beautiful examples of evolution's adaptive process, but they don't lend themselves to easy explanation. The rhythms and cycles flowing through an economy, like the rhythms and cycles of an ecology, are too complex to fully understand, too powerful to ignore, and too wonderful and fascinating not to appreciate. The physicist Rolf Landauer put it well when he said, "A complex system is exactly that; there are many things going on simultaneously. If you search carefully, you can find your favorite toy: fractals, chaos, self-organized criticality, phase transition analogies, Lotka-Volterra predator-prey oscillations, etc., in some corner, in a relatively well-developed and isolated way. But do not expect any single insight to explain it all."[1]

What we do know is that, driven by the engine of energy, knowledge, and competition, evolution's economies will keep delivering more value to customers as organizations continue to innovate and create knowledge. As each fresh ino is expressed, the economy adapts new forms and capabilities for improving our condition. The increasing material wealth produced by this process is no guarantee for cultural progress or a sustainable equitable future, for those matters lie beyond economy. But material wealth and progress do provide us with more choices for how we treat each other and the most vulnerable among us.

Capital Allocation Is the Quest for Truth over the Horizon

To be right. To find and express valued true knowledge. This is the quest of scientists, artists, economists, and capital allocators. Every capital allocation is based on the premise that value in the form of capital spent today will return as greater value tomorrow. The complexity associated with the nature of value promises one thing—that there is no fixed truth or absolute guarantee of wealth, value, or riches, although there are patterns and behaviors in the adaptive network that may recur. Allocators must continuously learn, spotting new patterns and behaviors, and be able to recognize strange new creatures and summon the courage to divine some idea of their nature—whether they be survivor, thriver, or extinct dead end.

Economic value is ultimately measured in human terms. Prioritizing the value of friends, family, and freedoms ensures that the wealth of a lifetime will be correctly measured in the creation of memories, loving relationships, and a reputation for integrity. Never compromise these forms of value for mere money.

Notes

Chapter 1

1. A microsecond is 1 millionth of a second. There are 350,000 microseconds in the blink of an eye. In 2012, some exchanges were measuring trade and message latency at 120 microseconds.

2. Entropy in this context refers to an increase in the Kolmogorov complexity of the price return series as measured by a Kolmogorov or related measure of statistical complexity.

3. Processes causing increased statistical entropy are axiomatically obvious when viewed from the perspective of physical thermodynamic laws, but these traits become interesting when looked at from an adaptive framework with propensities over time.

4. The efficient market hypothesis is still taught with many caveats. It is a broken and dangerous theory. Price reflects all of the beliefs and opinions about expected value, but doesn't reflect actual value.

5. Over the years, weak, semistrong, and other variations of the efficient market hypothesis have been put bravely forward. These variants are equivalent to putting epicycles onto a Euclidian model of the solar system in order to make a beautiful theory stretch over the ugly, awkward truth presented by the data.

6. Risk is formally described as a probable set of expectations or outcomes. Most price movement falls outside of normal statistical measurements of risk and into a realm formally known as uncertainty or ignorance. Unfortunately, the ease of applying basic statistical distributions to future prices, no matter how ill-fitting, hasn't stopped most professional financial

practitioners from accepting and thereby confusing statistical price risk with real economic value at risk.

7. Most financial asset prices move in patterns approximating a statistical process known as GARCH (generalized autoregressive conditional hetero-skedasticity). This concept is derived from an idea put forward on the blog Deus Ex Macchiato at blog.rivast.com on September 3, 2011.

8. This is best avoided by always applying a mental model of the value-creating process using nonprice inputs and asking what limits the process (how high is the sky and why?). The popular Fama-French three and four factor equity models use price momentum as one of the factors.

9. Charles Kindelberger's *Manias, Panics and Crashes* or Edward Chancellor's *Devil Take the Hindmost: A History of Financial Speculation* are excellent books on all-too-common bubbles and crashes.

10. Innovation in finance is almost always disastrous. Pure financial innovation usually involves new ways of temporarily hiding risk. Financial innovation is rarely beneficial in the long term.

Chapter 2

1. Brooks, Daniel R., and E. O. Wiley. 1988. *Evolution as Entropy*. Chicago: University of Chicago Press.

2. Darwin's theory wasn't popular. According to David Hull, a philosopher of science, only 75% of scientists agreed with Darwin ten years after *On the Origin of Species'* publication.

3. "Literary Notices," *Popular Science Monthly*, 2, February 1873.

4. Marshall, Alfred. 1890. *Principles of Economics*. London: Macmillan.

5. Kümmel, Reiner. 2011. *The Second Law of Economics: Energy, Entropy, and the Origins of Wealth*. New York: Springer.

6. Ayres, Robert U. 1987. *Manufacturing and Human Labor as Information Processes*. Edward Elgar.

7. Ayres, Robert U. 2010. *The Economic Growth Engine: How Energy and Work Drive Material Prosperity*. Cheltenham, UK: Edward Elgar.

8. In 1938, overlooked economist John Burr Williams correctly saw organizations as being made of value flows when he wrote, "The value of any stock, bond or business today is determined by the cash inflows and outflows—discounted at an appropriate interest rate—that can be expected to occur during the remaining life of the asset." John Burr Williams. 1997. *The Theory of Investment Value*. Cambridge: Harvard University Press.

9. International Geary-Khamis dollars 1990.

10. Physicist and Nobel Laureate P.W. Anderson offers a compelling explanation to the limits of reductionism, the emergence of information via symmetry breaking and hierarchies in his excellent paper "More Is Different," *Science*, 177, 1972, pp. 393–396.

11. Knowledge is the selected information (genetic, etc.) that has been selected and likely to replicate and amplify itself. Knowledge has a propensity for self-amplification. The concept of propensity is taken from Karl Popper's use of the term, in which finite probabilities are skewed toward an outcome due to a conditional context. Popper's perspective was that probabilities and finite state determinism are not statistically robust, and that propensities more accurately reflect long-term skews or trajectories. It can be argued that selected knowledge in DNA or INO forms constantly adjust their Bayesian priors as context for their own successful propagation and selection.

Chapter 3

1. Lotka, A. J. 1922. "Contribution to the Energetics of Evolution." *Proceedings of the National Academy of Sciences*, 8: 147–151.

2. Bejan, Adrian, and Sylvie Lorente. 2008. *Design with Constructal Theory*. Wiley.

3. An erg is the amount of work done by a force of one dyne exerted for a distance of one centimeter. 1 erg = 1 g·cm²/s².

4. Nicolas and Prigogine. 1977. *Self-Organization in Nonequilibrium Systems: From Dissipative Structures to Order through Fluctuations*. Wiley.

5. Eric D. Schneider, Dorion Sagan. 2006. *Into the Cool: Energy Flow, Thermodynamics, and Life*. Chicago: University of Chicago Press.

6. Kelly, Kevin. 2010. *What Technology Wants*. New York: Viking Adult.

7. Technically speaking, enzymes and bacteria in animal stomachs perform the initial metabolic reducing functions. Without the adapted symbiogenetically evolved network of the Kingdoms Bacteria and Proctista, there would be no animals. Symbiogenesis was originally put forth as an idea by Heinrich Anton de Bary 1831–1888 and re-emphasized by Lynn Margulis. Symbiosis is the living together of "differently named organisms."

8. Ecological niches can be thought of as networks defined by energy and resource transfer relationships between evolution's metabolizers.

9. Russian-born American economist Wassily Leontief created the input and output tables that became metrics and methods for calculating national GDP in the 1920s. In an ironic twist of fate, many ecologists are now turning

to some of the math and methods created by Leontief to assess ecological throughput and energy analysis in the biosphere.

10. Economies not only get more efficient, but they grow. Ecologist Robert Ulanowicz created an important adaptive thermodynamic concept known as ascendency. Ascendency includes growth and efficiency of adaptive systems measured in robust physical and informational terms. Economy has its own ascendant traits as indicated in the previous charts.

Chapter 4

1. Note the distinction that making a better mousetrap (adaptation alone) doesn't matter. Selling the better mousetrap for a profitable ROC is what matters, and what drives the selective process allowing ino and knowledge replication.

2. Williams, Wayne. 2012. "10 Interesting Things We've Learned from the Apple vs. Samsung Trial (So Far)." Betanews. http://betanews.com/2012/08/08/10-interesting-things-weve-learned-from-the-apple-vs-samsung-trial-so-far/?utm_source=feedburner&utm_medium=feed&utm_campaign=Feed+-+bn+-+Betanews+Full+Content+Feed+-+BN. Camm-Jones, Ben. 2011. "Apple by the Numbers: Sales, Stores, Staff All Grew in 2011." *MAC World*.

3. Quoted in Lamont, David. "What Percentage of Gross Revenues Should Be Allocated to the Marketing Budget?" Marketingsage.http://marketingsage.com/marketing-budget/.

4. Adaptation can occur even faster in the economy by swapping and exchanging whole sets of capabilities. Strategic partnerships, acquisitions, and mergers can all be considered symbiotic means of co-opting an entire organization's capability sets.

5. Bak, Per. *How Nature Works: The Science of Self-Organized Criticality.* Copernicus, 1999, p. 60.

6. Bifurcation into changes of form and structure allow for greater system flow and/or efficiency. The term "bifurcation" was created by mathematician Henri Poincaré in 1885.

7. Bejan, Adrian. 1997. *Advanced Engineering Thermodynamics*, 2nd ed. New York: Wiley.

8. Plants and animals also follow basic mathematical rules of scaling and structural change. For instance, the quarter-power law governing body size dictates that as animals get bigger, their life spans get longer, their pulse slows, and they burn energy less rapidly. From Johnson, George. "Of Mice and Elephants: a Matter of Scale." *The New York Times*, January 12, 1999.

Chapter 5

1. Keeley, Larry, Ryan Pikkel, Brian Quinn, and Helen Walters. 2013. *Ten Types of Innovation: The Discipline of Building Breakthroughs*. New York: Wiley.

2. Keeley, Larry, et al. 2013. *Ten Types of Innovation*, p. 83.

3. To understand this perspective more empirically in ecology and economics read Ulanowicz, Robert E. 1997. *Ecology, The Ascendent Perspective*. New York: Columbia University Press.

4. Wright, T. P. 1936. "Factors Affecting the Cost of Airplanes." *Journal of Aeronautical Sciences* 3 (4): 122–128.

5. Utterback, James M. 1996. *Mastering the Dynamics of Innovation*. Boston: Harvard Business Review Press, p. 222.

6. Henderson Rebecca, and Kim Clark. 1990. "Architectural Innovation: The Reconfiguration of Existing Product Technologies and the Failure of Established Firms," *Administrative Science Quarterly* 35 (1): 9.

7. Uncertainty is being used in the Knightian sense in which no probability can be assigned due to an inability to properly characterize the nature or likelihood of traditional risk or outcomes.

Chapter 6

1. The book *Hidden Champions of the Twenty-First Century: The Success Strategies of Unknown World Market Leaders* by Hermann Simon (2009, Springer) provides excellent insight into smaller-sized specialty firms that globally dominate niche markets in this way.

2. It should be acknowledged that Kodak was an innovator in digital technology, creating the QuickTake digital camera with Apple in 1992.

Chapter 7

1. OK. The Elvis Chia pet doesn't exist yet, but the Daffy Duck and Bugs Bunny ones do.

2. "Spaces" in this context is used within the mathematical concept of potential constrained area or location potential solution variables may occupy. The survival space for an elephant could be plotted on the dimensions of the viable body mass relative to its ambient environmental temperature.

3. There are 10 trillion human cells in the average person; each human cell holds roughly 23,000 genes. Human cells are organized into 220 types

to form the body's organs and systems. The human body is also home to a huge microbiome of 100 trillion bacteria cells with an estimated +3,000,000 genes. The human body could be considered to have its own ecology spread across the flora and fauna of the gut out to every available surface with each cell located only five cells away from the circulatory system.

4. For the mathematically inclined, the best way to plot the filled-in boundaries is as a bounded Voronoi tessellation.

5. Paradigm here is being used in Thomas Kuhn's true original sense of the word, not the "new and improved" cheapened version thrown around by consultants.

Chapter 8

1. James M. Utterback. 1996. *Mastering the Dynamics of Innovation*, 2nd edition. Harvard Business Review Press.

2. Krug, Steve. 2005. *Don't Make Me Think: A Common Sense Guide to Web Usability*. Indianapolis, IN: New Riders Publishing.

3. The architecture of the automobile has evolved to achieve greater capacity for energy throughput per unit of cost, all while increasing in system structural complexity. This increased system complexity has delivered improved engine performance per unit of mass and overall system efficiency, while the quality delivered on many dimensions of value has increased as relative cost has declined. These aspects of adaptive system evolution will be discussed later, during further explorations into the trends of accumulated knowledge, increased energy throughput density, and adapted trends in economic and ecological evolution.

4. Moore, Geoffrey, Paul Johnson, and Tom Kippola. 1999. *The Gorilla Game: Picking Winners in High Technology*. HarperBusiness.

5. Innosight report, 2012. Richard N. Foster, coauthor of *Creative Destruction* and author of *Innovation: The Attacker's Advantage*.

6. Warren Buffett famously practiced allocation discipline when he refused to invest in capital improvements for the textile manufacturing business of Berkshire Hathaway, correctly realizing the returns on capital to this fading sector would be low or negative.

Chapter 9

1. The term "cash cow" was used by the Boston Consulting Group (BCG) to refer to a high-margin slow-growth firm or business unit. Applying the

term to a cluster is a reference to the cluster's competitive traits and maturity. Some firms within the cash cow cluster will likely have cash cow characteristics associated with the familiar BCG usage of the term.

2. Seven years is a subjective number, but generally there is an advantage to thinking longer term than other investors. The inability to see beyond seven years correctly knocks out many fast capability-cycle industries and firms from consideration unless one is paying significantly below book value as a margin of safety.

3. Meeker, Mary, and Brian Fitzgerald. 2003. *The Technology IPO Yearbook: 9th Edition—23 Years of Technology Investing*. Morgan Stanley Equity Research, North America.

4. Van Valen, L. 1973. "A New Evolutionary Law." *Evolutionary Theory* 1: 1–30.

5. Steward, R.C. 1977. *"Industrial and Non-Industrial Melanism in the Peppered Moth Biston betularia (L.)."* Ecological Entomology 2 (3): 231–243. doi:10.1111/j.1365–2311.1977.tb00886.x

6. Baker, Nardin L., and Robert A. Haugen. "Low Risk Stocks Outperform within All Observable Markets of the World." Paper, April 12, 2012.

7. The flawed overattribution of business outcomes to CEOs is highlighted well in the important book *The Halo Affect* by Phil Rosenzweig (Fresh Press, 2007). This attribution flaw assigning mythical power to CEOs is a contributing factor to the vulgar overpayment of many corporate CEOs.

8. Warren Buffet has been known to carry a set of nontransitive dice to challenge opponents with. Nontransitive dice have a winning strategy assuming one knows the competitor's dice choice in advance. According to Janet Lowe's book *Bill Gates Speaks: Insight from the World's Greatest Entrepreneur* (Wiley, 1998), Warren Buffett offered Bill Gates the chance to play a game with the dice. Bill asked to see the dice first and then correctly suggested Buffett select a dice first. It seems billionaires think strategically about game theory and when not to compete.

9. Southwest and other budget or niche airlines are held up as counterexamples to this. The fact remains that, taken in aggregate, the airline cluster has destroyed net shareholder value.

10. Book value is a helpful starting point to value a firm. Book value is calculated as the Assets – Liabilities. Goodwill is a useful accounting fiction often used to reflect acquisition costs over book value. After the original goodwill entry is made its value is highly subjective and dependent on the asset's value-generating capability more than its accounting treatment and balance sheet representation.

11. For those interested in the how and why of biological and economic systems acting as transmission mechanisms for adaptive innovations, Richard Dawkins's, *The Selfish Gene* (Oxford University Press, 1989), Eric D. Schneider and Dorian Sagan's *Into the Cool* (University of Chicago Press, 2006), or Kevin Kelley's *What Technology Wants* (Penguin Books, 2011) are highly recommended.

12. Super brands demonstrate the concept of positioning, put forth by 1980s marketing gurus Al Ries and Jack Trout in their book *Positioning: The Battle for Your Mind* (McGraw-Hill, 2000). The thinking was that each product category had one to three important brands that could be recalled by consumers. Other brands faded into noise. Many brand managers recognized this as true and a proliferation of category bifurcation has ensued ever since in which ever more specialized clusters are targeted to niche needs, whether the needs are real or imagined.

13. See's Candy is used as an example due to its familiarity to value investors and readily available write-ups by Warren Buffett, for those interested in further research.

14. It is worthwhile to read Charlie Munger's book *Poor Charlie's Almanack* (The Donning Company, 2005), where he explains Lollapalooza and shares many other important lessons.

15. Lowe's mega hardware stores started filling in the economy and combined with The Home Depot, filling the entire economic cluster. As the carrying capacity limit was approached, margins and growth declined, reflecting a more mature cluster when looked at from the scale of economy.

16. *Built from Scratch: How a Couple of Regular Guys Grew The Home Depot from Nothing to $30 Billion* (Crown Business, 2001), by Bernie Marcus and Arthur Blank is a useful book on The Home Depot written by its founders.

Chapter 10

1. Marn, Michael V., Eric V. Roegner, and Craig C. Zawada. 2003. "The Power of Pricing." *The McKinsey Quarterly* 1: 26–39.

2. Coke (KO) focuses on branding and manufacturing concentrated syrup. The syrup is then sold to bottlers and distributors.

3. As of 2013.

4. Price to earnings ratio. The reciprocal provides an earnings yield.

5. Price to book value ratio.

Chapter 11

1. Value delivered must be perceived as greater than competing choices.

2. http://www.interbrand.com/Libraries/Press_Release/BGB_Press_Release_FINAL.sflb.ashx

3. Ries, Al, and Jack Trout. 2000. *Positioning: The Battle for Your Mind*. New York: McGraw-Hill.

Chapter 12

1. To be fair to CEOs, many activist shareholders and lawyers happily sue and win over actions that depress share prices and so CEOs are forced to play this role, due to the public's gross misunderstanding of short-term price changes versus the long-term nature of value creation.

2. Abbot Payson Usher, an economic historian at Harvard, advocated an economic model of growth based on a smooth gradual rate of innovative progress in contrast to the radical innovation espoused by Schumpeter. (Abbot Payson Usher. 1929. *A History of Mechanical Inventions*. New York: McGraw-Hill.)

3. Blaise Pascal. 1670. *Pensees*, 3rd edition. À Paris, chez Guillaume Desprez, rue Saint Jacques, à Saint Prosper. M. DC. LXX.

4. For insight into the power of intrinsically motivated performance psychology read Carol Dweck's book *Mindset*. (Carol Dweck. 2006. *Mindset: The New Psychology of Success*. Random House.)

5. Many firms argue they will use an IRR hurdle rate approach that covers ROE, but in many cases the target IRR hurdle used is below 15 percent or isn't declared in filings or reports to shareholders.

6. It should be noted that in risk-taking industries like insurance and banking, the risk cycle is longer than the typical annual ROE or revenue growth metric. This means careful analysis should be given to these sectors because they are structurally prone to short-term adverse selection, with dangerously destructive managers showing the best numbers during boom times.

Chapter 13

1. I encourage readers interested in learning more about evolutionary contingency to explore Stephen Jay Gould's writings on it.

2. All economic and ecological organized systems fail and get replaced by other organized forms. In books like *How Nature Works: The Science of Self-Organized Criticality* (Copernicus, 1999), the late theoretical physicist Per Bak showed how power law relationships occur across most complex systems, including ecologies, wars, and biological extinction events. Power law relationships are also seen in growing systems' structural properties, capabilities, and flow capacities via the Constructal theory put forth by Bejan.

3. Stephen Jay Gould. 1990. "Wonderful Life: The Burgess Shale and the Nature of History." 7.

4. The Human Development index focuses on measuring human potential in terms of health and education capabilities that are individually realized in an economy.

5. Counterintuitively, easily extractable oil or minerals may not contribute to economic development across an economy's human condition as measured in infant mortality, literacy rates, and life expectancy. This situation is referred to by development economists as the resource curse, whereby easily extractable and controlled resources such as minerals or fossil fuels form a narrow dominant segment of an economy that may be controlled and extracted exclusively for elites to retain patronage and power networks. Corrupt extractive regimes controlling this extractable wealth may not lead to knowledge creation and broad human development across an economy.

6. Karl Popper, in a lecture delivered to the London School of Economics in 1988 entitled "Towards an Evolutionary Theory of Knowledge," discussed innate animal behaviors that conferred a positive survival bias to be knowledge. This knowledge could be innate and visceral responsive or a conditioned and learned response conferring competitive survival advantage to the possessor of the knowledge or capacity for learning and retaining knowledge.

Popper then elaborated how information measured statistically or mechanically in Shannonian forms was uninteresting, but that an interesting subset of information, namely knowledge, was information organized such that it might itself alter or allow for an informationally reproductive cycle.

The argument put forth was that genetic information contained the knowledge required to replicate itself in the future through means of various expressed mechanisms such as protein expression and higher level biological functions all the way up to human behavior and the capacity for storing symbolic information (memory and language).

7. *Why Nations Fail* (Crown Business, 2012) by Daron Acemoglu and James Robinson provides an excellent history of extractive versus inclusive models of economy and the outcomes for social development and material economic progress they foster. *Why Nations Fail* compares extractive

regimes using historical and contemporary examples ranging from Latin America to the original American colonies. Most economies are organized mixes of these with predominant features defined by polities and culturally normative behaviors.

8. For those looking into the relationship between the Gini coefficient and entropy metrics, Thiel's index (http://utip.gov.utexas.edu/papers/utip_14.pdf) or Atkinson's research metric (http://www.sciencedirect.com/science/article/pii/0022053170900396) may be of particular interest.

9. Negative growth can occur when resources are actually wasted as value is destroyed by the economy or SPICE (Social, Political, Innovation, Cultural, or Ecological) factors. Value destruction can include domestic resource wastage or external foreign direct investment (FDI) and monetary aid intended for development extracted by a polity of enfranchised elites.

10. The costs of low GDP show up in increased infant and child mortality, reduced life expectancy, and many other health and socioeconomic factors. The lost human potential associated with poverty and under-education hinders knowledge and economic development and innovation for humanity.

11. This aid and development debate is best characterized by Jeffrey Sachs, who wants to apply more input resources to development, versus William Easterly, who advocates studying local causes and local actors' real needs against outcomes. William Easterly's insightful book *The White Man's Burden* (Penguin Press, 2006) is recommended reading for those interested in understanding development that really helps the poor. MIT economist Esther Duflo does commendable work on researching the outcomes and social payoffs the poor receive from development aid using randomized trials.

12. Examples of economic systemic brittleness associated with corruption or failed services often show up poignantly during natural disasters which are ecological system stressors. Earthquakes in countries or regions with corrupt or dysfunctional building permitting and land titling suffer greater damage. Failure in delivering water and utilities increases death rates associated with water-borne diseases such as cholera epidemics during floods or other crises. According to economist Amartya Sen, widespread famines are exclusively the result of market failures related to corrupt or extractive economic policies such as those seen during the potato famine in Ireland and parts of India during the period of English rule.

13. The territories and colonies referred to are the early U.S. colonies, which make an excellent example of the developing world's development success. Hernando de Soto's *The Mystery of Capital: Why Capitalism Works in the West* (Basic Books, 2000) tells the story well.

Chapter 14

1. Most economics books state incorrectly that money functions "as a store of value," ignoring the fact that most forms of money are mostly electronic blips, bulk metals, or pieces of paper with pictures of old men and government buildings on them. Money isn't a store of value; it is believed to be a store of value. That is, it is a representational belief system which functions best when it believed to be a store of value. Most forms of money have almost zero value if the belief system in them fails. This includes physical gold, which has limited functional utility based on its physical properties.

2. Spanish dollars circulated among the thirteen colonies easily and were legal tender in Virginia.

3. Preston, Martin, and Lita Epstein. 2003. *The Complete Idiot's Guide to the Federal Reserve*. New York: Alpha.

4. Furness, W. H. 1910. *The Island of Stone Money: Uap of the Carolines*, and Anthropologist Scott Fitzpatrick NPR interview, Dec 10, 2010.

5. Friedman, Milton. 1991. *The Island of Stone Money*. Stanford, CA: Hoover Institute Working Papers in Economics, pp. E-91–93.

6. The U.S. Federal Reserve has a dual mandate of maximizing employment and maintaining price stability. Generally it is believed that the Fed targets a stable 2 percent inflation rate. These dual goals are supposed to ensure optimal long-term economic growth.

7. Central banks primarily only purchase government debt and the most secure assets in order to maintain "faith" in their assets. During World War II to 1951 the Fed bought treasury bonds, never allowing their yield to exceed 2.5 percent. Recently the U.S. central bank has bought mortgage-backed securities among other things. During an equity crisis in 1998, the Hong Kong central bank purchased shares outright. Central banks also speculate in the value of their own currencies, such as the Bank of England's trading disaster in 1992.

8. Housing is ultimately a positional good and has a historical 3:1 income to value ratio. The $6.6 trillion factor is calculated using the median home value to income ratio variance from this historic average.

9. Metabolism is derived from the ancient Greek meaning "change" and "out-throw," which seems suitable for evolution's many expressed forms across physical, ecological, economic, and symbolic domains.

10. Note that China's inflation has ranged from −2 percent to +8 percent during its amazing 2000–2012 growth period.

11. Interestingly there isn't a known single cause associated with the Permian extinction. Theories include meteorite impact, vulcanism, methane hydrate releases, climate change, or a mix of these things.

12. Calculated using real 2005 dollars.

13. Zimbabwe's main stock index was up over 12,000 percent in 12 months in 2007.

14. Hanke, Steve H., and Nicholas Krus. 2012. "World Hyperinflations." Cato working paper #8. The world record holder for hyperinflation is Hungary, from August 1945 to July 1946, which saw prices doubling every fifteen hours measured in Pengos.

15. *When Money Dies: The Nightmare of Deficit Spending, Devaluation, and Hyperinflation in Weimar Germany* (Kimber, 1975) by Adam Fergusson provides an excellent view of hyperinflation from unique inside perspectives.

16. For comparison, in 2012, the United States had a debt to GDP ratio close to 1.1:1.0; Japan's is 2.0:1.0. Economic scholars Carmen Reinhart and Kenneth Rogoff estimate that a ratio of 0.9:1.0 is a dangerous tipping point for debt levels in their book, *This Time Is Different: Eight Centuries of Financial Folly* (Princeton University Press, 2011).

17. 1986 Cruzado, 1987 Bresser, 1989 Summer, 1990 Collar 1, 1991 Collar 2, 1995 Real.

18. "How Fake Money Saved Brazil," NPR radio, Oct 4, 2010, Robert Siegel and Mary Louise Kelly with Chana Joffe-Walt: http://www.npr.org/templates/transcript/transcript.php?storyId=130329523.

19. It has been argued by Charles P. Kindelberger that the Federal Reserve was hampered by the loss of its chairman Benjamin Strong in 1928. Kindelberger argues that without Strong the Fed's actions and inactions in the 1930s amplified the money (credit) contraction and related value flow problem.

20. http://eh.net/encyclopedia/deflation/.

21. Ayres, Robert, and Benjamin Warr. 2009. *Economic Growth Engine: How Energy and Work Drive Material Prosperity*, p. 34. Edward Elgar.

22. It should be noted that a handful of developing countries are inclusive economies making strides, but too many are perpetual poverty traps suffering from extractive patronage-based versus rule of law political regimes. Often these regimes are indirectly facilitated or supported by well-meaning multinational development projects. Without local political change these extractive governments can deplete any and all external resources poured into them. Wasted human potential and suffering is an ongoing tragedy, which will likely be resolved with domestic political change and a wider understanding of the costs of corruption and extractive politics.

23. This occurred with canal mania in the 1790s, railway shares in the 1840s, large-scale diffusion of automobiles, telephones, and electricity, creating unprecedented industrial growth in the 1920s, and of course Internet/telecom shares in 1995–2000, to name a few.

24. Real cost refers to an inflation adjusted cost. Nominal cost is the displayed or quoted price of an item. Real (inflation adjusted) purchasing power of income is typically used to show how an economy's internal price relationships change after a period of price inflation.

25. Relative price is the item's comparative price to similar or substitute quality goods.

26. This assumes debt and associated monies at the macroeconomic level are sustainable and bear a reasonable relationship to value and wealth within the economy on a go-forward basis. Large debt to excess value-creating abilities can be unsustainable, leading to defaults, political or monetary instabilities, or even collapses.

27. This is a yield curve.

28. A familiar example of monoculture and monocrop failure is the Irish potato famine. Thirty percent of the Irish people depended on potatoes for food. A blight wiped out the crop, killing 1 million people and forcing another estimated 1 million to leave the island. These changes caused Ireland's population to shrink an estimated 20 to 25 percent in seven years from 1845 to 1852.

29. Asset bubbles involve the creation of excess money acting as a direct claim on an asset class used to purchase more of the same asset, pushing up the asset class's price far beyond value. Cheap money and price re-inforce each other, as people confuse price with the value-creating ability of the asset class. The creation of money (usually debt) allocated to the asset feeds a mania of senseless price increases until the whole charade collapses in a panic, destroying the created money and often depreciating the real value of the original asset because of resource over allocation. If the money created debt or equity is not forgiven or destroyed, the ongoing debt service relative to the "under-water" post crash assets, drains other forms of money flow from the economy as the underlying assets go "under-water." This aggregate far money contraction creates recessions as value flows shrink to service the now relatively expensive money, measured in debt to asset ratios.

30. *Resilience Thinking: Sustaining Ecosystems and People in a Changing World* (Island Press, 2006), by Brian Walker and David Salt, is an excellent learning resource for learning about ecological resilience.

31. Cash means immediately transactible currency and not so-called cash equivalents. In 2007 many found out that cash equivalent money market instruments and auction rate securities liquidity disappeared just as it was needed most. Like so many financial innovations, the extra yield measured as a few basis points turned out to be junk. The instant convertibility of cash is a valuable financial option costing a few basis points of forgone allocation to near cash equivalents.

32. Low rates of inflation may strengthen a firm's goodwill, depending on the source of the firm's goodwill. A strong brand and distribution network advantage allows for relative premium pricing versus other goods. During inflationary periods this premium pricing may efficiently expand value, but not the balance sheet representation of the goodwill asset. The goodwill stays fixed in nominal terms on the balance sheet even while its contribution to ROC margins and intrinsic and book value increase as the moat works its magic. The nature of value and the accounting conventions associated with goodwill can be at odds with each other. If the firm is not a fad and has a genuine branded moat, then marketing costs going forward may shrink as a percentage of per-customer revenue. This means richly expanded returns on working capital.

Chapter 15

1. ICI Factbook, 2012; http://www.ici.org/pdf/2012_factbook.pdf.

2. The outcome will depend on the index rebalancing strategy, a detail often left out of "beta" conversations dealing with entering and exiting firms in the index.

3. The truth in academic economics comes in shades of gray. Beta depends on how things are weighted and so on, and most research is U.S.-based or suffers economy-wide survivorship bias. Like the bogus equity risk premium concept, don't look at beta too closely or it melts into a big mess.

4. This model ignores the slight effects of momentum.

5. Trading in HHH stopped on December 23, 2011.

6. Not all countries will be effective economies for an index approach. The economy in question must follow the rule of law with minimal corruption and not be subject to capricous taxation or regulatory powers. The economic governance and legal systems are also required to be fair and independent for equity shareholders for such an approach to be valid.

Chapter 16

1. Phillip Ball. 1999. *The Self-Made Tapestry: Pattern Formation in Nature.* Oxford: Oxford University Press.

Index

Accenture, 3, 4
adaptation: bifurcation in firms, 67–68;
   cluster, 106–8, 116–17; evolution
   and, 39–44, 65, 66, 102–3, 148–49;
   of new inos, 65; organization, 66–67.
   See also ecological adaptation
adaptive change: adaptive economy and,
   25, 26; of clusters, 137; ecology and,
   25–26; knowledge and, 60; network,
   224–25; panarchy and, 30, 32. *See*
   also evolution
adaptive complex systems, 68; adaptive
   economies as, 24, 28; ecology as, 24,
   28; feedback loops, 29; growth of,
   106; as networked, 28–29; overview,
   24; predictability of, 221; selective
   feedback, 102. *See also* panarchy
adaptive economy: adaptive change and,
   25, 26; as adaptive complex system,
   24, 28; bifurcation in, 65–67; capabilities and, 322n4; competition in,
   65; cycles, 103; ecological adaptation
   and, 19–24, 32, 229; evolution and,
   20–21, 23–24, 32; life and, 19; overview, 19, 229; selection in, 65; selective feedback in, 65; value and, 19
adaptive flow, complexity and efficiency,
   23–28

adaptive selection, 103; adaptive selective
   feedback, 30, 33, 65, 102
adaptive systems, 32; evolutionary, 221,
   222, 227–28, 324n3; growth of, 106.
   See also adaptive complex systems
agriculture, mono-crop, 278, 332n28
aircraft, 128–29; taxonomy, 67, 68
airline industry, 154, 325n9
allocations: as bets, 86–87, 323n7;
   capability assessment and, 95–97;
   cash cow cluster, 159–61; cluster,
   141, 153, 209; economy types and
   allocators, 235–42; firms unique
   capability mix and, 89–98; inflation
   and, 282–89, 297; innovation and,
   157; lottery cluster, 146; management and, 208–9; moated firms and,
   208–9, 295, 295–97; money shocks
   and, 244–98; MV=P equation and,
   290–96, 291; negative optionality and, 84–88; as quest for true
   knowledge, 318; Red Queen clusters,
   153–57; stable cluster, 157–65. *See*
   also nature of value allocation
Amazon, 139, 145, 156, 196–97
amplification: economic predictability and
   knowledge, 232–33, 328n6;
   evolutionary, 39–41; selective